VOLUME 578

NOVEMBER 2001

THE ANNALS

of The American Academy *of* Political
and Social Science

ALAN W. HESTON, *Editor*
NEIL A. WEINER, *Assistant Editor*

WHAT WORKS IN PREVENTING CRIME?
SYSTEMATIC REVIEWS
OF EXPERIMENTAL AND
QUASI-EXPERIMENTAL RESEARCH

Special Editors of this Volume

DAVID P. FARRINGTON
University of Cambridge
BRANDON C. WELSH
University of Massachusetts Lowell

 Sage Publications   *THOUSAND OAKS   LONDON   NEW DELHI*

The American Academy of Political and Social Science

c/o Fels Center of Government, University of Pennsylvania, 3814 Walnut Street, Philadelphia, PA 19104; (215) 746-6500; (215) 898-1202 (fax); www.1891.org

Origin and Purpose. The Academy was organized December 14, 1889, to promote the progress of political and social science, especially through publications and meetings. The Academy does not take sides in controverted questions, but seeks to gather and present reliable information to assist the public in forming an intelligent and accurate judgment.

Meetings. The Academy occasionally holds a meeting in the spring extending over two days.

Publications. THE ANNALS of the American Academy of Political and Social Science is the bimonthly publication of The Academy. Each issue contains articles on some prominent social or political problem, written at the invitation of the editors. Also, monographs are published from time to time, numbers of which are distributed to pertinent professional organizations. These volumes constitute important reference works on the topics with which they deal, and they are extensively cited by authorities throughout the United States and abroad. The papers presented at the meetings of The Academy are included in THE ANNALS.

Membership. Each member of The Academy receives THE ANNALS and may attend the meetings of The Academy. Membership is open only to individuals. Annual dues: $65.00 for the regular paperbound edition (clothbound, $100.00). For members outside the U.S.A., add $12.00 (surface mail) or $24.00 (air mail) for shipping of your subscription. Members may also purchase single issues of THE ANNALS for $20.00 each (clothbound, $30.00).

Subscriptions. THE ANNALS of the American Academy of Political and Social Science (ISSN 0002-7162) is published six times annually—in January, March, May, July, September, and November. Institutions may subscribe to THE ANNALS at the annual rate: $375.00 (clothbound, $425.00). Add $12.00 per year for subscriptions outside the U.S.A. Institutional rates for single issues: $70.00 each (clothbound, $75.00).

Periodicals postage paid at Thousand Oaks, California, and at additional mailing offices.

Single issues of THE ANNALS may be obtained by individuals who are not members of The Academy for $30.00 each (clothbound, $40.00). Single issues of THE ANNALS have proven to be excellent supplementary texts for classroom use. Direct inquiries regarding adoptions to THE ANNALS c/o Sage Publications (address below).

All correspondence concerning membership in The Academy, dues renewals, inquiries about membership status, and/or purchase of single issues of THE ANNALS should be sent to THE ANNALS c/o Sage Publications, 2455 Teller Road, Thousand Oaks, CA 91320. Telephone: (800) 818-SAGE (7243) and (805) 499-9774; FAX/Order line: (805) 375-1700. *Please note that orders under $30 must be prepaid.* Sage affiliates in London and India will assist institutional subscribers abroad with regard to orders, claims, and inquiries for both subscriptions and single issues.

Printed on recycled, acid-free paper

THE ANNALS

© 2001 *by* The American Academy *of* Political *and* Social Science

Editorial Office: Fels Center of Government, University of Pennsylvania, 3814 Walnut Street, Philadelphia, PA 19104-6197.

For information about membership* (individuals only) and subscriptions (institutions), address:

SAGE PUBLICATIONS
2455 Teller Road
Thousand Oaks, CA 91320

Sage Production Staff: BARBARA CORRIGAN, SCOTT SPRINGER, and ROSE TYLAK

From India and South Asia, write to:		*From Europe, the Middle East, and Africa, write to:*
SAGE PUBLICATIONS INDIA Pvt. Ltd		SAGE PUBLICATIONS LTD
P.O. Box 4215		6 Bonhill Street
New Delhi 110 048		London EC2A 4PU
INDIA		UNITED KINGDOM

*Please note that members of The Academy receive THE ANNALS with their membership.
International Standard Serial Number ISSN 0002-7162
International Standard Book Number ISBN 0-7619-2569-4 (Vol. 578, 2001 paper)
International Standard Book Number ISBN 0-7619-2568-6 (Vol. 578, 2001 cloth)
Manufactured in the United States of America. First printing, November 2001.

The articles appearing in THE ANNALS are abstracted or indexed in *Academic Abstracts, Academic Search, America: History and Life, Asia Pacific Database, Book Review Index, CAB Abstracts Database, Central Asia: Abstracts & Index, Communication Abstracts, Corporate ResourceNET, Criminal Justice Abstracts, Current Citations Express, Current Contents: Social & Behavioral Sciences, e-JEL, EconLit, Expanded Academic Index, Guide to Social Science & Religion in Periodical Literature, Health Business FullTEXT, HealthSTAR FullTEXT, Historical Abstracts, International Bibliography of the Social Sciences, International Political Science Abstracts, ISI Basic Social Sciences Index, Journal of Economic Literature on CD, LEXIS-NEXIS, MasterFILE FullTEXT, Middle East: Abstracts & Index, North Africa: Abstracts & Index, PAIS International, Periodical Abstracts, Political Science Abstracts, Sage Public Administration Abstracts, Social Science Source, Social Sciences Citation Index, Social Sciences Index Full Text, Social Services Abstracts, Social Work Abstracts, Sociological Abstracts, Southeast Asia: Abstracts & Index, Standard Periodical Directory (SPD), TOPICsearch, Wilson OmniFile V,* and *Wilson Social Sciences Index/Abstracts,* and are available on microfilm from University Microfilms, Ann Arbor, Michigan.

Information about membership rates, institutional subscriptions, and back issue prices may be found on the facing page.

Advertising. Current rates and specifications may be obtained by writing to THE ANNALS Advertising and Promotion Manager at the Thousand Oaks office (address above).

Claims. Claims for undelivered copies must be made no later than six months following month of publication. The publisher will supply missing copies when losses have been sustained in transit and when the reserve stock will permit.

Change of Address. Six weeks' advance notice must be given when notifying of change of address to ensure proper identification. Please specify name of journal. **POSTMASTER:** Send address changes to: THE ANNALS of the American Academy of Political and Social Science, c/o Sage Publications, 2455 Teller Road, Thousand Oaks, CA 91320.

THE ANNALS

of The American Academy *of* Political
and Social Science

ALAN W. HESTON, *Editor*
NEIL A. WEINER, *Assistant Editor*

FORTHCOMING

DRUG POLICY
Special Editors: Peter Reuter
and Robert J. MacCoun

Volume 579   January 2002

FIXITY OF EXCHANGE RATES
Special Editors: Michael K. Ulan
and George Tavlas

Volume 580   March 2002

GLOBAL DEMOCRACY
Special Editor: R. Munck

Volume 581   May 2002

See page 2 for information on Academy membership and
purchase of single volumes of **The Annals.**

CONTENTS

BOOK DEPARTMENT CONTENTS

UNITED STATES

SOCIOLOGY

ECONOMICS

PREFACE

The main aims of this special issue of *The Annals* are to examine the systematic review method and to report on some of its contributions to evidence-based crime prevention. The main title of this issue, "What Works in Preventing Crime?" signals our primary interest in identifying those interventions that are effective in preventing crime and offending and that ultimately may lead to more effective crime prevention policy and practice. The issue's subtitle, "Systematic Reviews of Experimental and Quasi-Experimental Research," signals our interest in using the most rigorous methods of research synthesis and only the highest-quality research designs to evaluate the effectiveness of criminological interventions.

Systematic reviews have received increased attention in recent years in the social sciences generally and in criminology and criminal justice specifically. This is part of the broader interest in evidence-based policy and practice in public services (Davies, Nutley, and Smith 2000) and evidence-based crime prevention (Sherman et al. 1997, forthcoming).

At the forefront of the development of systematic reviews is the newly formed Campbell Collaboration. Named after the influential experimental psychologist Donald T. Campbell (1969), this was set up for the purpose of preparing, maintaining, and disseminating evidence-based research on the effects of interventions in the fields of education, social welfare, and crime and justice. Its Crime and Justice Group aims to prepare and maintain systematic reviews of criminological interventions and to make them accessible electronically to scholars, practitioners, policy makers, and the general public. The present work, although not officially carried out under the auspices of the Campbell Collaboration, represents an important contribution to its Crime and Justice Group, and the four systematic reviews reported here are undergoing review by the Campbell Collaboration; it is hoped that they will be approved and disseminated as Campbell reviews in due course.

This issue of *The Annals* introduces the path-breaking work of the Campbell Collaboration and its Crime and Justice Group, examines key methodological issues facing systematic reviews of criminological interventions, reports on four original systematic reviews of the effects of different interventions on crime and offending, and makes progress toward an evidence-based approach to preventing crime and offending. Throughout this issue, *crime prevention* is defined as any program or policy that causes a lower number of crimes to occur in the future than would have occurred without that program or policy.

This special issue originated with the 2001 Jerry Lee Crime Prevention Symposium, a 2-day conference on systematic reviews of criminological interventions, held in early April at the University of Maryland, College Park, and at the U.S. capitol building in Washington, D.C. Convened by the University of Maryland's Department of Criminology and Criminal Justice and sponsored by the Jerry Lee Foundation,[1] the conference brought together leading researchers in the fields of crime prevention, experimental criminology, and research synthesis. The conference also benefited from the participation of directors of governmental and nongovernmental research units, criminal justice policy makers, and journalists specializing in crime and justice. Five countries were represented: Australia, Canada, Israel, the United Kingdom, and the United States. Papers on substantive issues relating to methods and findings of systematic reviews of criminological interventions were presented and discussed. Subsequently the papers were revised in light of editorial comments, and they are now presented here.

METHODS AND PERSPECTIVES

Four articles examine methods of conducting systematic reviews of criminological interventions. Important in each of these articles, and to this special issue as a whole, is the need for systematic reviews to include only those studies with the highest quality research designs to evaluate the impact of prevention programs on crime and offending. In the case of criminology and criminal justice, this means experimental (randomized and nonrandomized) and quasi-experimental designs. Ideally we would have been able to limit studies in systematic reviews to only those that used randomized experimental designs, as this is the most convincing method of evaluating crime prevention programs (Farrington 1983). However, for systematic reviews of criminological interventions, this is rarely feasible, largely because there is not a long history of experimental evaluations in criminology and this would result in the complete exclusion of area-level studies (as opposed to individual-level studies), such as the effects of closed circuit television and many types of community crime prevention programs. In area-level studies, the best and most feasible design usually involves before and after measures of crime in comparable experimental and control conditions, together with statistical control of extraneous variables.

In the first article, by Anthony Petrosino, Robert Boruch, Haluk Soydan, Lorna Duggan, and Julio Sanchez-Meca, the authors discuss the growing interest in and challenges facing an evidence-based approach to the development of public policy and practice. Some of these challenges, which take the form of political and policy efforts to maintain the status quo (see Davies, Nutley, and Smith 1999) as well as the quality of the evaluation evidence, can be overcome through the use of systematic reviews.

In the second article, by David Farrington and Anthony Petrosino, the authors describe in detail the methodology of systematic reviews to investigate the effectiveness of interventions to prevent crime and criminal offending. Also delineated are the many challenges facing the Campbell Collaboration Crime and Justice Group. In the context of discussing the most important of these challenges—the criterion of methodological quality to be used for including studies—the authors review some of the theoretical underpinnings of evaluation methodology.

In light of the need for systematic reviews of criminological interventions to include studies with different high-quality research designs, instead of being limited to studies with only randomized experimental designs, an important question is, Does the research design affect study outcomes? This is the focus of the third article by David Weisburd, Cynthia Lum, and Anthony Petrosino. The authors begin with a review of the methods literature on this topic and report on key studies in medicine and the social sciences that have investigated the subject of research design's affecting study outcomes. For their study—the first of its kind focused specifically on criminological and criminal justice interventions—the authors draw on a recent, encyclopedic review of the crime prevention evidence that was commissioned by the National Institute of Justice and carried out by Lawrence Sherman and his colleagues (1997). Weisburd and his colleagues find that there is a "moderate inverse relationship" between research design and study outcomes. The main implication of this finding, despite the authors' noting that their work is preliminary and hence that it should be interpreted with caution, is that the findings of systematic reviews may be biased by the inclusion of nonrandomized studies.

In the final article in this section, David Wilson reviews the methodology of the quantitative data synthesis technique of meta-analysis (the statistical analysis of the results of prior research studies), examines some of its strengths and limitations as a method for assessing the effectiveness of criminological interventions, and discusses the importance of its use in systematic reviews. As noted in the article by David Farrington and Anthony Petrosino and elsewhere (for example, Farrington and Petrosino 2000; Farrington, Petrosino, and Welsh 2001), quantitative techniques (for example, meta-analysis) should be used, when appropriate and feasible, in summarizing results as part of systematic reviews. The appropriateness and feasibility of doing a meta-analysis as part of a systematic review depend, in large part, on the need to have a reasonable number of intervention studies (from which effect sizes can be calculated) and to have studies that are sufficiently similar to be grouped together. These points notwithstanding, the inclusion of a meta-analysis in a systematic review (when done with full integrity, of course) has the capacity to produce the most rigorous summary assessment of the effectiveness of a criminological intervention based on a number of evaluation studies.

RESEARCH FINDINGS FROM PREVENTION
AND INTERVENTION STUDIES

The systematic review and the meta-analytic review are the most rigorous methods for assessing the effectiveness of criminological interventions and have the most to offer to evidence-based crime prevention.[2]

Systematic reviews use rigorous methods for locating, appraising, and synthesizing evidence from prior evaluation studies, and they are reported with the same level of detail that characterizes high-quality reports of original research. They have explicit objectives, explicit criteria for including or excluding studies, extensive searches for eligible evaluation studies from around the world, careful extraction and coding of key features of studies, and a structured and detailed report of the methods and conclusions of the review. All of this contributes greatly to the ease of their replication by other researchers.

Four articles report on systematic reviews of the effects of different interventions in preventing crime or offending: parent training and support programs, hot spots policing, correctional boot camps, and cognitive-behavioral programs. Each follows as closely as possible the methodology for conducting systematic reviews that has been specified by the Campbell Collaboration.

In the first article of this section, Odette Bernazzani, Catherine Côté, and Richard Tremblay report on a systematic review of parent training and support before age 3. Seven studies are reviewed, and effectiveness is assessed on the outcome measures of disruptive behavior (for example, opposition to adults, truancy, aggression) and delinquency. The authors find that the evidence on effectiveness is mixed: three studies report some beneficial effects (with one reporting some harmful effects), and the other four studies report no evidence of effectiveness. The authors call for caution in interpreting the results (for example, due to modest effect sizes of the beneficial studies) and recommend further intervention studies in these areas.

In the second article, Anthony Braga reviews the effects of hot spots policing to reduce crime. This form of policing involves the targeting of police enforcement measures in high-crime areas. Nine studies are reviewed, and effectiveness is assessed on the outcome measures of crime and disorder. Braga also examines the effects of the studies on the displacement of crime (an unintended increase in crime, for example, in a different location) and the diffusion of crime control benefits (an unintended decrease in crime in a different location). He finds evidence that targeted police actions can prevent crime and disorder in hot spots, that displacement is rare, and that some programs produce unintended crime prevention benefits.

The third article, by Doris MacKenzie, David Wilson, and Suzanne Kider, reports on a systematic review—incorporating meta-analytic techniques—of the effects of correctional boot camps (otherwise known as shock or intensive incarceration) on offending. Forty-four studies are reviewed, and effectiveness is assessed according to recidivism. The systematic review reveals varied effects on recidivism: 9 studies report beneficial effects, 8 report harmful effects, and 27 report no effects. Overall the meta-analysis finds evidence of no effect. MacKenzie and her colleagues conclude that boot camps are an ineffective correctional treatment to reduce future offending.

In the final article in this section, Mark Lipsey, Gabrielle Chapman, and Nana Landenberger report on a systematic review—incorporating meta-analytic techniques—of cognitive-behavioral programs for offenders. Fourteen of the highest quality studies with outcome measures of recidivism are reviewed. Lipsey and his colleagues find strong evidence that cognitive-behavioral programs are effective in reducing recidivism.

FUTURE DIRECTIONS

In the final article in this collection, we bring together the main conclusions from the individual articles and identify priorities for moving toward an evidence-based approach to preventing crime.

The Campbell Collaboration Crime and Justice Group has begun the important task of preparing systematic reviews of the effectiveness of a wide range of criminological interventions and will soon be in a position to make them accessible to researchers, policy makers, practitioners, and the general public. We argue that alongside the Campbell effort, a program of research of new crime prevention and intervention experiments and quasi-experiments must be initiated. These need to be evaluated using the most rigorous research designs, involve large samples, have long-term follow-up periods, and include cost-benefit or cost-effectiveness analyses. These new studies should be initiated in many Western countries.

It is a well-known fact that having convincing research evidence and having it influence policy and practice are two very different matters. How to overcome some of the misconceived political and policy barriers to get more of what works in preventing crime into policy and practice is by no means an easy task, but fortunately it has received some attention in various academic disciplines, criminology included.

In the final analysis, a great deal of work needs to be done—by researchers, policy makers, practitioners, and politicians (in no order of importance)—to achieve the well-intentioned yet lofty goal of using the highest-quality scientific evidence in the development of public policy and practice for the prevention of crime. We view this special issue of *The Annals* as an important step toward this goal. Of course, should it spur academic interest, encourage more systematic reviews, inspire further innovation among policy makers and practitioners, and ignite the interest of politicians, these too will be important effects.

DAVID P. FARRINGTON
BRANDON C. WELSH

Notes

1. We wish to personally thank Jerry Lee not only for his sponsorship of this important event but also for his unwavering support of an evidence-based approach to preventing crime and building safer communities. We are grateful to Lawrence Sherman for helping to organize this event (with David Farrington) and to Charles Wellford and his staff (especially Cynthia Mewborn) for their top-rate coordination and administration of the conference. Special thanks

also to Senator Barbara Mikulski and the Consortium of Social Science Associations for their assistance.

2. We discuss here only the systematic review method because systematic reviews employ meta-analysis when appropriate and possible.

References

Campbell, Donald T. 1969. Reforms as Experiments. *American Psychologist* 24:409-29.

Davies, Huw T. O., Sandra M. Nutley, and Peter C. Smith. 1999. Editorial: What Works? The Role of Evidence in Public Sector Policy and Practice. *Public Money & Management* 19:3-5.

Davies, Huw T. O., Sandra M. Nutley, and Peter C. Smith, eds. 2000. *What Works? Evidence-Based Policy and Practice in Public Services*. Bristol, UK: Policy Press.

Farrington, David P. 1983. Randomized Experiments on Crime and Justice. In *Crime and Justice: An Annual Review of Research*. Vol. 4, ed. Michael Tonry and Norval Morris. Chicago: University of Chicago Press.

Farrington, David P. and Anthony Petrosino. 2000. Systematic Reviews of Criminological Interventions: The Campbell Collaboration Crime and Justice Group. *International Annals of Criminology* 38:49-66.

Farrington, David P., Anthony Petrosino, and Brandon C. Welsh. 2001. Systematic Reviews and Cost-Benefit Analyses of Correctional Interventions. *The Prison Journal* 81:338-58.

Sherman, Lawrence W., David P. Farrington, Brandon C. Welsh, and Doris Layton MacKenzie, eds. Forthcoming. *Evidence-Based Crime Prevention*. London: Routledge.

Sherman, Lawrence W., Denise C. Gottfredson, Doris Layton MacKenzie, John E. Eck, Peter Reuter, and Shawn D. Bushway. 1997. *Preventing Crime: What Works, What Doesn't, What's Promising*. Washington, DC: U.S. Department of Justice, National Institute of Justice.

ANNALS, *AAPSS*, **578**, November 2001

Meeting the Challenges of Evidence-Based Policy: The Campbell Collaboration

By ANTHONY PETROSINO, ROBERT F. BORUCH, HALUK SOYDAN, LORNA DUGGAN, and JULIO SANCHEZ-MECA

ABSTRACT: Evidence-based policy has much to recommend it, but it also faces significant challenges. These challenges reside not only in the dilemmas faced by policy makers but also in the quality of the evaluation evidence. Some of these problems are most effectively addressed by rigorous syntheses of the literature known as systematic reviews. Other problems remain, including the range of quality in systematic reviews and their general failure to be updated in light of new evidence or disseminated beyond the research community. Based on the precedent established in health care by the international Cochrane Collaboration, the newly formed Campbell Collaboration will prepare, maintain, and make accessible systematic reviews of research on the effects of social and educational interventions. Through mechanisms such as rigorous quality control, electronic publication, and worldwide coverage of the literature, the Campbell Collaboration seeks to meet challenges posed by evidence-based policy.

Anthony Petrosino is a research fellow at the Center of Evaluation, American Academy of Arts and Sciences and coordinator for the Campbell Crime and Justice Group.

Robert F. Boruch is University Trustee Professor at the University of Pennsylvania Graduate School of Education and cochair of the Campbell Collaboration Steering Group.

Haluk Soydan is the director of the Center for Evaluation at the Center for Evaluation, Swedish National Board of Health and Welfare and a cochair of the Campbell Collaboration Steering Group.

Lorna Duggan is a forensic psychiatrist in the United Kingdom and reviewer for the Cochrane Collaboration.

Julio Sanchez-Meca is a psychology professor at the University of Murcia in Spain and the director of the Unit for Meta-Analysis.

NOTE: We appreciate the assistance of Maureen Matkovich and colleagues at the National Criminal Justice Reference Service who supplied the data in Figure 1. The first author's work was supported by grants from the Mellon Foundation to the Center for Evaluation and from the Home Office to Cambridge University. Thanks to Brandon C. Welsh for his comments on earlier drafts of the article.

DONALD Campbell (1969) was an influential psychologist who wrote persuasively about the need for governments to take evaluation evidence into account in decisions about social programs. He also recognized, however, the limitations of the evidence-based approach and the fact that government officials would be faced with a number of political dilemmas that confined their use of research. The limits of evidence-based policy and practice, however, reside not only in the political pressures faced by decision makers when implementing laws and administrative directives or determining budgets; they also reside in problems with the research evidence.

Questions such as, What works to reduce crime in communities? are not easily answered. The studies that bear on these questions are often scattered across different fields and written in different languages, are sometimes disseminated in obscure or inaccessible outlets, and can be of such questionable quality that interpretation is risky at best. How can policy and practice be informed, if not persuaded, by such a fragmented knowledge base comprising evaluative studies that range in quality? Which study, or set of studies, if any at all, ought to be used to influence policy? What methods ought to be used to appraise and analyze a set of separate studies bearing on the same question? And how can the findings be disseminated in such a way that the very people Donald Campbell cared about—the decision makers in government and elsewhere—receive findings from these analyses that they trust were not the product of advocacy?

Donald Campbell unfortunately did not live long enough to bear witness to the creation of the international collaboration named in his honor that ambitiously attempts to address some of the challenges posed by evidence-based policy. The Campbell Collaboration was created to prepare, update, and disseminate systematic reviews of evidence on what works relevant to social and educational intervention (see http://campbell.gse.upenn.edu). The target audience will include decision makers at all levels of government, practitioners, citizens, media, and researchers.

This article begins with a discussion of the rationale for the Campbell Collaboration. We then describe the precedent established by the Cochrane Collaboration in health care. This is followed by an overview of the advent and early progress of the Campbell Collaboration. We conclude with the promise of the Campbell Collaboration in meeting the challenges posed by evidence-based policy.

RATIONALE

*Surge of interest in
  evidence-based policy*

There are many influences on decisions or beliefs about what ought to be done to address problems like crime, illiteracy, and unemployment. Influential factors include ideology, politics, costs, ethics, social background, clinical experience, expert opinion, and anecdote (for example,

Lipton 1992). The evidence-based approach stresses moving beyond these factors to also consider the results of scientific studies. Although few writers have articulated the deterministic view that the term "evidence-based" suggests, it is clear that the vast majority of writers argue that decision makers need to—at the very least—be aware of the research evidence that bears on policies under consideration (for example, Davies, Nutley, and Smith 2000). Certainly the implicit or explicit goal of research-funding agencies has always been to influence policy through science (Weiss and Petrosino 1999), and there have always been individuals who have articulated the need for an evidence-based approach (for example, Fischer 1978). But there has been a surge of interest, particularly in the 1990s, in arguments for research-, science-, or evidence-based policy (for example, Amann 2000; Boruch, Petrosino, and Chalmers 1999; Nutley and Davies 1999; Wiles 2001).

One indirect gauge of this surge is the amount of academic writing on the topic. For example, in Sherman's (1999) argument for evidence-based policing, decisions about where to target police strategies would be based on epidemiological data about the nature and scope of problems. The kinds of interventions employed, and how long they were kept in place, would be guided by careful evaluative studies, preferably randomized field trials. Cullen and Gendreau (2000) and MacKenzie (2000) are among those who made similar arguments about correctional treatment. Davies (1999), Fitz-

Gibbon (1999), MacDonald (1999), and Sheldon and Chilvers (2000), among others, articulated views about evidence-based education and social welfare.

A more persuasive indicator that evidence-based policy is having some impact is initiatives undertaken by governments since the late 1990s. Whether due to growing pragmatism or pressures for accountability on how public funds are spent, the evidence-based approach is beginning to take root. For example, the United Kingdom is promoting evidence-based policy in medicine and the social sectors vigorously (for example, Davies, Nutley, and Smith 2000; Wiles 2001). In 1997, its Labour government was elected using the slogan, "What counts is what works" (Davies, Nutley, and Smith 2000). The 1998 U.K. Crime Reduction Programme was greatly influenced by both the University of Maryland report to Congress on crime prevention (Sherman et al. 1997) and the Home Office's own syntheses (Nuttall, Goldblatt, and Lewis 1998). In Sweden, the National Board of Health and Welfare was commissioned by the government to draft a program for advancing knowledge in the social services to ensure they are evidence based (National Board of Health and Welfare 2001).

In the United States, the Government Performance and Review Act of 1993 was implemented to hold federal agencies responsible for identifying measurable objectives and reaching them. This has led to the development of performance indicators to assess whether there is value added by agencies. The 1998 reauthorization of the Safe and Drug Free Schools and Communities Act required that programs funded under the law be research based. The news media now commonly ask why police are not using research-based eyewitness identification techniques (Gawande 2001) or why schools use ineffective drug prevention programs (for example, Cohn 2001).

All of these signs seem to indicate more than a passing interest in evidence-based policy. As Boruch (1997) noted, different policy questions require different types of scientific evidence. To implement the most effective interventions to ameliorate problems, careful evaluations are needed. An evidence-based approach to what works therefore requires that these evaluations be gathered, appraised, and analyzed and that the results be made accessible to influence relevant decisions whenever appropriate and possible.

Challenges to evidence-based policy: Evaluation studies

If evidence-based policy requires that we cull prior evaluation studies, researchers face significant challenges in doing so. For one, the relevant evaluations are not tidily reported in a single source that we can consult. Instead they are scattered across different academic fields. For example, medical, psychological, educational, and economic researchers more routinely include crime measures as dependent variables in their studies (for example, Greenberg and Shroder 1997). These evaluations are as relevant as those reported in justice journals.

Coinciding with fragmentation, evaluation studies are not regularly published in academic journals or in outlets that are readily accessible. Instead a large percentage of evaluative research resides in what Sechrest, White, and Brown (1979) called the fugitive literature. These are government reports, dissertations and master's theses, conference papers, technical documents, and other literature that is difficult to obtain. Lipsey (1992), in his review of delinquency prevention and treatment studies, found 4 in 10 were reported in this literature. Although some may argue that unpublished studies are of lesser quality because they have not been subjected to blind peer review as journal articles are, this is an empirical question worthy of investigation. Such an assertion, at the very least, ignores the high-quality evaluations done by private research firms. Evaluators in such entities do not have organizational incentives to publish in peer-reviewed journals, as professors or university-based researchers do.

Relevant studies are not reported solely within the confines of the United States or other English-speaking nations. Recently the Kellogg Foundation supported an international project that has identified more than 30 national evaluation societies, including those in Brazil, Ghana, Korea, Sri Lanka, Thailand, and Zimbabwe (see http://home.wmis.net/~russon/icce/eorg.htm). One argument is that it is not important to consider evaluations conducted outside of one's jurisdiction because the cultural context will be very different. This is

FIGURE 1
CUMULATIVE GROWTH OF EVALUATION STUDIES:
NATIONAL CRIMINAL JUSTICE REFERENCE SERVICE DATABASE

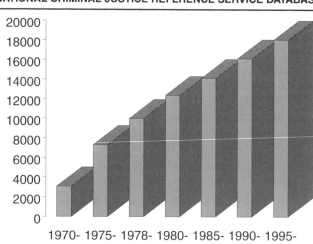

SOURCE: The National Criminal Justice Reference Service (www.ncjrs.org).

another assertion worthy of empirical test. Harlen (1997) noted that many in education believe evaluative studies and findings from different jurisdictions are not relevant to each other. This ignores the reality that interventions are widely disseminated across jurisdiction without concern for context. For example, the officer-led drug prevention program known as D.A.R.E. (Drug Abuse Resistance Education) is now in 44 nations (Weiss and Petrosino 1999). Harlen (1997) suggested that we must investigate the role of context across these evaluations. This is most effectively done through rigorous research reviews. Such reviews, however, are difficult with international literature without translation capabilities.

Another challenge to gathering evaluative studies is that there is no finite time by which the production of this evidence stops. Research, including evaluation, is cumulatively increasing (Boruch, Petrosino, and Chalmers 1999). An example is provided in Figure 1. Consider the cumulative growth of studies indexed either as evaluation or as evaluative study by the National Criminal Justice Reference Service for its database of abstracts. The data underscore the challenge faced in coping with the burgeoning evaluation literature.

It would be good to identify and acquire all relevant evaluations and keep abreast of new studies as they become available. It would be even better if all evaluations were of similar methodological quality and came to the same conclusion about the effectiveness of the intervention. Unfortunately not all evaluations are created equal. The results across studies of the same intervention will often differ, and sometimes those differences will be related to the quality of the methods used (see Weisburd, Lum, and Petrosino 2001). This highlights the importance of appraising evaluation studies for methodological quality.

Challenges to evidence-based policy: Reviewing methods

But what is the best way to draw upon these existing evaluation studies to understand what works and develop evidence-based policy? Certainly, relying on one or a few studies when others are available is very risky because it ignores evidence. For example, relying on one study if five relevant studies have been completed means that we ignore 80 percent of the evidence (Cook et al. 1992). It is true that the one study we pick may be representative of all the other studies, but as mentioned previously, studies in an area often conflict rather than converge. Evaluation studies themselves are part of a sampling distribution and may differ because of chance probability. Until we do a reasonable job of collecting those other studies, an assertion of convergence based on an inadequate sampling of studies is unsupported.

Criminologists have generally understood the problem of drawing conclusions from incomplete evidence and have a half century's experience in conducting broad surveys of the literature to identify relevant evaluations (for example, Bailey 1966; Kirby 1954; Lipton, Martinson, and Wilks 1975; Logan 1972; Witmer and Tufts 1954). Although a few of these earlier syntheses were remarkably exhaustive, the science of reviewing that developed in the 1970s focused attention on the methods used in reviews of research.

Methods for analyzing separate but similar studies have a century of experience (Chalmers, Hedges, and Cooper in press), but it was not until the 1970s that reviews became scrutinized like primary reports of surveys and experiments. This was ironic, as some of the most influential and widely cited articles across fields were literature reviews (Chalmers, Hedges, and Cooper in press). Beginning in the 1970s, not only were the traditional reviews of evaluations under attack, but the modern statistical foundation for meta-analysis or quantitative analysis of study results was also being developed (for example, Glass, McGaw, and Smith 1981; Hedges and Olkin 1985). Research confirmed that traditional reviews, in which researchers make relative judgments about what works by using some unknown and inexplicit process of reasoning, were fraught with potential for bias (Cooper and Hedges 1994). Quinsey (1983) underscored how such bias could affect conclusions about research following his review of research on sex offender treatment effects: "The difference in recidivism across these studies is truly remarkable; clearly by selectively contemplating the various studies, one can conclude anything one wants" (101).

One major problem noted with regard to traditional reviews was their lack of explicitness about the methods used, such as why certain studies were included, the search methods used, and how the studies were analyzed. This includes the criteria used to judge whether an intervention was effective or not. Consider the debate over the conclusions in the Lipton, Martinson, and Wilks (1975) summary of more than 200 correctional program evaluations, briskly reported first by Martinson (1974). Despite finding that nearly half of the evaluations reported in Martinson's article had at least one statistically significant finding in favor of treatment, his overall conclusions were gloomy about the prospects of correctional intervention. The criterion for success was not readily apparent, but it must have been strict (Palmer 1975).

These earlier reviews, like Martinson's (1974), were also problematic because they seemed to rely on statistical significance as the criterion for judging whether an intervention was successful. This later proved to be problematic, as research showed that statistical significance is the function not only of the size of the treatment effect but of methodological factors such as sample size (for example, Lipsey 1990). For example, large and meaningful effects reported in studies with small samples would be statistically insignificant; the investigator and traditional reviewer would consider the finding evidence that treatment did not succeed. Given that most social science research uses small samples, moderate and important intervention effects have often been interpreted as statistically insignificant and therefore as treatment failures.

Systematic reviews

Evidence-based policy requires overcoming these and other problems with the evaluation studies and methods for reviewing them. There is consensus among those who advocate evidence-based policy that systematic reviews are an important tool in this process (Davies 1999; Nutley, Davies, and Tilley 2000). In systematic reviews, researchers attempt to gather relevant evaluative studies, critically appraise them, and come to judgments about what works using explicit, transparent, state-of-the-art methods. Systematic reviews will include detail about each stage of the decision process, including the question that guided the review, the criteria for studies to be included, and the methods used to search for and screen evaluation reports. It will also detail how analyses were done and how conclusions were reached.

The foremost advantage of systematic reviews is that when done well and with full integrity, they provide the most reliable and comprehensive statement about what works. Such a final statement, after sifting through the available research, may be, "We know little or nothing—proceed with caution." This can guide funding agencies and researchers toward an agenda for a new generation of evaluation studies. This can also include feedback to funding agencies where additional process, implementation, and theory-driven studies would be critical to implement.

Systematic reviews, therefore, are reviews in which rigorous methods are employed regardless of whether meta-analysis is undertaken to summarize, analyze, and combine study findings. When meta-analysis is used, however, estimates of the average impact across studies, as well as how much variation there is and why, can be provided. Meta-analysis can generate clues as to why some programs are more effective in some settings and others are not. Meta-analysis is also critical in ruling out the play of chance when combining results (Hedges and Olkin 1985).

Systematic reviews have other byproducts. They can reconcile differences between studies. Because each study document is scrutinized, systematic reviews can underscore deficiencies in report writing and lead to better systems for collecting data required by reviewers. Reviews also ensure that relevant evaluations—which may have been ignored and long forgotten—are eternally utilized. It is satisfying to investigators to find their studies still considered 20 years or more after completion (Petrosino forthcoming).

Systematic reviews have been influential. This is understandable, as Weiss (1978) predicted that policy makers would find good syntheses of research compelling because they would reconcile conflicting studies when possible and provide a comprehensive resource for their aides to consult. Hunt (1997) discussed how the results from meta-analysis contradicted conclusions in earlier traditional reviews, in areas such as psychotherapy, class size, and school funding. Palmer (1994) noted that meta-analyses like Lipsey's (1992) helped to counter the prevailing pessimism about the efficacy of correctional treatment generated by earlier reviews.

Challenges to evidence-based policy: Current systematic reviews

There seems to be growing convergence among researchers and others that systematic reviews are a critical tool for evidence-based policy (for example, Nutley, Davies, and Tilley 2000). This is reflected in the decision by the United Kingdom's most prestigious social science funding agency, the Economic and Social Research Council, to support an evidence-based policy and practice initiative featuring systematic reviews (see http://www.esrc.ac.uk/EBPesrcUKcentre.htm). On closer scrutiny, however, we find that there are some challenges to the use of systematic reviews in evidence-based policy as they are currently done.

One problem is that there is often a lack of transparency in the review process. Completed syntheses are generally submitted to peer-reviewed journals, long after the research question has been determined and the methods selected. Except for rare occasions in which reviewers submit a grant proposal for funding, researchers do not a priori describe why they are doing the review and what methods they will employ. Without transparent processes from beginning to end, ex post facto decisions that can influence a review and slant it knowingly or unknowingly toward one conclusion or another are possible. This is especially important in persuading policy makers who want to be sure that research is not the product of slick advocacy.

Because there is no uniform quality control process, systematic reviews, like evaluations, range on a continuum of quality. In some cases, the quality is due to the methods employed. Some reviewers may use meta-analytic methods but inadequately describe their decision process. Other reviews may detail exhaustive search processes but then use questionable methods for analysis. It is difficult for even the discerning reader to know how trustworthy the findings are from a particular review. In other cases, the quality of the review is due to the way it is reported. Sometimes the nature of the outlet dictates how explicit and transparent the reviewers can be. Some reviews, particularly those prepared for academic print journals with concerns about page lengths, are briskly written. Dissertations and technical reports are usually very detailed but are less accessible to readers. Systematic reviews may all contain Materials and Methods sections, but the level of detail in each may vary depending on the dissemination outlet.

Policy makers and other interested users of research have a wide range of questions about what works to which they want answers. Although funding agencies will sponsor reviews at times to meet these information needs, reviews are generally conducted because of the interests of individual researchers. For example, in criminology, offender treatment has been a controversial and popular topic and the target of most systematic review activity (Petrosino 2000). Other important areas for review such as police training, services for crime victims, court backlog interventions, and so on have been inadequately covered. Evidence-based policy requires that evaluations in these areas be synthesized, even if they are less relevant to longstanding criminological debates.

Even if reviews did cover many more questions than they currently do, they are often not disseminated in such ways that decision makers and the public can get them. All too often, reviews are published by academics in peer-reviewed journals, outlets that are not consulted by policy makers. In fact, decision makers often get their information about research from news media, which can selectively cover only a few of the thousands of evaluative studies relevant to crime and justice reported each year (Weiss and Singer 1988). Tyden (1996) wrote that publishing an academic paper to disseminate to policy makers was akin to shooting it over a wall, blindly, into water. The path to utilization by decision makers was haphazard at best.

To examine dissemination further, we analyzed the citations for 302 meta-analyses reported by Lipsey and Wilson (1993) of psychological and educational treatment studies. Nearly two-thirds listed in the reference section were published in academic journals. These were scattered across 93 journals during the years covered (1977-1991). Only the *Review of Educational Research* published an average of one review or more per year. Unless researchers were using other unknown mechanisms such as oral briefings and internal memos to communicate to decision makers, it seems very unlikely that this evidence got into the hands of anyone other than research specialists working in narrow areas.

Most systematic reviews also tend to be one-off exercises, conducted only as funding, interest, or time permits. Rarely are they updated to take into account new studies that are relevant to the review, a challenge that is more significant given the cumulative growth of evaluation reports highlighted in Figure 1. Yet years may go by before an investigator pursues funding to update an existing review. The methodology and statistical foundation for meta-analysis is still rapidly evolving, with improved techniques and new software being developed to solve data problems. It is rare to find reviews that take into account these new techniques, conducting analyses to determine if results using different methods converge.

Some reviewers publish in print journals, an inefficient method for disseminating reviews. Because print journals find them too costly, cases in which reviewers take into account cogent criticisms by others and conduct reanalysis are rarely reported. Unlike medical journals, criminological journals do not have a strong tradition in routinely printing letters to the editor that respond to criticisms with additional analyses.

Some journals also have lengthy lag times between submission and publication, delaying the dissemination of evidence even further.

THE COCHRANE COLLABORATION

Are there ways of overcoming challenges to using systematic reviews in evidence-based policy? A precedent for doing so was established in the health care field. Archie Cochrane was a noted epidemiologist who wrote persuasively about the need for medical practitioners to take scientific evidence into account in their practice. Cochrane (1972) lamented the fact that although randomized trials had shown some practices to be effective and others harmful, clinical practitioners and medical schools were ignoring the information. He later (Cochrane 1979) wondered why the medical sciences had not yet organized all relevant trials into subspecialties so that decision makers could take such evidence into account. A protégé of Cochrane, an obstetrician turned researcher named Iain Chalmers, soon identified and reviewed randomized trials relevant to childbirth and prenatal interventions (see www.cochrane.org).

In the early 1990s, the U.K. National Health Service (NHS), under the direction of Sir Michael Peckham, initiated the Research and Development Programme with the goal of establishing an evidence-based resource for health care. Because of the success of their earlier project on childbirth and pregnancy studies, Chalmers and his colleagues were asked to extend this effort to all areas of health care intervention. The U.K. Cochrane Centre was established, with core funding from the NHS, to begin the work. It soon became clear that the amount of work far surpassed the capacity of one center or one nation to take into account. In 1993, in honor of his mentor, Chalmers and his colleagues launched the international Cochrane Collaboration to "help people make well-informed decisions about healthcare by preparing, maintaining and promoting the accessibility of systematic reviews of the effects of healthcare interventions." In just 8 years, the Cochrane Collaboration has been able to organize thousands of individuals worldwide to contribute to its work. Much more information about the Cochrane Collaboration can be found at its Web site, www.cochrane. org. But the Cochrane Collaboration, in a very brief time, established a number of mechanisms to address challenges to using systematic reviews in evidence-based health care policy.

For example, collaborative review groups (CRGs) are responsible for the core work of systematic reviewing. CRGs are international networks of individuals interested in particular health areas such as breast cancer, epilepsy, injuries, and stroke. Each CRG has an editorial board, generally comprising persons with scientific or practical expertise in the area, who are responsible for quality control of protocols (plans) and completed drafts of reviews.

It is useful to examine how a Cochrane review is prepared. First, individuals approach the CRG in which the intended topic area seems appropriate. Once a title for the proposed review is agreed on, it is circulated to ensure that no other similar reviews are being prepared by reviewers from other CRGs. Reducing overlap and duplication is a crucial goal for the Cochrane Collaboration, as scarce resources must be used judiciously. Reviews are needed in so many areas of health care that wide coverage is a priority. Once the title is agreed on, the reviewers must then submit a protocol for the review. The protocol is a detailed plan that spells out a priori the question to be answered, the background to the issue, and the methods to be employed. The protocol then goes through a round or two of criticism by the CRG editors. It must conform to a certain template to facilitate electronic publication using the Cochrane Collaboration's software, *Review Manager*, or *RevMan*. Once the protocol is approved, it is published in the next edition of the quarterly electronic publication, the *Cochrane Library*, and made available to all subscribers for comment and criticism. The editorial board must decide which criticisms should be taken into account.

The reviewers then prepare the review according to the protocol. Although deviation from the plan is sometimes necessary, the protocol forces a prospective, transparent process. Post hoc changes are readily detected, and analyses can be done to determine if they altered findings. After the reviewers conduct the review and write up a draft, it too is submitted to the CRG editorial board. Once the review draft is completed, the editors critique it again. It is also sent to external readers, including researchers as well as practitioners and patients. This round of criticism is designed to improve the methods in the review and to ensure that the final review is written as accessibly as possible to a nonresearch audience, including health care patients, providers, and citizens. For each completed Cochrane review, the Cochrane Consumer Network crafts a one-page synopsis written accessibly for patients and other consumers and posts the synopses at its Web site (see http://www.cochrane.org/cochrane/consumer.htm). Once the review is approved, it is published in the next issue of the *Cochrane Library* and again made available for external criticism by subscribers. Again the editors and the reviewers have to determine which of these criticisms ought to be taken into account in a subsequent review update. Cochrane reviews must be updated every 2 years, to take into account new studies meeting eligibility criteria.

Another important mechanism for the Cochrane Collaboration is the methods groups. These are international networks of individuals who conduct systematic reviews focused on the methods used in systematic reviews and primary studies. For example, a methods group might collect all systematic reviews in which randomized trials are compared to nonrandomized trials. In this review, they would seek to determine if there is a consistent relationship between the reporting of random assignment and results. Their objective is to make sure that decisions in reviews, such as setting eligibility criteria, be informed as much as possible by evidence. The Cochrane Collaboration is also facilitated by 15 centers around the world; they promote the interests of the collaboration within host countries, train people in doing systematic reviews, and identify potential collaborators and end users. Finally Cochrane fields and networks, such as the Cochrane Consumer Network, focus on dimensions of health care other than health problems and work to ensure that their priorities are reflected in systematic reviews.

The main product of the Cochrane Collaboration is the *Cochrane Library*. This electronic publication is updated quarterly and made available via the World Wide Web or through CD-ROMs mailed to subscribers. The January 2001 issue contained 1000 completed reviews and 832 protocols (or plans for a review) in one central location using the same format. Wolf (2000) noted that the uniformity allows the reader to understand and find all of the necessary information in each review, facilitating training and use. Another important feature of the *Cochrane Library* is the *Cochrane Controlled Trials Register* (*CCTR*). The *CCTR* has more than a quarter million citations to randomized trials relevant to health care, an important resource in assisting reviewers find studies so they can prepare and maintain their reviews.

Empirical studies have reported that Cochrane syntheses are more rigorous than non-Cochrane systematic reviews and meta-analyses published in medical journals. For example, Jadad and his colleagues (1998) found that Cochrane reviews provided more detail, were more likely to test for methodological effects, were less likely to be restricted by language barriers, and were updated more than print journal reviews. The *Cochrane Library* is quickly becoming recognized as the best single source of evidence on the effectiveness of health care interventions (Egger and Davey-Smith 1998). Reviews by the Cochrane Collaboration are frequently used to generate and support guidelines by government agencies such as the National Institute for Clinical Excellence (for example, see Chalmers, Hedges, and Cooper in press). In 1999, the U.S. National Institutes of Health made the *Cochrane Library* available to all 16000 of its employees. It is now accessible by all doctors in Brazil, the U.K. NHS, and all U.K. universities (Mark Starr, personal communication, 2001). Finally the queen recognized Iain Chalmers for his efforts with the United Kingdom's greatest honor: knighthood!

Thus the Cochrane Collaboration has been able to meet many of the challenges posed by evidence-based policy in health care. By requiring detailed protocols, the Cochrane Collaboration addresses the lack of transparency in most systematic reviews of research. Through rigorous quality control, they produce commendable reviews. By publishing electronically, dissemination is quickened, and the ability to update and correct the reviews in light of new evidence is realized. By provid-ing an unbiased, single source for evidence and producing reviews, abstracts, and synopses for different audiences, they facilitate utilization.

THE CAMPBELL
COLLABORATION

With the success of the Cochrane Collaboration, the same type of organization was soon suggested for reviewing social and educational evaluations. Adrian Smith (1996), president of the Royal Statistical Society, issued a challenge when he said,

As ordinary citizens . . . we are, through the media, confronted daily with controversy and debate across a whole spectrum of public policy issues. Obvious topical examples include education—what does work in the classroom?—and penal policy—what is effective in reducing reoffending? Perhaps there is an opportunity . . . *to launch a campaign directed at developing analogues to the Cochrane Collaboration, to provide suitable evidence bases in other areas besides medicine* [emphasis added]. (378)

A number of individuals across different fields and professions organized and met to determine how best to meet this challenge. Several exploratory meetings were held during 1999, including two headed by the School of Public Policy at University College–London, and one organized in Stockholm by the National Board of Health and Welfare. These meetings, which included researchers and members of the policy and practice communities, provided evidence that the development of an infrastructure similar to Cochrane's for social and educational intervention including criminal justice should be vigorously pursued (Davies, Petrosino, and Chalmers 1999; www.ucl.ac.uk/spp/publications/campbell.htm).

Early days and progress

The Campbell Collaboration was officially inaugurated in February 2000 at a meeting in Philadelphia, with more than 80 individuals from 12 nations participating. The Campbell Collaboration was founded on nine principles developed first by the Cochrane Collaboration (see Table 1). At the February 2000 inaugural meeting, it was agreed that the headquarters (secretariat) should reside at the University of Pennsylvania. An international eight-member steering group was officially designated to guide its early development.

The first three Campbell coordinating groups (similar to Cochrane's CRGs) were created to facilitate systematic reviews in their areas: education, social welfare, and crime and justice. The Campbell Education Coordinating Group is focused on developing protocols and reviews in the following critical areas: truancy, mathematics learning, science learning, information technology learning, work-related learning and transferable skills, assessment and learning, comprehensive school reform, school leadership and management, professional education, and economics and education. The Campbell Social Welfare Coordinating Group has also organized itself into several areas: social work, transportation, housing, social casework with certain ethnic clientele, child welfare, and

employment programs within the welfare system. The early progress of the Campbell Crime and Justice Coordinating Group is described elsewhere in this issue (see Farrington and Petrosino 2001).

The Campbell Collaboration Methods Group was developed to increase the precision of Campbell reviews by conducting reviews to investigate the role of methodological and statistical procedures used in systematic reviews, as well as characteristics in original studies (see http://web.missouri.edu/~c2method). Three methods subgroups were created during the past year, including statistics, quasi-experiments, and

TABLE 1
PRINCIPLES OF THE CAMPBELL COLLABORATION

Collaborating by fostering open communication, cooperation, and transparency

Building on the enthusiasm of individuals by involving and supporting people of different skills and backgrounds

Avoiding unnecessary duplication by coordinating and maximizing economy of effort

Minimizing bias by maximizing scientific rigor, assuring broad participation, and avoiding conflicts of interest

Keeping current by ensuring that systematic reviews are kept up to date through incorporation of new evidence

Ensuring relevance by promoting reviews that use outcomes that matter to people making choices

Promoting access by widely disseminating the collaboration's products and taking advantage of strategic alliances

Ensuring quality by inviting critical comment, applying advances in methodology, and developing systems for quality improvement

Continuing to renew by updating reviews, editorial processes, and key functions and by engaging new collaborators

SOURCE: C2 Steering Group (2001).

FIGURE 2
C2-SPECTR

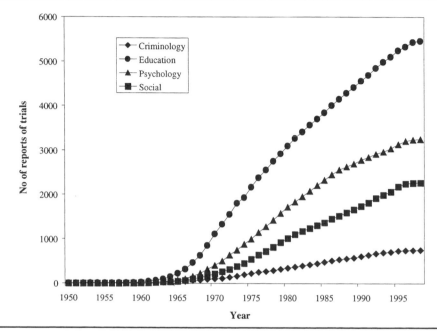

SOURCE: Petrosino et al. (2000).

process and implementation sub-groups. In conjunction with the Campbell secretariat and the coordinating groups, the methods group has taken the lead in developing a preliminary quality control process based on the Cochrane model (see Appendix A). The Campbell Communication and Dissemination Group will develop best practice in translating results to a variety of end users, including policy makers, practitioners, media, and the public.

To facilitate the work of reviewers, the *Campbell Collaboration Social, Psychological, Educational and Criminological Trials Register* (*C2-SPECTR*) is in development. As

Figure 2 shows, preliminary work toward *C2-SPECTR* has already identified more than 10000 citations to randomized or possibly randomized trials (Petrosino et al. 2000), and this has now been augmented with new additions to the data file. Like the *CCTR* in health care, *C2-SPECTR* should serve as a productive resource and facilitate preparation and maintenance of reviews. Plans to build a complimentary database of nonrandomized evaluations are being discussed.

During 2000, Campbell and Cochrane groups mutually participated in the NHS Wider Public Health Project (see www.york.ac.uk/

crd/publications/wphp.htm), an attempt to collate evidence from systematic reviews relevant to the United Kingdom's intended health policies. As the NHS now considers education, social welfare, and criminal justice directly or indirectly related to public health, Campbell groups were involved (for example, Petrosino 2000). Several hundred systematic—or possibly systematic—reviews were identified in these areas and can now be used to help us map the terrain and identify target areas where high-quality reviews are needed.

Funding from the Ministry of Social Affairs of Denmark has been acquired to establish a Campbell Center in Copenhagen to facilitate efforts in the Nordic region. Resources have also been secured to create the Meta-Analysis Unit at the University of Murcia in Spain (see http://www.um.es/sip/unidadmal. html), the first step in developing a Campbell Center for Mediterranean nations. Objectives of these centers include facilitating reviews through training, identifying end users and collaborators, and promoting dissemination and utilization.

These are just a few of the many developments in the early days of the Campbell Collaboration. Although the collaboration anticipates creating an electronic publication that will make available C2-SPECTR and other helpful resources, its critical product will be high-quality systematic reviews. For the Campbell Collaboration to achieve the kind of success Cochrane has obtained in the health care field, it will have to ensure that these reviews are as unbiased and technically sound as possible. Appendix B provides a preliminary model of stages in a Campbell review.

CONCLUSION

Donald Campbell articulated an evidence-based approach before the methods of systematic reviewing and meta-analysis became staples of empirical inquiry. Still we think he would be pleased with the efforts of hundreds of individuals who are working worldwide to advance the international collaboration that bears his name.

The challenges of evidence-based policy are many. We think the Campbell Collaboration will help to meet some of them. For example, with rigorous quality control and protocols, the Campbell Collaboration will attempt to produce the same level of transparency with unbiased reviews for which the Cochrane Collaboration is lauded. Through electronic publication of reviews in a single source (that is, *Campbell Library*), it will attempt to extend beyond communicating with researchers and facilitate dissemination and utilization by decision makers and ordinary citizens. Maintaining reviews, taking into account evidence worldwide, and preparing reviews using the best science available should enhance the use of Campbell reviews.

Systematic reviews are certainly an important tool for evidence-based policy, but like Campbell before us, we do not wish to zealously oversell scientific evidence. Systematic reviews will not resolve all enduring political and academic conflicts, nor will they often—if at all—provide neat and tidy prescriptions to decision makers on what they ought to do. In their proper role in evidence-based policy, they will enlighten by explicitly revealing what is known from scientific evidence and what is not. They will also generate more questions to be resolved. One unanticipated benefit in the short life of the Campbell Collaboration is the sustained forum it provides for discussions about evaluation design and how to engage people from around the world.

Criminology is a noble profession because it aims to reduce the misery stemming from crime and injustice. To the extent that this collaboration can fulfill Don Campbell's vision of assisting people in making well-informed decisions, it will help criminologists stay true to criminology's original and noble intent.

APPENDIX A
A FLOW CHART OF THE STEPS IN THE CAMPBELL REVIEW QUALITY CONTROL PROCESS

Reviewer defines the research question or topic
↓
Reviewer submits the title and expected completion date to the relevant area coordinator
↓
Coordinator and committee chair assign project to a primary editor
↓
Reviewer begins the literature search with assistance from the primary editor
↓
Reviewer develops the review protocol
↓
Editorial team (including a methodologist and external reviewer[s]) reviews the protocol
↓
Editorial team submits the protocol to the Campbell Database
↓
Reviewer completes the literature searching, quality assessment of primary studies, data extraction, and analysis
↓
Reviewer writes and submits a draft review to primary editor
↓
Reviewer receives and incorporates feedback from the editorial team
↓
Reviewer submits a second draft
↓
Primary editor obtains external reviews of second draft
↓
Reviewer incorporates feedback from external reviewer
↓
Reviewer submits final review
↓
Review is published

SOURCE: C2 Steering Group (2001).

APPENDIX B
STAGES OF A CAMPBELL SYSTEMATIC REVIEW

1. Formulate review questions
2. Define inclusion and exclusion criteria
   · Participants
   · Interventions and comparisons
   · Outcomes
   · Study designs and methodological quality
3. Locate studies; develop search strategy considering the following sources:
   · C2-SPECTR
   · Electronic databases and trials registers not covered by C2-SPECTR
   · Checking of reference lists

- Hand searching of key journals
- Personal communication with experts in the field
4. Select studies
    - Have eligibility checked by more than one observer
    - Develop strategy to resolve disagreements
    - Keep log of excluded studies, with reasons for exclusions
5. Assess study quality
    - Consider assessment by more than one observer
    - Use simple checklists rather than quality scales
    - Assess handling of attrition
    - Consider blinding assessors to authors, institutions, and journals
    - Assess randomization and power
6. Extract data
    - Design and pilot data extraction form
    - Consider data extraction by more than one extractor
    - Consider blinding of extractors to authors, institutions, and journals
7. Analyze and present results
    - Tabulate results from individual studies
    - Examine plots
    - Explore possible sources of heterogeneity
    - Consider meta-analysis of all trials or subgroups of trials
    - Perform sensitivity analyses, examine funnel plots
    - Make list of excluded studies available to interested readers
    - Examine process/implementation of interventions
8. Interpret results
    - Consider limitations, including publication and related biases
    - Consider strength of evidence
    - Consider applicability
    - Consider statistical power
    - Consider economic implications
    - Consider implications for future research

SOURCE: C2 Steering Group (2001).

References

Amann, Ron. 2000. Foreword. In *What Works? Evidence-Based Policy and Practice in Public Services*, ed. Huw T. O. Davies, Sandra Nutley, and Peter C. Smith. Bristol, UK: Policy Press.

Bailey, William C. 1966. Correctional Outcome: An Evaluation of 100 Reports. *Journal of Criminal Law, Criminology and Police Science* 57:153-60.

Boruch, Robert F. 1997. *Randomized Experiments for Planning and Evaluation: A Practical Guide*. Thousand Oaks, CA: Sage.

Boruch, Robert F., Anthony Petrosino, and Iain Chalmers. 1999. The Campbell Collaboration: A Proposal for Multinational, Continuous and Systematic Reviews of Evidence. In *Proceedings of the International Meeting on Systematic Reviews of the Effects of Social and Educational Interventions July 15-16*, ed. Philip Davies, Anthony Petrosino, and Iain Chalmers. London: University College–London, School of Public Policy.

Campbell, Donald T. 1969. Reforms as Experiments. *American Psychologist* 24:409-29.

Chalmers, Iain, Larry V. Hedges, and Harris Cooper. In press. A Brief History of Research Synthesis. *Evaluation & the Health Professions*.

Cochrane, Archie L. 1972. *Effectiveness and Efficiency. Random Reflections on Health Services*. London: Nuffield Provincial Hospitals Trust.

———. 1979. 1931-1971: A Critical Review, with Particular Reference to the Medical Profession. In *Medicines for the Year 2000*. London: Office of Health Economics.

Cohn, Jason. 2001. Drug Education: The Triumph of Bad Science. *Rolling Stone* 869:41-42, 96.

Cook, Thomas D., Harris Cooper, David S. Cordray, Heidi Hartmann, Larry V. Hedges, Richard J. Light, Thomas A.

Louis, and Frederick Mosteller, eds. 1992. *Meta-Analysis for Explanation*. New York: Russell Sage.

Cooper, Harris C. and Larry V. Hedges, eds. 1994. *The Handbook of Research Synthesis*. New York: Russell Sage.

C2 Steering Group. 2001. *C2: Concept, Status, Plans. Overarching Grant Proposal*. Philadelphia: Campbell Collaboration Secretariat.

Cullen, Francis T. and Paul Gendreau. 2000. Assessing Correctional Rehabilitation: Policy, Practice, and Prospects. In *Policies, Processes, and Decisions of the Criminal Justice System, Criminal Justice 2000*, vol. 3, ed. Julie Horney. Washington, DC: National Institute of Justice.

Davies, Huw T. O., Sandra M. Nutley, and Peter C. Smith, eds. 2000. *What Works? Evidence-Based Policy in Public Services*. Bristol, UK: Policy Press.

Davies, Phillip. 1999. What Is Evidence-Based Education? *British Journal of Educational Studies* 47:108-21.

Davies, Philip, Anthony Petrosino, and Iain Chalmers, eds. 1999. *Proceedings of the International Meeting on Systematic Reviews of the Effects of Social and Educational Interventions, July 15-16*. London: University College–London, School of Public Policy.

Egger, Matthias and George Davey-Smith. 1998. Bias in Location and Selection of Studies. *British Medical Journal* 316:61-66.

Farrington, David P. and Anthony Petrosino. 2001. The Campbell Collaboration Crime and Justice Group. *Annals of the American Academy of Political and Social Science* 578:35-49.

Fischer, Joel. 1978. Does Anything Work? *Journal of Social Service Research* 1:215-43.

Fitz-Gibbon, Carol. 1999. Education: The High Potential Not Yet Realized. *Public Money & Management* 19:33-40.

Gawande, Atul. 2001. Under Suspicion. The Fugitive Science of Criminal Justice. *New Yorker*, 8 Jan., 50-53.

Glass, Gene V., Barry McGaw, and Mary L. Smith. 1981. *Meta-Analysis in Social Research*. London: Sage.

Greenberg, David and Mark Shroder. 1997. *The Digest of Social Experiments*. 2d ed. Washington, DC: Urban Institute Press.

Harlen, Wynne. 1997. Educational Research and Educational Reform. In *The Role of Research in Mature Educational Systems*, ed. Seamus Hegarty. Slough, UK: National Foundation for Educational Research.

Hedges, Larry V. and Ingram Olkin. 1985. *Statistical Methods for Meta-Analysis*. New York: Academic Press.

Hunt, Morton. 1997. *The Story of Meta-Analysis*. New York: Russell Sage.

Jadad, Alejandor R., Deborah J. Cook, Alison Jones, Terry P. Klassen, Peter Tugwell, Michael Moher, and David Moher. 1998. Methodology and Reports of Systematic Reviews and Meta-Analyses: A Comparison of Cochrane Reviews with Articles Published in Paper-Based Journals. *Journal of the American Medical Association* 280:278-80.

Kirby, Bernard C. 1954. Measuring Effects of Criminals and Delinquents. *Sociology and Social Research* 38:368-74.

Lipsey, Mark W. 1990. *Design Sensitivity: Statistical Power for Experimental Research*. Newbury Park, CA: Sage.

———. 1992. Juvenile Delinquency Treatment: A Meta-Analytic Inquiry into the Variability of Effects. In *Meta-Analysis for Explanation*, ed. Thomas D. Cook, Harris Cooper, David S. Cordray, Heidi Hartmann, Larry V. Hedges, Richard J. Light, Thomas A. Louis, and Frederick Mosteller. New York: Russell Sage.

Lipsey, Mark W. and David B. Wilson. 1993. The Efficacy of Psychological,

Educational and Behavioral Treatment: Confirmation from Meta-Analysis. *American Psychologist* 48:1181-209.

Lipton, Douglas S. 1992. How to Maximize Utilization of Evaluation Research by Policymakers. *Annals of the American Academy of Political and Social Science* 521:175-88.

Lipton, Douglas S., Robert Martinson, and Judith Wilks. 1975. *The Effectiveness of Correctional Treatment.* New York: Praeger.

Logan, Charles H. 1972. Evaluation Research in Crime and Delinquency: A Reappraisal. *Journal of Criminal Law, Criminology and Police Science* 63:378-87.

MacDonald, Geraldine. 1999. Evidence-Based Social Care: Wheels Off the Runway? *Public Money & Management* 19:25-32.

MacKenzie, Doris Layton. 2000. Evidence-Based Corrections: Identifying What Works. *Crime & Delinquency* 46:457-71.

Martinson, Robert. 1974. What Works? Questions and Answers About Prison Reform. *Public Interest* 10:22-54.

National Board of Health and Welfare. 2001. *A Programme of National Support for the Advancement of Knowledge in the Social Services.* Stockholm: Author.

Nutley, Sandra and Huw T. O. Davies. 1999. The Fall and Rise of Evidence in Criminal Justice. *Public Money & Management* 19:47-54.

Nutley, Sandra, Huw T. O. Davies, and Nick Tilley. 2000. Letter to the Editor. *Public Money & Management* 20:3-6.

Nuttall, Christopher, Peter Goldblatt, and Chris Lewis, eds. 1998. *Reducing Offending: An Assessment of Research Evidence on Ways of Dealing with Offending Behaviour.* London: Home Office.

Palmer, Ted. 1975. Martinson Revisited. *Journal of Research in Crime and Delinquency* 12:133-52.

———. 1994. *A Profile of Correctional Effectiveness and New Directions for Research.* Albany: State University of New York Press.

Petrosino, Anthony. 2000. Crime, Drugs and Alcohol. In *Evidence from Systematic Reviews of Research Relevant to Implementing the "Wider Public Health" Agenda*, Contributors to the Cochrane Collaboration and the Campbell Collaboration. York, UK: NHS Centre for Reviews and Dissemination.

———. Forthcoming. *What Works to Reduce Offending? A Systematic Review of 300 Randomized Field Trials in Crime Reduction.* New York: Oxford University Press.

Petrosino, Anthony, Robert F. Boruch, Cath Rounding, Steve McDonald, and Iain Chalmers. 2000. The Campbell Collaboration Social, Psychological, Educational and Criminological Trials Register (C2-SPECTR) to Facilitate the Preparation and Maintenance of Systematic Reviews of Social and Educational Interventions. *Evaluation Research in Education* 14:293-307.

Quinsey, Vernon L. 1983. Prediction of Recidivism and the Evaluation of Treatment Programs for Sexual Offenders. In *Sexual Aggression and the Law*, ed. Simon N. Verdun-Jones and A. A. Keltner. Burnaby, Canada: Simon Fraser University Criminology Research Centre.

Sechrest, Lee, Susan O. White, and Elizabeth D. Brown, eds. 1979. *The Rehabilitation of Criminal Offenders: Problems and Prospects.* Washington, DC: National Academy of Sciences.

Sheldon, Brian and Roy Chilvers. 2000. *Evidence-Based Social Care: A Study of Prospects and Problems.* Dorset, UK: Russell House.

Sherman, Lawrence W. 1999. Evidence-Based Policing. In *Ideas in American Policing*. Washington, DC: Police Foundation.

Sherman, Lawrence W., Denise C. Gottfredson, Doris Layton MacKenzie, John E. Eck, Peter Reuter, and Shawn D. Bushway. 1997. *Preventing Crime: What Works, What Doesn't, What's Promising*. Washington, DC: U.S. Department of Justice, National Institute of Justice.

Smith, Adrian. 1996. Mad Cows and Ecstasy: Chance and Choice in an Evidence-Based Society. *Journal of the Royal Statistical Society* 159:367-83.

Tyden, Thomas. 1996. The Contribution of Longitudinal Studies for Understanding Science Communication and Research Utilization. *Science Communication* 18:29.

Weisburd, David, Cynthia M. Lum, and Anthony Petrosino. 2001. Does Research Design Affect Study Outcomes? Findings from the Maryland Report Criminal Justice Sample. *Annals of the American Academy of Political and Social Science* 578:50-70.

Weiss, Carol Hirschon. 1978. Improving the Linkage Between Social Research and Public Policy. In *Knowledge and Policy: The Uncertain Connection*, ed. L. E. Lynn. Washington, DC: National Academy of Sciences.

Weiss, Carol Hirschon and Anthony Petrosino. 1999. Improving the Use of Research: The Case of D.A.R.E. Unpublished grant proposal to the Robert Wood Johnson Foundation, Substance Abuse Policy Research Program. Cambridge, MA: Harvard Graduate School of Education.

Weiss, Carol Hirschon and Eleanor Singer. 1988. *The Reporting of Social Science in the National Media*. New York: Russell Sage.

Wiles, Paul. 2001. Criminology in the 21st Century: Public Good or Private Interest? Paper presented at the meeting of the Australian and New Zealand Society of Criminology, University of Melbourne, Australia, Feb.

Witmer, Helen L. and Edith Tufts. 1954. *The Effectiveness of Delinquency Prevention Programs*. Washington, DC: U.S. Department of Health, Education and Welfare, Social Security Administration, Children's Bureau.

Wolf, Frederic M. 2000. Lessons to be Learned from Evidence-Based Medicine: Practice and Promise of Evidence-Based Medicine and Evidence-Based Education. *Medical Teacher* 22:251-59.

ANNALS, *AAPSS*, **578**, November 2001

The Campbell Collaboration Crime and Justice Group

By DAVID P. FARRINGTON and ANTHONY PETROSINO

ABSTRACT: Systematic reviews use rigorous methods for locating, appraising, and synthesizing evidence from prior evaluation studies. They have explicit objectives, explicit criteria for including or excluding studies, and a structured and detailed report. The Campbell Collaboration Crime and Justice Group aims to prepare and maintain systematic reviews of criminological interventions and to make them accessible electronically to scholars, practitioners, policy makers, and the general public. The major challenges include setting methodological criteria for including studies in reviews, securing continued funding, academics needing publications in scholarly journals, and coping with the volume of work needed to maintain high standards, including refereeing proposals and final reviews and dealing with correspondence and unsolicited proposals. The aim of making the best knowledge about the effectiveness of criminological interventions immediately available to everyone is ambitious and very important.

David P. Farrington is Professor of Psychological Criminology at the University of Cambridge and Jerry Lee Research Professor of Criminology at the Department of Criminology and Criminal Justice, University of Maryland.

Anthony Petrosino is a research fellow at the Center for Evaluation, Initiative for Children Program at the American Academy of Arts and Sciences and a research associate at Harvard University. He is also the coordinator of the Campbell Crime and Justice Coordinating Group.

NOTE: We are very grateful to the Home Office and to Paul Wiles, its director of research and statistics, for supporting the work of the Campbell Crime and Justice Coordinating Group. Anthony Petrosino was also supported by a Mellon Foundation grant to the Center for Evaluation, Initiative for Children Program.

WHAT works to reduce crime? How should offenders be dealt with so that they do not reoffend? What methods of preventing crime are most cost-effective? These are all questions to which citizens, as well as government officials, policy makers, practitioners, researchers, teachers, and the news media, deserve good answers. All such persons should have ready access to the most rigorous and up-to-date evidence on the effects of interventions designed to reduce crime and offending. The best evidence on what works should be quickly accessible to those who need it.

In recent years, a number of systematic reviews and meta-analyses have been carried out to discover what works to reduce crime. This article describes systematic reviews and then discusses a newly formed international network that will facilitate the production and accessibility of rigorous and continually updated evidence on what works in crime and justice: the Campbell Collaboration Crime and Justice Group. This network of researchers, policy makers, practitioners, and others from around the world will collaborate in preparing systematic reviews of high-quality research on the effects of criminological interventions.

These systematic reviews will be maintained and updated in light of new studies, cogent criticisms, or new methodological developments. They will be made readily accessible through the use of electronic publishing, the Internet and the World Wide Web, and traditional publishing methods. Through international collaboration, the Campbell Crime and Justice Group will ensure that relevant evaluation studies conducted all over the world will be taken into account in its systematic reviews and that the evidence from such reviews will be made accessible globally through language translation and worldwide dissemination.

CHARACTERISTICS OF
SYSTEMATIC REVIEWS

What are systematic reviews? These are reviews that use rigorous methods for locating, appraising, and synthesizing evidence from prior evaluation studies. They contain Methods and Results sections and are reported with the same level of detail that characterizes high-quality reports of original research. Other features of systematic reviews include the following:

1.   Objectives are explicit. The rationale for conducting the review is made clear.

2.   Eligibility criteria are explicit. The reviewers specify in detail why they included certain studies and rejected others. What was the minimum level of methodological quality? Did they consider only a particular type of evaluation design such as randomized experiments? Did the studies have to include a certain type of participant such as children or adults? What types of interventions were included? What kinds of outcome data had to be reported in the studies? All criteria or rules used in selecting eligible studies should be explicitly stated in the final report.

3. The search for studies is designed to reduce potential bias. There are many potential ways in which bias can compromise the results of a review. The reviewers must explicitly state how they conducted their search of potential studies to reduce such bias. How did they try to locate studies reported outside scientific journals? How did they try to locate studies in foreign languages? All bibliographic databases that were searched should be made explicit so that potential gaps in coverage can be identified.

4. Each study is screened according to eligibility criteria, with exclusions justified. The searches will undoubtedly locate many citations to and abstracts of potentially relevant studies. Each of the reports of these potentially relevant studies must be screened to determine if it meets the eligibility criteria for the review. A full listing of all excluded studies and the justifications for exclusion should be made available to readers.

5. The most complete data possible are assembled. The systematic reviewer will generally try to obtain all relevant evaluations meeting the eligibility criteria. In addition, all data relevant to the objectives of the review should be carefully extracted from each eligible report and coded and computerized. Sometimes original study documents lack important information. When possible, the systematic reviewer will attempt to obtain this data from the authors of the original report.

6. Quantitative techniques are used, when appropriate and possible, in analyzing results. Although there is still some confusion about the meaning of these terms, it is useful to distinguish between a systematic review and a meta-analysis. A meta-analysis involves the statistical or quantitative analysis of the results of prior research studies. Since it involves the statistical summary of data (for example, effect sizes), it requires a reasonable number of intervention studies that are sufficiently similar to be grouped together. For example, there may be little point in reporting a mean effect size based on a very small number of studies. Nevertheless quantitative methods can be very important in helping the reviewer determine the average effect of a particular intervention.

A systematic review may or may not include a meta-analysis. For example, a reviewer may find only a few studies meeting the eligibility criteria. Those studies may differ just enough in the operational definition of the intervention or in the way they were conducted to make formal meta-analysis inappropriate and potentially misleading. Another possibility is that a researcher may carry out a meta-analysis adequately but use inexplicit and potentially biased methods in conducting the search for relevant studies. In this case, the review would not be systematic.

7. The report is structured and detailed. The final report of a systematic review is structured and detailed so that the reader can understand each phase of the research, the decisions that were made, and the conclusions that were reached.

SYSTEMATIC REVIEWS IN CRIMINOLOGY

Petrosino (2000) was commissioned by the U.K. National Health Service to identify, retrieve, and summarize systematic reviews of research on the effects of interventions relevant to crime and drug or alcohol abuse. He used a variety of techniques to locate relevant reviews. He conducted electronic searches of 18 bibliographic databases and the World Wide Web, searched for citations from the reference lists of existing reviews, and contacted researchers for their own reviews or those of others in their files. Especially useful was his scrutiny of reviews already gathered and analyzed by other researchers such as Lipsey and Wilson (1993), Lösel (1995), and Palmer (1994).

Petrosino (2000) located 205 citations to systematic or possibly systematic reviews of research on the effects of interventions relevant to crime, drugs, or alcohol. These reviews were categorized into the following groups: preventive interventions for crime, drugs, or alcohol (84); programs designed to treat or control crime, drugs, or alcohol (95); improving the criminal or mental health systems (12); interventions for crime victims (12); and reviews addressing more than one of these areas (2). As many as 72 of the prevention/control reviews were relevant to what works in corrections, which was by far the most common area. Consequently, we will concentrate on this area in very briefly discussing the recent history and influence of systematic reviews in criminology.

The meta-analysis carried out by Andrews and his colleagues (1990) has been particularly influential in North America. They classified correctional treatment as appropriate or inappropriate; appropriate treatment involved delivery of service to higher risk cases, targeting of criminogenic needs, and use of techniques (for example, cognitive-behavioral) matched to the needs of clients. They found that appropriate treatment was effective, while criminal sanctions and inappropriate techniques had negative effects (that is, the controls did better). Among agencies influenced by this research was the U.S. National Institute of Corrections, in its technical advice to jurisdictions implementing correctional programs.

Similarly, Redondo, Sanchez-Meca, and Garrido (1999) in Spain identified 32 European studies between 1980 and 1991 that tested the effects of some treatment on subsequent criminal offending. They reported an average 12 percent reduction in recidivism when compared to a quasi-experimental comparison group or the pretest period. Interestingly no randomized experiments were included in their sample of 32 studies. Nonetheless their overall results are typical of most of the meta-analyses reported to date in showing that correctional intervention is generally effective in reducing reoffending. Furthermore they and most other reviewers (for example, Antonowicz and Ross 1994; Lipsey and Wilson 1998) concluded that the most effective type of correctional treatment was cognitive-behavioral skills training.

THE CAMPBELL COLLABORATION

The success of the Cochrane Collaboration in reviewing health care interventions stimulated international interest in establishing a similar infrastructure for conducting systematic reviews of research on the effects of social and educational interventions. Following several exploratory meetings in London and elsewhere, the Campbell Collaboration (named after the psychologist Donald T. Campbell) was officially founded at a meeting of more than 80 persons from 12 countries in Philadelphia in February 2000. Professor Robert Boruch of the University of Pennsylvania was appointed chair of the Campbell Collaboration's Steering Group. More information on the Steering Group, as well as on the background and progress of the Campbell Collaboration, can be found at http://www.campbell.gse.upenn.edu.

Following the example of the Cochrane Collaboration, the Campbell Collaboration will prepare rigorous and systematic reviews of high-quality evidence about what works. Recognizing that evidence is changing all the time, these reviews will be updated on a periodic basis, taking account of new studies, cogent criticisms, and methodological advances. The Campbell Collaboration will go beyond traditional dissemination in scientific journals and will use a variety of methods including the World Wide Web, to promote rapid access to evidence of all interested persons—and not just the research community.

Through international networking, the Campbell Collaboration will ensure that relevant evaluation studies conducted around the world will be taken into account in its systematic reviews and that evidence from such reviews will be made accessible globally through language translation and worldwide dissemination. Consumers of Campbell Collaboration products should include the general public, practitioners, funding organizations, professional associations, policy makers, and teachers and their students. The reviews will be nonpartisan and objective, using methods that are defensible and explicit.

THE CAMPBELL CRIME AND JUSTICE COORDINATING GROUP (CJCG)

At that February 2000 meeting, the Campbell Collaboration appointed its CJCG to coordinate the work of the Crime and Justice Group. The broad mission of the CJCG is to oversee the preparation, maintenance, and accessibility of systematic reviews of research on the effects of criminological and criminal justice interventions. The main emphasis is on reviews of interventions designed to prevent or reduce crime or delinquency. Broadly, the CJCG will include systematic reviews of research on the effects of interventions delivered by the courts, police, probation or parole agencies, prisons, and community groups; for more information about the Campbell Crime and Justice Group, see Farrington and Petrosino (2000).

Persons who contribute systematic reviews to the Campbell Collaboration must agree to the following requirements:

1. A commitment to conduct updates of the systematic review to incorporate new evidence, respond to criticisms, or use more advanced methods, on a regular basis (for example, every 2 years).

2. A commitment to undergo a rigorous editorial review process from not only researchers but also policy makers, practitioners, and citizens to ensure that the review meets high scientific standards and is also written to be understandable to nonacademic audiences.

3. A commitment to maintain transparent and open review processes so that users can comment and criticize each stage of the review, from its proposal through to its completion.

4. A commitment to use the most rigorous search methods available to ensure that all relevant studies are considered for inclusion or exclusion and not just those reported in easily accessible journals and books.

5. A commitment to cover literature from around the world and not just the English-speaking world.

6. A commitment to code and computerize key features of each evaluation study reviewed (so that anyone accessing the review can organize the studies according to such features as sample size, design, and effect size).

7. A commitment to explicitly report the final review so that readers can understand decisions made at each stage, justifications for those decisions, and how conclusions were reached.

8. A commitment to make the review available to broader audiences than readerships of peer-reviewed academic journals through electronic publication and dissemination into policy, practice, and media outlets.

The CJCG consists of 14 members from 10 countries: David P. Farrington (United Kingdom, chair), Ulla V. Bondeson (Denmark), Vicente Garrido (Spain), Peter Grabosky (Australia), Jerry Lee (United States), Mark W. Lipsey (United States), Friedrich Lösel (Germany), Joan McCord (United States), Anthony Petrosino (United States), Lawrence W. Sherman (United States), Chuen-Jim Sheu (Taiwan), Richard E. Tremblay (Canada), Hiroshi Tsutomi (Japan), and David L. Weisburd (Israel). Anthony Petrosino was appointed part-time coordinator for the CJCG, and Joan McCord was appointed to liaise with the Campbell Collaboration Steering Group. It was also decided that the institutional base for the Crime and Justice Group should be the Jerry Lee Center of Criminology at the Fels Center of Government, University of Pennsylvania, under the direction of Lawrence Sherman. Since the British government in general and the Home Office in particular are increasingly committed to evidence-based policy and practice, David Farrington applied to the Home Office for funding and obtained support for the first 2 years of the CJCG, beginning in April 2000.

To encourage international participation, the first meeting of the CJCG was held in Paris in May 2000, coinciding with meetings of the

International Society of Criminology (ISC). It was hoped that ISC members, who are drawn from all over the world, would help this venture, especially since Lawrence Sherman is the current president of the ISC. At the Paris meeting, it was decided that systematic reviews should be solicited on 15 key topics, examining the effects on crime of the following: restorative justice, parent education programs, child skills training, juvenile curfews, juvenile boot camps, electronic monitoring, cognitive-behavioral programs for offenders, faith-based programs for prisoners, length of imprisonment, community service orders, treatment of psychopaths, closed-circuit television, improved street lighting, neighborhood watch, and hot spots policing.

The CJCG decided initially to take a proactive approach in soliciting reviews rather than a reactive approach (responding to unsolicited proposals) for four main reasons. The first was to ensure that early reviews targeted areas that were especially important to policy, practice, or research. At the first meeting of the CJCG, we benefited from a great deal of advice from Paul Wiles of the Home Office. The second was to control the amount of work and flow of correspondence in light of the limited resources available to deal with it. We were worried about being overwhelmed by correspondence and e-mail. The third was to establish the early reputation of the Crime and Justice Group by getting well-known researchers to do the first reviews. The fourth was to ensure that some reviews were completed in a timely fashion. We were conscious of the need for quick results to demonstrate the value of this effort. In general, the aim was to select a narrow topic for each review, where there was likely to be only a small number of high-quality evaluations—of the order of 20 rather than hundreds. Together, the reviews would cover a wide range of criminological interests.

Potential reviewers were asked to complete proposals for their reviews specifying the following: the background to the reviews (hypotheses tested, operational definitions of independent and dependent variables, interventions); objectives of the reviews; strategies for searching the literature; selection criteria for including or excluding studies; and strategies for data extraction, coding, and analysis. This was modeled on the protocol for Cochrane reviews; the Campbell Collaboration developed its own standards for a proposal in January 2001.

Potential reviewers were also sent a draft checklist for data extraction suggesting that they code and computerize the following topics for each study: principal investigators; full citations to all evaluation reports; funding; publication dates; design of the study; characteristics of experimental units (for example, age and sex of individuals, prior crime rates of areas); sample size, hypotheses, and interventions; implementation details; how independent and extraneous variables were controlled so that it was possible to disentangle the impact of the intervention; who were the program delivery personnel; what were the control conditions (since it was rarely possible to have a truly untreated control group); who knows what about the intervention (since double blind trials were ideal); measurement of dependent variables (for example, official records of crime or self-reports of offending); before and after measures of crime or offending; and follow-up period after the intervention.

SUBSEQUENT DEVELOPMENTS

The CJCG met for the second time in San Francisco in November 2000, coinciding with the American Society of Criminology meetings. At this meeting, more topics for review were proposed, including repeat victimization programs; treatment of sex offenders; domestic violence interventions; reentry programs for incarcerated offenders; sports/recreation–based programs; aftercare treatment for juvenile offenders; drug courts; prison-based drug treatment; interventions for serious, violent youth; and interventions for gun violence.

Anthony Petrosino constructed a brochure for the Crime and Justice Group, which is being used to respond to enquiries and to circulate at meetings. A Web site for the Crime and Justice Group has been constructed by John Myrtle and Peter Levan of the Australian Institute of Criminology. It has been decided to house a central registry of studies at the Fels Center of Government in Philadelphia. This requires the development of a core coding system for every study.

More than 120 people from 16 countries have written to express interest in the Crime and Justice Group, many of whom wish to help in conducting reviews or reviewing proposals. These people are being kept informed about all developments. An informal advisory board of 30 persons has also been created. The members of the board have been asked to suggest topics for review and to identify funding opportunities. The Jerry Lee Crime Prevention Symposium in April 2001, titled Systematic Reviews of Criminological Interventions, can be regarded as the official launching meeting of the Crime and Justice Group.

The next meeting of the CJCG was in Paris in May 2001. The work of the Crime and Justice Group will be publicized at the American Society of Criminology meeting in Atlanta, Georgia, in November 2001. Plans include having a panel session on systematic reviews and also a workshop (sponsored by the Division of Sentencing and Corrections) providing training on systematic reviews and meta-analyses. There are also plans to have the next Jerry Lee Crime Prevention Symposium, titled Systematic Reviews of Criminological Interventions, in April 2002 and to publish the proceedings of this conference in the first 2003 issue of *The Annals*.

KEY CHALLENGES

Several major challenges were identified. The first (perhaps most important and controversial) is what criterion of methodological quality should be set for including evaluation studies in systematic reviews. Several CJCG members argued that only randomized experiments should be reviewed since these were able to demonstrate effects most convincingly (with highest internal validity). However, setting the gold standard of randomized experiments would inevitably exclude almost all evaluations based on areas (as opposed to individuals), covering the effects of interventions such as neighborhood watch or closed-circuit television. Also, when David Farrington, Anthony Petrosino, and Lawrence Sherman made a presentation to the Committee of Directors of Criminological Institutes in November 2000, some of those present were concerned that the methodological standard should not be set so high that important evaluations were excluded. Directors said that they needed the best available evidence and that conclusions saying "we know nothing because all studies are flawed" were very unhelpful.

Intervention studies differ in methodological quality. Two of the most important features of methodological quality are internal and external validity (Cook and Campbell 1979). Internal validity refers to how well the study unambiguously demonstrates that an intervention (for example, restorative justice) had an effect on an outcome (for example, offending). External validity refers to how well the effect of an intervention on an outcome is generalizable or replicable in different conditions: different operational definitions of the intervention and various outcomes, different persons, different environments, and so on. Each reviewer is ultimately responsible for determining criteria for inclusion or exclusion of studies in a systematic review. However, it is expected that the selection of studies for detailed consideration in systematic reviews of criminological interventions for the Campbell Collaboration Crime and Justice Group will be influenced by the methodological quality of the studies. Criteria for inclusion and standards for methodological quality have yet to be recommended by the Campbell Collaboration Methods Group, whose conclusions are likely to be influential for all Campbell reviews.

Internal validity is maximized (or conversely, threats to internal validity are minimized) in a randomized experiment. The randomization maximizes the chance that experimental units (for example, persons or areas) receiving the intervention are comparable in all respects to those units (controls) that do not receive the intervention. Of course, randomized experiments are only the gold standard if implemented with full integrity. To the extent that there are implementation problems (for example, problems of maintaining random assignment, differential attrition, crossover between control and experimental conditions), internal validity could be reduced in them. It is expected that reviewers will code such implementation problems and will attempt to answer questions such as which types of project management techniques are most likely to avoid implementation problems.

Other things being equal, an intervention study in which experimental and control units are matched or statistically equated (for example, using a prediction score) prior to the intervention has less internal validity than a randomized experiment. An intervention study with no control group has even less internal validity since it fails to address many threats to internal validity (for example, history, that is, the idea that changes in the outcome might be attributable to events other than the intervention; maturation or the continuation of preexisting trends; testing or instrumentation effects; and regression to the mean).

Different considerations apply to intervention studies based on areas compared to intervention studies based on individuals. Randomized experiments can rarely be carried out to evaluate area-based interventions. It is rarely feasible to allocate at random a sufficiently large number of areas (for example, at least 100) to experimental or control conditions in order to equate these conditions on all possible extraneous variables before the intervention (within the limits of statistical fluctuation).

In area-based studies, internal validity is usually maximized by having before and after measures of an outcome (for example, crime) in comparable experimental and control areas. Even better, the effect of an intervention on crime can be investigated after controlling (for example, in a regression equation) not only for prior crime but also for other factors that influence crime. Another possibility is to match two areas and then to choose one at random to be the experimental area. Of course, several pairs of areas would be better than only one pair. An intervention study with no comparable control area (merely measuring crime before and after an intervention, as in a one-group pre-post design) has low

internal validity because of its failure to tackle the threats mentioned above. An interrupted time series study is more convincing than a one-group pre-post design, especially if an experimental time series is compared with a control time series.

It is expected that persons conducting systematic reviews of interventions will select studies with high internal validity for detailed consideration and inclusion in systematic reviews. However, studies with lower internal validity may also be listed in less detail in the review, together with summary information about them (for example, sample size, design, effect size). This will permit others to argue that these studies should have been included in the expected dialogue between reviewers and others that will be facilitated by the electronic publication of systematic reviews. The plan is that reviews should be continually updated in light of new studies, relevant criticisms, and methodological developments. This updating may well change the studies that are included or excluded.

External validity will be measured according to the extent to which the selected studies report similar results. It is important to determine how well interventions do or do not work within different contexts or boundary conditions. Other types of validity (for example, construct validity, statistical conclusion validity) will also be summarized by the reviewers for each study, who also may try to draw conclusions about what is the "active ingredient" of an intervention or about causal pathways between interventions and outcomes. In addition, reviewers should consider how well the program is described in detail and whether there is information about the reliability and validity of outcome measures.

The statement that reviewers will select studies with high internal validity does not imply that reviewers will select only randomized experiments. This might possibly be the case for an intervention where there are many randomized experiments (for example, cognitive-behavioral skills training). However, randomized experiments to evaluate criminological interventions are relatively uncommon. If reviews were restricted to randomized experiments, they would be relevant to only a small fraction of the key questions for policy and practice in criminology. Where there are few randomized experiments, it is expected that reviewers will select both randomized and nonrandomized studies for inclusion in detailed reviews, possibly reporting different types of research design in different sections of the review.

For area-based interventions, it is unlikely that reviewers will be able to review any randomized experiments. In this case, it is expected that reviewers will select the highest quality quasi-experimental intervention studies for detailed consideration, such as those with before and after measures of the outcome in experimental and control areas. However, they may also provide a summary list of before and after studies with noncomparable or no control areas in their systematic review.

One of the main aims of conducting a systematic review is to draw conclusions about the best available knowledge about the effects of a criminological intervention, possibly accompanied by methodological caveats or "health warnings." To the extent that existing research is inadequate, in internal validity or in any other feature, this should be stated by the reviewer, and recommendations should be made about needed research in the future. It is hoped that systematic reviews will identify gaps in knowledge and key questions that need addressing and also that they will lead to increased attention to methodological issues and to an improvement in the methodological quality of intervention research in criminology.

The second challenge is funding. The very welcome Home Office funding covers the salary of the part-time coordinator and some CJCG meeting expenses but not the cost of reviews. The Jerry Lee Crime Prevention Program generously sponsored the 2001 conference. Without funding, it was thought likely that reviewers would not give Campbell reviews high priority. Already one potential reviewer has responded that he thinks the systematic review is very important and would love to do it but cannot without resources. It is hoped that further funding will be received from other sources, including the U.S. National Institute of Justice and the Smith-Richardson Foundation, and that the Canadian Department of Justice will fund Canadian reviewers. Funding is needed not only for reviews and meeting expenses but also for refereeing proposals and completed reviews, administrative and organizational support, translation costs, and setting up a registry of studies. Of course, efforts are being made concurrently to obtain funding for the larger Campbell Collaboration, and some of this funding may yet trickle down to the Crime and Justice Group.

A third challenge, related to incentives for reviewers, is the worry that academics will not give Campbell reviews high priority if they do not produce publications. Academics need publications in scholarly journals to get tenure, promotion, and fame. It was therefore suggested that reviewers be encouraged to complete not only a detailed electronic Campbell review but also an (inevitably less detailed) review for a scholarly journal. Of course, this raises problems of copyright and duplication that need to be resolved. Journal editors may be reluctant to publish systematic reviews if a more detailed version is available on the Web. On the other hand, many journals are now being published on the Web. It is hoped that in due course Campbell reviews on the Web will have sufficient prestige themselves to carry weight in tenure and promotion decisions.

A fourth challenge is the coordination of reviews, both with other parts of the Campbell Collaboration and with the Cochrane Collaboration. Anthony Petrosino met with representatives of the Campbell Collaboration Methods Group in July 2000 to discuss standards for proposals and other methodological issues. The Crime and Justice Group has moved forward very quickly; we could not afford to wait for these topics to be resolved by the Campbell Collaboration. There is also the problem that similar topics are being reviewed by the Cochrane Developmental, Psychosocial and Learning Problems Group, such as the treatment of sex offenders. We decided to go ahead with our own reviews and to see how they differed from Cochrane reviews, which focus more on medical and health care issues.

The fifth challenge is how the CJCG can cope with the work needed to maintain the high quality of systematic reviews. This involves refereeing both proposals and final versions of reviews, as well as building up the network and infrastructure of the Crime and Justice Group. Already, organizing the CJCG has generated an enormous amount of day-to-day work for both of us, as all the different activities have built up. This is why we decided to move forward initially with a relatively small number of reviews and to learn from experience. We are concerned that large-scale publicity, inviting people to volunteer to do particular reviews, might open the floodgates and unleash a monster that we cannot cope with. However, we have to open things up and move to unsolicited review proposals and wider participation by the research community as soon as possible.

The sixth challenge is how to regularize the CJCG, which was essentially appointed on an ad hoc basis for three years (until August 2003). The overall Campbell Collaboration Steering Committee needs to work out procedures for appointing and replacing CJCG members and the chair, ensuring that the CJCG includes a wide variety of expertise and countries and that it has the capacity to supervise reviews and reviewers effectively.

A seventh challenge is that the people who are most knowledgeable and motivated to carry out a systematic review are often those who have worked on the particular topic, but arguably they are not unbiased and may have a stake in the conclusions. One way of dealing with this challenge is to encourage collaborations between reviewers who have and have not previously worked on a particular topic. Also, there is a need for workshops to train people in how to do systematic reviews.

There are other issues to be resolved. For example, most of the persons who have so far been asked to do systematic reviews are located in the United States. It is important to solicit more reviews and more contributions to reviews (possibly involving translation) from persons in other countries. To build up a registry of studies, it is necessary to agree on a common core of items to be coded and computerized in all reviews. Another issue is how far all reviewers should be encouraged to carry out a meta-analysis or other quantitative summary of conclusions. Ideally cost-benefit information should be included in all reviews, where available. Ideally the CJCG should develop a master plan (a systematic classification and organization of all possible intervention topics for review) and aim to fill the gaps with solicited reviews.

Another issue is how far Campbell reviews should include policy recommendations. These would be useful for funding agencies, but some members of the CJCG feel that systematic reviews should be restricted to scientific conclusions. An issue for the future is how to ensure that systematic reviews are understandable to a wide audience. This will probably involve soliciting comments on reviews from members of the public as well as from policy makers and practitioners. So far, we have focused on reviews of interventions designed to reduce crime and offending. In the future, we might aim to commission reviews on interventions designed to improve the management or operations of the criminal justice system. Also, we could expand our remit to systematic reviews of the strength of relationships between particular risk factors and offending or of tests of particular criminological theories. However, it might be better to establish new crime and justice committees to cover both of these topics.

CONCLUSION

It is hoped that systematic reviews will improve on previous influential comprehensive reviews of criminological interventions by the U.S. National Academy of Sciences and others (for example, Nuttall, Goldblatt, and Lewis 1998; Sherman et al. 1997) in a number of ways. Systematic reviews describe their methods more explicitly, search the literature more extensively and more internationally, and provide more information about criteria for inclusion or exclusion and about sources searched. They include more detailed tables and codings of studies. They are subject to rigorous quality control, are revised in light of cogent criticisms, are regularly updated, and are speedily disseminated. Best of all, systematic reviews are immediately available electronically to everyone. They should be used in the future by reviewers for the U.S. National Academy of Sciences and other agencies.

The Campbell Collaboration CJCG has made enormous progress in a very short time. We are proud to have received the first Donald Campbell Award from the Campbell Collaboration in 2000 to recognize our outstanding progress. Nevertheless, we anticipate that the majority of reviews of criminological interventions will always be carried out outside the Campbell Collaboration. By setting and maintaining high standards, we hope that Campbell reviews will become recognized as the best available. We also hope that reviewers outside the Campbell Collaboration will be influenced to carry out systematic reviews and that the greater use of systematic reviews will lead to improvements in the reporting of intervention studies. While the work ahead is daunting, systematic reviews of criminological interventions have enormous potential both to advance knowledge and to make policy and practice more effective in the future. The aim of making the best knowledge about the effectiveness of interventions to reduce crime immediately available to everyone is ambitious and very important and would benefit everyone in all countries.

References

Andrews, Donald A., Ivan Zinger, Robert D. Hoge, James Bonta, Paul Gendreau, and Francis T. Cullen. 1990. Does Correctional Treatment Work? A Clinically Relevant and Psychologically Informed Meta-analysis. *Criminology* 28:369-404.

Antonowicz, Daniel H. and Robert R. Ross. 1994. Essential Components of Successful Rehabilitation Programs for Offenders. *International Journal of Offender Therapy and Comparative Criminology* 38:97-104.

Cook, Thomas D. and Donald T. Campbell. 1979. *Quasi-Experimentation: Data and Analysis Issues for Field Settings.* Chicago: Rand McNally.

Farrington, David P. and Anthony Petrosino. 2000. Systematic Reviews of Criminological Interventions: The Campbell Collaboration Crime and Justice Group. *International Annals of Criminology* 38:49-66.

Lipsey, Mark W. and David B. Wilson. 1993. The Efficacy of Psychological, Educational, and Behavioral Treatment: Confirmation from Meta-Analysis. *American Psychologist* 48:1181-209.

———. 1998. Effective Intervention for Serious Juvenile Offenders: A Synthesis of Research. In *Serious and Violent Juvenile Offenders: Risk Factors and Successful Interventions*, ed. Rolf Loeber and David P. Farrington. Thousand Oaks, CA: Sage.

Lösel, Friedrich. 1995. Increasing Consensus in the Evaluation of Offender Rehabilitation? Lessons from Recent Research Syntheses. *Psychology, Crime and Law* 2:19-39.

Nuttall, Christopher, Peter Goldblatt, and Chris Lewis, eds. 1998. *Reducing Offending: An Assessment of Research Evidence on Ways of Dealing with Offending Behaviour.* London: Home Office.

Palmer, Ted. 1994. *A Profile of Correctional Effectiveness and New Directions for Research*. Albany: State University of New York Press.

Petrosino, Anthony. 2000. Crime, Drugs and Alcohol. In *Evidence from Systematic Reviews of Research Relevant to Implementing the "Wider Public Health" Agenda*, Contributors to the Cochrane Collaboration and the Campbell Collaboration. York, UK: NHS Centre for Reviews and Dissemination. Retrieved August 2000 from http://www.york.ac.uk/inst/crd/wph. htm.

Redondo, Santiago, Julio Sanchez-Meca, and Vicente Garrido. 1999. The Influence of Treatment Programmes on the Recidivism of Juvenile and Adult Offenders: A European Meta-Analytic Review. *Psychology, Crime and Law* 5:251-78.

Sherman, Lawrence W., Denise C. Gottfredson, Doris Layton MacKenzie, John E. Eck, Peter Reuter, and Shawn D. Bushway. 1997. *Preventing Crime: What Works, What Doesn't, What's Promising*. Washington, DC: U.S. Department of Justice, National Institute of Justice.

ANNALS, *AAPSS*, **578**, November 2001

Does Research Design Affect Study Outcomes in Criminal Justice?

By DAVID WEISBURD, CYNTHIA M. LUM, and ANTHONY PETROSINO

ABSTRACT: Does the type of research design used in a crime and justice study influence its conclusions? Scholars agree in theory that randomized experimental studies have higher internal validity than do nonrandomized studies. But there is not consensus regarding the costs of using nonrandomized studies in coming to conclusions regarding criminal justice interventions. To examine these issues, the authors look at the relationship between research design and study outcomes in a broad review of research evidence on crime and justice commissioned by the National Institute of Justice. Their findings suggest that design does have a systematic effect on outcomes in criminal justice studies. The weaker a design, indicated by internal validity, the more likely a study is to report a result in favor of treatment and the less likely it is to report a harmful effect of treatment. Even when comparing randomized studies with strong quasi-experimental research designs, systematic and statistically significant differences are observed.

David Weisburd is a senior research fellow in the Department of Criminology and Criminal Justice at the University of Maryland and a professor of criminology at the Hebrew University Law School in Jerusalem.

Cynthia M. Lum is a doctoral student in the Department of Criminology and Criminal Justice at the University of Maryland.

Anthony Petrosino is a research fellow at the Center for Evaluation, Initiative for Children Program at the American Academy of Arts and Sciences and a research associate at Harvard University. He is also the coordinator of the Campbell Crime and Justice Coordinating Group.

NOTE: We are indebted to a number of colleagues for helpful comments in preparing this article. We especially want to thank Iain Chalmers, John Eck, David Farrington, Denise Gottfredson, Doris MacKenzie, Joan McCord, Lawrence Sherman, Brandon Welsh, Charles Wellford, and David Wilson.

THERE is a growing consensus among scholars, practitioners, and policy makers that crime control practices and policies should be rooted as much as possible in scientific research (Cullen and Gendreau 2000; MacKenzie 2000; Sherman 1998). This is reflected in the steady growth in interest in evaluation of criminal justice programs and practices in the United States and the United Kingdom over the past decade and by large increases in criminal justice funding for research during this period (Visher and Weisburd 1998). Increasing support for research and evaluation in criminal justice may be seen as part of a more general trend toward utilization of scientific research for establishing rational and effective practices and policies. This trend is perhaps most prominent in the health professions, where the idea of evidence-based medicine has gained strong government and professional support (Millenson 1997; Zuger 1997), though the evidence-based paradigm is also developing in other fields (see Nutley and Davies 1999; Davies, Nutley, and Smith 2000).

A central component of the movement toward evidence-based practice and policy is reliance on systematic review of prior research and evaluation (Davies 1999). Such review allows policy makers and practitioners to identify what programs and practices are most effective and in which contexts. The Cochrane Collaboration, for example, seeks to prepare, maintain, and make accessible systematic reviews of research on the effects of health care interventions (see Chalmers and Altman 1995; www.cochrane.org.) The *Cochrane Library* is now widely recognized as the single best source of evidence on the effectiveness of health care and medical treatments and has played an important part in the advancement of evidence-based medicine (Egger and Smith 1998). More recently, social scientists following the Cochrane model established the Campbell Collaboration for developing systematic reviews of research evidence in the area of social and educational interventions (see Boruch, Petrosino, and Chalmers 1999). In recognition of the growing importance of evidence-based policies in criminal justice, the Campbell Collaboration commissioned a coordinating group to deal with crime and justice issues. This group began with the goal of providing the best evidence on "what works in crime and justice" through the development of "systematic reviews of research" on the effects of crime and justice interventions (Farrington and Petrosino 2001 [this issue]).

In the Cochrane Collaboration, and in medical research in general, clinical trials that randomize participants to treatment and control or comparison groups are considered more reliable than studies that do not employ randomization. And the recognition that experimental designs form the gold standard for drawing conclusions about the effects of treatments or programs is not restricted to medicine. There is broad agreement among social and behavioral scientists that randomized experiments provide the best method for drawing causal inferences between treatments and programs and their outcomes (for example, see Boruch, Snyder, and DeMoya 2000; Campbell and Boruch 1975; Farrington 1983; Feder, Jolin, and Feyerherm 2000). Indeed, a task force convened by the Board of Scientific Affairs of the American Psychological Association to look into statistical methods concluded that "for research involving causal inferences, the assignments of units to levels of the causal variable is critical. Random assignment (not to be confused with random selection) allows for the strongest possible causal inferences free of extraneous assumptions" (Wilkinson and Task Force on Statistical Inference 1999).

While reliance on experimental studies in drawing conclusions about treatment outcomes has become common in the development of evidence-based medicine, the Campbell Collaboration Crime and Justice Coordinating Group has concluded that it is unrealistic at this time to restrict systematic reviews on the effects of interventions relevant to crime and justice to experimental studies. In developing its *Standards for Inclusion of Studies in Systematic Reviews* (Farrington 2000), the group notes that it does not require that reviewers select only randomized experiments:

This might possibly be the case for an intervention where there are many randomized experiments (e.g. cognitive-behavioral skills training). However, randomized experiments to evaluate criminological interventions are relatively uncommon. If reviews were restricted to randomized experiments, they

would be relevant to only a small fraction of the key questions for policy and practice in criminology. Where there are few randomized experiments, it is expected that reviewers will select both randomized and non-randomized studies for inclusion in detailed reviews. (3)

In this article we examine a central question relevant both to the Campbell Collaboration crime and justice effort and to the more general emphasis on developing evidence-based practice in criminal justice: Does the type of research design used in a crime and justice study influence the conclusions that are reached? Assuming that experimental designs are the gold standard for evaluating practices and policies, it is important to ask what price we pay in including other types of studies in our reviews of what works in crime and justice. Are we likely to overestimate or underestimate the positive effects of treatment? Or conversely, might we expect that the use of well-designed nonrandomized studies will lead to about the same conclusions as we would gain from randomized experimental evaluations?

To examine these issues, we look at the relationship between research design and study outcomes in a broad review of research evidence on crime and justice commissioned by the National Institute of Justice. Generally referred to as the Maryland Report because it was developed in the Department of Criminology and Criminal Justice at the University of Maryland at College Park, the study was published under the title *Preventing Crime: What Works, What*

Doesn't, What's Promising (Sherman et al. 1997). The Maryland Report provides an unusual opportunity for assessing the impact of study design on study outcomes in crime and justice both because it sought to be comprehensive in identifying available research and because the principal investigators of the study devoted specific attention to the nature of the research designs of the studies included. Below we detail the methods we used to examine how study design affects study outcomes in crime and justice research and report on our main findings. We turn first, however, to a discussion of why randomized experiments as contrasted with quasi-experimental and non-experimental research designs are generally considered a gold standard for making causal inferences. We also examine what prior research suggests regarding the questions we raise.

WHY ARE RANDOMIZED EXPERIMENTS CONSIDERED THE GOLD STANDARD?

The key to understanding the strength of experimental research designs is found in what scholars refer to as the internal validity of a study. A research design in which the effects of treatment or intervention can be clearly distinguished from other effects has high internal validity. A research design in which the effects of treatment are confounded with other factors is one in which there is low internal validity. For example, suppose a researcher seeks to assess the effects of a specific drug treatment program on recidivism. If at the end of the evaluation the researcher can present study results and confidently assert that the effects of treatment have been isolated from other confounding causes, the internal validity of the study is high. But if the researcher has been unable to ensure that other factors such as the seriousness of prior records or the social status of offenders have been disentangled from the influence of treatment, he or she must note that the effects observed for treatment may be due to such confounding causes. In this case internal validity is low.

In randomized experimental studies, internal validity is developed through the process of random allocation of the units of treatment or intervention to experimental and control or comparison groups. This means that the researcher has randomized other factors besides treatment itself, since there is no systematic bias that brings one type of subject into the treatment group and another into the control or comparison group. Although the groups are not necessarily the same on every characteristic—indeed, simply by chance, there are likely to be differences—such differences can be assumed to be distributed randomly and are part and parcel of the stochastic processes taken into account in statistical tests. Random allocation thus allows the researcher to assume that the only systematic differences between the treatment and comparison groups are found in the treatments or interventions that are applied. When the study is complete, the researcher can argue with confidence that if a difference has been observed between treatment and comparison groups, it is likely the result of the treatment itself (since randomization has isolated the treatment effect from other possible causes).

In nonrandomized studies, two methods may be used for isolating treatment or program effects. Quasi-experiments, like randomized experiments, rely on the design of a research study to isolate the effects of treatment. Using matching or other methods in an attempt to establish equivalence between groups, quasi-experiments mimic experimental designs in that they attempt to rule out competing causes by identifying groups that are similar except in the nature of the treatment that they receive in the study. Importantly, however, quasi-experiments do not randomize out the effects of other causes as is the case in randomized experimental designs; rather they seek to maximize the equivalence between the units studied through matching or other methods. Threats to internal validity in quasi-experimental studies derive from the fact that it is seldom possible to find or to create treatment and control groups that are not systematically different in one respect or another.

Nonexperimental studies rely primarily on statistical techniques to distinguish the effects of the intervention or treatment from other confounding causes. In practice, quasi-experimental studies often rely as well on statistical approaches to increase the equivalence of the comparisons made.[1] However, in nonexperimental studies, statistical controls are the primary method applied in attempts to increase the level of a study's internal validity. In this case, multivariate statistical methods are used to isolate the effects of treatment from that of other causes. This demands of course that the researcher clearly identify and measure all other factors that may threaten the internal validity of the study outcomes. Only if all such factors are included in the multivariate models estimated can the researcher be confident that the effects of treatment that have been reported are not confounded with other causes.

In theory, the three methods described here are equally valid for solving the problem of isolating treatment or program effects. Each can ensure high internal validity when applied correctly. In practice, however, as Feder and Boruch (2000) note, "there is little disagreement that experiments provide a superior method for assessing the effectiveness of a given intervention" (292). Randomization, according to Kunz and Oxman (1998), "is the only means of controlling for unknown and unmeasured differences between comparison groups as well as those that are known and measured" (1185). While random allocation itself ensures high internal validity in experimental research, for quasi-experimental and nonexperimental research designs, unknown and unmeasured causes are generally seen as representing significant potential threats to the internal validity of the comparisons made.[2]

INTERNAL VALIDITY
AND STUDY OUTCOMES
IN PRIOR REVIEWS

While there is general agreement that experimental studies are more likely to ensure high internal validity than are quasi-experimental or nonexperimental studies, it is difficult to specify at the outset the effects that this will have on study outcomes. On one hand, it can be assumed that weaker internal validity is likely to lead to biases in assessment of the effects of treatments or interventions. However, the direction of that bias in any particular study is likely to depend on factors related to the specific character of the research that is conducted. For example, if nonrandomized studies do not account for important confounding causes that are positively related to treatment, they may on average overestimate program outcomes. However, if such unmeasured causes are negatively related to treatment, nonrandomized studies would be expected to underestimate program outcomes. Heinsman and Shadish (1996) suggested that whatever the differences in research design, if nonrandomized and randomized studies are equally well designed and implemented (and thus internal validity is maximized in each), there should be little difference in the estimates gained. Much of what is known empirically about these questions is drawn from reviews in such fields as medicine, psychology, economics, and education (for example, see Burtless 1995; Hedges 2000; Kunz and Oxman 1998; Lipsey and Wilson 1993). Following, what one would expect in theory, a general conclusion that can be reached from the literature is that there is not a consistent bias that results from use of nonrandomized research designs. At the same time, a few studies suggest that differences, in whatever direction, will be smallest when nonrandomized studies are well designed and implemented.

Kunz and Oxman (1998), for example, using studies drawn from the Cochrane database, found varying results when analyzing 18 meta-analyses (incorporating 1211 clinical trials) in the field of health care. Of these 18 systematic reviews, 4 found randomized and higher-quality studies[3] to give higher estimates of effects than nonrandomized and lower-quality studies, and 8 reviews found randomized or high-quality studies to produce lower estimates of effect sizes than nonrandomized or lower-quality studies. Five other reviews found little or inconclusive differences between different types of research designs, and in one review, low-quality studies were found to be more likely to report findings of harmful effects of treatments.

Mixed results are also found in systematic reviews in the social sciences. Some reviews suggest that nonrandomized studies will on average underestimate program effects. For example, Heinsman and Shadish (1996) looked at four meta-analyses that focused on interventions in four different areas: drug use, effects of coaching on Scholastic Aptitude Test performance, ability grouping of pupils in secondary schools, and psychosocial interventions for postsurgery outcomes. Included in their analysis were 98 published and unpublished studies. As a whole, randomized experiments were found to yield larger effect sizes than studies where randomization was not used. In contrast, Friedlander and Robins (2001), in a review of social welfare programs, found that nonexperimental statistical approaches often yielded estimates larger than those gained in randomized studies (see also Cox, Davidson, and Bynum 1995; LaLonde 1986).

In a large-scale meta-analysis examining the efficacy of psychological, educational, and behavioral treatment, Lipsey and Wilson (1993) suggested that conclusions reached on the basis of nonrandomized studies are not likely to strongly bias conclusions regarding treatment or program effects. Although studies varied greatly in both directions as to whether nonrandomized designs overestimated or underestimated effects as compared with randomized designs, no consistent bias in either direction was detected. Lipsey and Wilson, however, did find a notable difference between studies that employed a control/comparison design and those that used one-group pre and post designs. The latter studies produced consistently higher estimates of treatment effects.

Support for the view that stronger nonrandomized studies are likely to provide results similar to randomized experimental designs is provided by Shadish and Ragsdale (1996). In a review of 100 studies of marital or family psychotherapy, they found overall that randomized experiments yielded significantly larger weighted average effect sizes than nonequivalent control group designs. Nonetheless, the difference

between randomized and nonrandomized studies decreased when confounding variables related to the quality of the design of the study were included.

Works that specifically address the relationship between study design and study outcomes are scarce in criminal justice. In turn, assessment of this relationship is most often not a central focus of the reviews developed, and reviewers generally examine a specific criminal justice area, most often corrections (for example, see Bailey 1966; MacKenzie and Hickman 1998; Whitehead and Lab 1989). Results of these studies provide little guidance for specifying a general relationship between study design and study outcomes for criminal justice research. In an early review of 100 reports of correctional treatment between 1940 and 1960, for example, Bailey (1966) found that research design had little effect on the claimed success of treatment, though he noted a slight positive relationship between the "rigor" of the design and study outcome. Logan (1972), who also reviewed correctional treatment programs, found a slight negative correlation between study design and claimed success.

Recent studies are no more conclusive. Wilson, Gallagher, and MacKenzie (2000), in a meta-analysis of corrections-based education, vocation, and work programs, found that run-of-the-mill quasi-experimental studies produced larger effects than did randomized experiments. However, such studies also produced larger effects than did low-quality designs that clearly lacked comparability among groups. In a review of

165 school-based prevention programs, Whitehead and Lab (1989) found little difference in the size of effects in randomized and non-randomized studies. Interestingly however, they reported that nonrandomized studies were much less likely to report a backfire effect whereby treatment was found to exacerbate rather than ameliorate the problem examined. In contrast, a more recent review by Wilson, Gottfredson, and Najaka (in press) found overall that nonrandomized studies yielded results on average significantly lower than randomized experiments' results, even accounting for a series of other design characteristics (including the overall quality of the implementation of the study). However, it should be noted that many of these studies did not include delinquency measures, and schools rather than individuals were often the unit of random allocation.[4]

THE STUDY

We sought to define the influence of research design on study outcomes across a large group of studies representing the different types of research design as well as a broad array of criminal justice areas. The most comprehensive source we could identify for this purpose has come to be known as the Maryland Report (Sherman et al. 1997). The Maryland Report was commissioned by the National Institute of Justice to identify "what works, what doesn't, and what's promising" in preventing crime. It was conducted at the University of Maryland's Department of Criminology and Criminal Justice over a yearlong period between 1996 and 1997. The report attempted to identify all available research relevant to crime prevention in seven broad areas: communities, families, schools, labor markets, places, policing, and criminal justice (corrections). Studies chosen for inclusion in the Maryland Report met minimal methodological requirements.[5]

Though the Maryland Report did not examine the relationship between study design and study outcomes, it did define the quality of the methods used to evaluate the strength of the evidence provided through a scientific methods scale (SMS). This SMS was coded with numbers 1 through 5, with "5 being the strongest scientific evidence" (Sherman et al. 1997, 2.18). Overall, studies higher on the scale have higher internal validity, and studies with lower scores have lower internal validity. The 5-point scale was broadly defined in the Maryland Report (Sherman et al. 1997) as follows:

1: Correlation between a crime prevention program and a measure of crime or crime risk factors.

2: Temporal sequence between the program and the crime or risk outcome clearly observed, or a comparison group present without the demonstrated comparability to the treatment group.

3: A comparison between two or more units of analysis, one with and one without the program.

4: Comparison between multiple units with and without the program, controlling for other factors, or a non-equivalent comparison group has only minor differences evident.

5: Random assignment and analysis of comparable units to program and comparison groups. (2.18-2.19)

A score of 5 on this scale suggests a randomized experimental design, and a score of 1 a nonexperimental approach. Scores of 3 and 4 may be associated with quasi-experimental designs, with 4 distinguished from 3 by a greater concern with control for threats to internal validity. A score of 2 represents a stronger nonexperimental design or a weaker quasi-experimental approach. However, the overall rating given to a study could be affected by other design criteria such as response rate, attrition, use of statistical tests, and statistical power. It is impossible to tell from the Maryland Report how much influence such factors had on each study's rating. However, correspondence with four of the main study investigators suggests that adjustments based on these other factors were uncommon and generally would result in an SMS decrease or increase of only one level.

Although the Maryland Report included a measure of study design, it did not contain a standardized measure of study outcome. Most prior reviews have relied on standardized effect measures as a criterion for studying the relationship between design type and study findings. Although in some of the area reviews in the Maryland Report, standardized effect sizes were calculated for specific studies, this was not the case for the bulk of the studies

reviewed in the report. Importantly, in many cases it was not possible to code such information because the original study authors did not provide the specific details necessary for calculating standardized effect coefficients. But the approach used by the Maryland investigators also reflected a broader philosophical decision that emphasized the bottom line of what was known about the effects of crime and justice interventions. In criminal justice, the outcome of a study is often considered more important than the effect size noted. This is the case in good part because there are often only a very small number of studies that examine a specific type of treatment or intervention. In addition, policy decisions are made not on the basis of a review of the effect sizes that are reported but rather on whether one or a small group of studies suggests that the treatment or intervention works.

From the data available in the Maryland Report, we developed an overall measure of study outcomes that we call the investigator reported result (IRR). The IRR was created as an ordinal scale with three values: 1, 0, and −1, reflecting whether a study concluded that the treatment or intervention worked, had no detected effect, or led to a backfire effect. It is defined by what is reported in the tables of the Maryland Report and is coded as follows:[6]

1: The program or treatment is reported to have had an intended positive effect for the criminal justice system or society. Outcomes in this case supported the position that interventions or treatments lead to reductions in crime, recidivism, or related measures.[7]

0: The program treatment was reported to have no detected effect, or the effect was reported as not statistically significant.

−1: The program or treatment had an unintended backfire effect for the criminal justice system or society. Outcomes in this case supported the position that interventions or treatments were harmful and lead to increases in crime, recidivism, or related measures.[8]

This scale provides an overall measure of the conclusions reached by investigators in the studies that were reviewed in the Maryland Report. However, we think it is important to note at the outset some specific features of the methodology used that may affect the findings we gain using this approach. Perhaps most significant is the fact that Maryland reviewers generally relied on the reported conclusions of investigators unless there was obvious evidence to the contrary.[9] This approach led us to term the scale the *investigator reported result* and reinforces the fact that we examine the impacts of study design on what investigators report rather than on the actual outcomes of the studies examined.

While the Maryland reviewers examined tests of statistical significance in coming to conclusions about which programs or treatments work,[10] they did not require that statistical tests be reported by investigators to support the specific conclusions reached in each study. In turn, the tables in the Maryland Report often do not note whether specific studies employed statistical tests of significance. Accordingly, in reviewing the Maryland Report studies, we cannot assess whether the presence or absence of such tests influences our conclusions. Later in our article we reexamine our results, taking into account statistical significance in the context of a more recent review in the corrections area that was modeled on the Maryland Report.

Finally, as we noted earlier, most systematic reviews of study outcomes have come to use standardized effect size as a criterion. While we think that the IRR scale is useful for gaining an understanding of the relationship between research design and reported study conclusions, we recognize that a different set of conclusions might have been reached had we focused on standardized effect sizes. Again, we use the corrections review referred to above to assess how our conclusions might have differed if we had focused on standardized effect sizes rather than the IRR scale.

We coded the Scientific Methods Scale and the IRR directly from the tables reported in *Preventing Crime: What Works, What Doesn't, What's Promising* (Sherman et al. 1997). We do not include all of the studies in the Maryland Report in our review. First, given our interest in the area of criminal justice, we excluded studies that did not have a crime or delinquency outcome measure. Second, we excluded studies that did not provide an SMS score (a feature of some

TABLE 1

STUDIES CATEGORIZED BY SMS

SMS	Studies	
	n	Percentage
1	10	3
2	94	31
3	130	42
4	28	9
5	46	15
Total	308	100

TABLE 2

STUDIES CATEGORIZED BY THE IRR

IRR	Studies	
	n	Percentage
−1	34	11
0	76	25
1	198	64
Total	308	100

tables in the community and family sections of the report). Finally, we excluded the school-based area from review because only selected studies were reported in tables.[11] All other studies reviewed in the Maryland Report were included, which resulted in a sample of 308 studies. Tables 1 and 2 display the breakdown of these studies by SMS and IRR.

As is apparent from Table 1, there is wide variability in the nature of the research methods used in the studies that are reviewed. About 15 percent were coded in the highest SMS category, which demands a randomized experimental design. Only 10 studies included were coded in the lowest SMS category, though almost a third fall in category 2. The largest category is score 3, which required simply a comparison between two units of analysis, one with and one without treatment. About 1 in 10 cases were coded as 4, suggesting a quasi-experimental study with strong attention to creating equivalence between the groups studied.

The most striking observation that is drawn from Table 2 is that almost two-thirds of the crime and justice studies reviewed in the Maryland Report produced a reported result in the direction of success for the treatment or intervention examined. This result is very much at odds with reviews conducted in earlier decades that suggested that most interventions had little effect on crime or related problems (for example, see Lipton, Martinson, and Wilks 1975; Logan 1972; Martinson 1974).[12] At the same time, a number of the studies examined, about 1 in 10, reported a backfire effect for treatment or intervention.

RELATING STUDY DESIGN
AND STUDY OUTCOMES

In Tables 3 and 4 we present our basic findings regarding the relationship between study design and study outcomes in the Maryland Report sample. Table 3 provides mean IRR outcome scores across the five SMS design categories. While the mean IRR scores in this case present a simple method for examining the results, we also provide an overall statistical measure of correlation, Tau-c (and the associated significance level), which is more appropriate for data of this type. In Table 4 we provide the

TABLE 3
**MEAN IRR SCORES
ACROSS SMS CATEGORIES**

SMS	Mean	n	Standard Deviation
1	.80	10	.42
2	.66	94	.63
3	.56	130	.67
4	.39	28	.83
5	.22	46	.70
Total	.53	308	.69

NOTE: Tau-c = −.181. $p < .001$.

cross-tabulation of IRR and SMS scores. This presentation of the results allows us to examine more carefully the nature of the relationship both in terms of outcomes in the expected treatment direction and outcomes that may be classified as backfire effects.

Overall Tables 3 and 4 suggest that there is a linear inverse relationship between the SMS and the IRR. The mean IRR score decreases with each increase in step in the SMS score (see Table 3). While fully nonexperimental designs have a mean IRR score of .80, randomized experiments have a mean of only .22. The run of the mill quasi-experimental designs represented in category 3 have a mean IRR score of .56, while the strongest quasi experiments (category 4) have a mean of .39. The overall correlation between study design and study outcomes is moderate and negative (−.18), and the relationship is statistically significant at the .001 level.

Looking at the cross-tabulation of SMS and IRR scores, our findings are reinforced. The stronger the method

in terms of internal validity as measured by the SMS, the less likely is a study to conclude that the intervention or treatment worked. The weaker the method, the less likely the study is to conclude that the intervention or treatment backfired.

While 8 of the 10 studies in the lowest SMS category and 74 percent of those in category 2 show a treatment impact in the desired direction, this was true for only 37 percent of the randomized experiments in category 5. Only in the case of backfire outcomes in categories 4 and 5 does the table not follow our basic findings, and this departure is small. Overall the relationship observed in the table is statistically significant at the .005 level.

Comparing the highest-quality nonrandomized studies with randomized experiments

As noted earlier, some scholars argue that higher-quality nonrandomized studies are likely to have outcomes similar to outcomes of randomized evaluations. This hypothesis is not supported by our data. In Table 5 we combine quasi-experimental studies in SMS categories 3 and 4 and compare them with randomized experimental studies placed in SMS category 5. Again we find a statistically significant negative relationship ($p < .01$). While 37 percent of the level 5 experimental studies show a treatment effect in the desired direction, this was true for 65 percent of the quasi-experimental studies.

Even if we examine only the highest-quality quasi-experimental studies as represented by category 4 and

TABLE 4
CROSS-TABULATION OF SMS AND IRR

| | SMS | | | | | | | | | |
| | 1 | | 2 | | 3 | | 4 | | 5 | |
IRR	n	Percentage	n	Percentage	n	Percentage	n	Percentage	n	Percentage
−1	0	0	8	9	13	10	6	21	7	15
0	2	20	16	17	31	24	5	18	22	48
1	8	80	70	74	86	66	17	61	17	37
Total	10	100	94	100	130	100	28	100	46	100

NOTE: Chi-square = 25.487 with 8 df ($p < .005$).

TABLE 5
COMPARING QUASI-EXPERIMENTAL
STUDIES (SMS = 3 OR 4) WITH
RANDOMIZED EXPERIMENTS (SMS = 5)

| | SMS | | | |
| | 3 or 4 | | 5 | |
IRR	n	Percentage	n	Percentage
−1	19	12	7	15
0	36	23	22	48
1	103	65	17	37
Total	158	100	46	100

NOTE: Chi-square = 12.971 with 2 df ($p < .01$).

TABLE 6
COMPARING HIGH-QUALITY QUASI-
EXPERIMENTAL DESIGNS (SMS = 4)
WITH RANDOMIZED DESIGNS (SMS = 5)

| | SMS | | | |
| | 4 | | 5 | |
IRR	n	Percentage	n	Percentage
−1	6	21	7	15
0	5	18	22	48
1	17	61	17	37
Total	28	100	46	100

NOTE: Chi-square = 6.805 with 2 df ($p < .05$).

compare these to the randomized studies included in category 5, the relationship between study outcomes and study design remains statistically significant at the .05 level (see Table 6). There is little difference between the two groups in the proportion of backfire outcomes reported; however, there remains a very large gap between the proportion of SMS category 4 and SMS category 5 studies that report an outcome in the direction of treatment effectiveness. While 61 percent of the category 4 SMS studies reported a positive treatment or intervention effect, this was true for only 37 percent of the randomized studies in category 5. Accordingly, even when comparing those nonrandomized studies with the highest internal validity with randomized experiments, we find significant differences in terms of reported study outcomes.

Taking into account tests of statistical significance

It might be argued that had we used a criterion of statistical significance, the overall findings would not have been consistent with the analyses reported above. While we cannot examine this question in the context of the Maryland Report, since statistical significance is generally not reported in the tables or the text of the report, we can review this concern in the context of a more recent review conducted in the corrections area by one of the Maryland investigators, which uses a similar methodology and reports Maryland SMS (see MacKenzie and Hickman 1998). MacKenzie and Hickman (1998) examined 101 studies in their 1998 review of what works in corrections, of which 68 are reported to have included tests of statistical significance.

Developing the IRR score for each of MacKenzie and Hickman's (1998) studies proved more complex than the coding done for the Maryland Report. MacKenzie and Hickman reported all of the studies' results, sometimes breaking up results by gender, employment, treatment mix, or criminal history, to list a few examples. Rather than count each result as a separate study, we developed two different methods that followed different assumptions for coding the IRR index.

The first simply notes whether any significant findings were found supporting a treatment effect and codes a backfire effect when there are statistically significant negative findings with no positive treatment effects (scale A).[13] The second (scale B) is more complex and gives weight to each result in each study.[14]

Taking this approach, our findings analyzing the MacKenzie and Hickman (1998) data follow those reported when analyzing the Maryland Report. The correlation between

TABLE 7
RELATING SMS AND IRR ONLY FOR STUDIES IN MacKENZIE AND HICKMAN (1998) THAT INCLUDE TESTS OF STATISTICAL SIGNIFICANCE

SMS	Scale A		Scale B	
	Mean	n	Mean	n
1		0		0
2	0.83	24	1.46	24
3	0.62	26	1.04	26
4	0.36	11	0.64	11
5	0.00	7	0.14	7
Total	.59	68	1.03	68

NOTE: Tau-c for scale A = $-.285$ ($p < .005$). Tau-c for scale B = $-.311$ ($p < .005$).

study design and study outcomes is negative and statistically significant ($p < .005$) irrespective of the approach we used to define the IRR outcome scale (see Table 7). Using scale A, the correlation observed is $-.29$, while using scale B, the observed correlation is $-.31$.

Comparing effect size and IRR score results

It might be argued that our overall findings are related to specific characteristics of the IRR scale rather than the underlying relationship between study design and study outcomes. We could not test this question directly using the Maryland Report data because, as noted earlier, standardized effect sizes were not consistently recorded in the report. However, MacKenzie and Hickman (1998) did report standardized effect size coefficients, and thus we are able to reexamine this question in the context of corrections-based criminal justice studies.

Using the average standardized effect size reported for each study reviewed by MacKenzie and Hickman (1998) for the entire sample (including studies where statistical significance is not reported), the results follow those gained from relating IRR and SMS scores using the Maryland Report sample (see Table 8). Again the correlation between SMS and study outcomes is negative; in this case the correlation is about −.30. The observed relationship is also statistically significant at the .005 level. Accordingly, these findings suggest that our observation of a negative relationship between study design and study outcomes in the Maryland Report sample is not an artifact of the particular codings of the IRR scale.

DISCUSSION

Our review of the Maryland Report Studies suggests that in criminal justice, there is a moderate inverse relationship between the quality of a research design, defined in terms of internal validity, and the outcomes reported in a study. This relationship continues to be observed even when comparing the highest-quality nonrandomized studies with randomized experiments. Using a related database concentrating only on the corrections area, we also found that our findings are consistent when taking into account only studies that employed statistical tests of significance. Finally, using the same database, we were able to examine whether our results would have differed had we used standardized effect size measures rather than the

TABLE 8

RELATING AVERAGE EFFECT SIZE AND SMS FOR STUDIES IN MacKENZIE AND HICKMAN (1988)

SMS	Effect Size Available from the Entire Sample	
	Mean	n
1		0
2	.29	39
3	.23	30
4	.19	13
5	.00	7
Total	.23	89
Missing values		12

NOTE: Correlation $(r) = -.296$ $(p < .005)$.

IRR index that was drawn from the Maryland Report. We found our results to be consistent using both methods. Studies that were defined as including designs with higher internal validity were likely to report smaller effect sizes than studies with designs associated with lower internal validity.

Prior reviews of the relationship between study design and study outcomes do not predict our findings. Indeed, as we noted earlier, the main lesson that can be drawn from prior research is that the impact of study design is very much dependant on the characteristics of the particular area or studies that are reviewed. In theory as well, there is no reason to assume that there will be a systematic type of bias in studies with lower internal validity. What can be said simply is that such studies, all else being equal, are likely to provide biased findings as compared with results drawn from randomized experimental designs. Why then do we find in reviewing a broad group of crime and justice studies what appears to be a systematic relationship between study design and study outcomes?

One possible explanation for our findings is that they are simply an artifact of combining a large number of studies drawn from many different areas of criminal justice. Indeed, there are generally very few studies that examine a very specific type of treatment or intervention in the Maryland Report. And it may be that were we able to explore the impacts of study design on study outcomes for specific types of treatments or interventions, we would find patterns different from the aggregate ones reported here. We think it is likely that for specific areas of treatment or specific types of studies in criminal justice, the relationship between study design and study outcomes will differ from those we observe. Nonetheless, review of this question in the context of one specific type of treatment examined by the Campbell Collaboration (where there was a substantial enough number of randomized and nonrandomized studies for comparison) points to the salience of our overall conclusions even within specific treatment areas (see Petrosino, Petrosino, and Buehler 2001). We think this example is particularly important because it suggests the potential confusion that might result from drawing conclusions from nonrandomized studies.

Relying on a systematic review conducted by Petrosino, Petrosino, and Buehler (2001) on Scared Straight and other kids-visit programs, we identified 20 programs that included crime-related outcome measures. Of these, 9 were randomized experiments, 4 were quasi-experimental trials, and 7 were fully nonexperimental studies. Petrosino, Petrosino, and Buehler reported on the randomized experimental trials in their Campbell Collaboration review. They concluded that Scared Straight and related programs do not evidence any benefit in terms of recidivism and actually increase subsequent delinquency. However, a very different picture of the effectiveness of these programs is drawn from our review of the quasi-experimental and nonexperimental studies. Overall, these studies, in contrast to the experimental evaluations, suggest that Scared Straight programs not only are not harmful but are more likely than not to produce a crime prevention benefit.

We believe that our findings, however preliminary, point to the possibility of an overall positive bias in nonrandomized criminal justice studies. This bias may in part reflect a number of other factors that we could not control for in our data, for example, publication bias or differential attrition rates across designs (see Shadish and Ragsdale 1996). However, we think that a more general explanation for our findings is likely to be found in the norms of criminal justice research and practice.

Such norms are particularly important in the development of nonrandomized studies. Randomized experiments provide little freedom to the researcher in defining equivalence between treatment and comparison groups. Equivalence in randomized experiments is defined simply through the process of randomization. However, nonrandomized studies demand much insight and knowledge in the development of comparable groups of subjects. Not only must the researcher understand the factors that influence treatment so that he or she can prevent confounding in the study results, but such factors must be measured and then controlled for through some statistical or practical procedure.

It may be that such manipulation is particularly difficult in criminal justice study. Criminal justice practitioners may not be as strongly socialized to the idea of experimentation as are practitioners in other fields like medicine. And in this context, it may be that a subtle form of creaming in which the cases considered most amenable to intervention are placed in the intervention group is common. In specific areas of criminal justice, such creaming may be exacerbated by self-selection of subjects who are motivated toward rehabilitation. Nonrandomized designs, even in relatively rigorous quasi-experimental studies, may be unable to compensate or control for why a person is considered amenable and placed in the intervention group. Matching on traditional control variables like age and race, in turn, might not identify the subtle components that make individuals amenable to treatment and thus more likely to be placed in intervention or treatment categories.

Of course, we have so far assumed that nonrandomized studies are biased in their overestimation of program effects. Some scholars might argue just the opposite. The inflexibility of randomized experimental designs has sometimes been seen as a barrier to development of effective theory and practice in criminology (for example, see Clarke and Cornish 1972; Eck 2001; Pawson and Tilley, 1997). Here it is argued that in a field in which we still know little about the root causes and processes that underlie phenomena we seek to influence, randomized studies may not allow investigators the freedom to carefully explore how treatments or programs influence their intended subjects. While this argument has merit in specific circumstances, especially in exploratory analyses of problems and treatments, we think our data suggest that it can lead in more developed areas of our field to significant misinterpretation and confusion.

CONCLUSION

We asked at the outset of our article whether the type of research design used in criminal justice influences the conclusions that are reached. Our findings, based on the Maryland Report, suggest that design does matter and that its effect in criminal justice study is systematic. The weaker a design, as indicated by internal validity, the more likely was a study to report a result in favor of treatment and the less likely it was to report a harmful effect of treatment. Even when comparing studies defined as randomized designs in the Maryland Report with strong quasi-experimental research designs, systematic and statistically significant differences were observed. Though our study should bscores e seen only as a preliminary step in understanding how research design affects study outcomes in criminal justice, it suggests that systematic reviews of what works in criminal justice may be strongly biased when including nonrandomized studies. In efforts such as those being developed by the Campbell Collaboration, such potential biases should be taken into account in coming to conclusions about the effects of interventions.

Notes

1. Statistical adjustments for random group differences are sometimes employed in experimental studies as well.

2. We should note that we have assumed so far that external validity (the degree to which it can be inferred that outcomes apply to the populations that are the focus of treatment) is held constant in these comparisons. Some scholars argue that experimental studies are likely to have lower external validity because it is often difficult to identify institutions that are willing to randomize participants. Clearly, where randomized designs have lower external validity, the assumption that they are to be preferred to nonrandomized studies is challenged.

3. Kunz and Oxman (1998) not only compared randomized and nonrandomized studies but also adequately and inadequately concealed randomized trials and high-quality versus low-quality studies. Generally, high-quality randomized studies included adequately concealed allocation, while lower-quality randomized trails were inadequately concealed. In addition, the general terms *high-quality trials* and *low-quality trials* indicate a difference where "the specific effect of randomization or allocation concealment could not be separated from the effect of other methodological manoeuvres such as double blinding" (Kunz and Oxman 1998, 1185).

4. Moreover, it may be that the finding of higher standardized effects sizes for randomized studies in this review was due to school-level as opposed to individual-level assignment. When only those studies that include a delinquency outcome are examined, a larger effect is found when school rather than student is the unit of analysis (Denise Gottfredson, personal communication, 2001).

5. As the following Scientific Methods Scale illustrates, the lowest acceptable type of evaluation for inclusion in the Maryland Report is a simple correlation between a crime prevention program and a measure of crime or crime risk factors. Thus studies that were descriptive or contained only process measures were excluded.

6. There were also (although rarely) studies in the Maryland Report that reported two findings in opposite directions. For instance, in Sherman and colleagues' (1997) section on specific deterrence (8.18-8.19), studies of arrest for domestic violence had positive results for employed offenders and backfire results for nonemployed offenders. In these isolated cases, the study was coded twice with the same scientific methods scores and each of the investigator-reported result scores (of 1 and –1) separately.

7. For studies examining the absence of a program (such as a police strike) where social conditions worsened or crime increased, this would be coded as 1.

8. For studies examining the absence of a program (such as a police strike) where social conditions improved or crime decreased, this would be coded as –1.

9. Only in the school-based area was there a specific criterion for assessing the investigator's conclusions. As noted below, however, the school-based studies are excluded from our review for other reasons.

10. For example, the authors of the Maryland Report noted in discussing criteria for deciding which programs work, "These are programs that we are reasonably certain of preventing crime or reducing risk factors for crime in the kinds of social contexts in which they have been evaluated, and for which the findings should be generalizable to similar settings in other places and times. Programs coded as 'working' by this definition must have at least two level 3 evaluations with statistical

significance tests showing effectiveness and the preponderance of all available evidence supporting the same conclusion" (Sherman et al. 1997, 2-20).

11. It is the case that many of the studies in this area would have been excluded anyway since they often did not have a crime or delinquency outcome measure (but rather examined early risk factors for crime and delinquency).

12. While the Maryland Report is consistent with other recent reviews that also point to greater success in criminal justice interventions during the past 20 years (for example, see Poyner 1993; Visher and Weisburd 1998; Weisburd 1997), we think the very high percentage of studies showing a treatment impact is likely influenced by publication bias. The high rate of positive findings is also likely influenced by the general weaknesses of the study designs employed. This is suggested by our findings reported later: that the weaker a research design in terms of internal validity, the more likely is the study to report a positive treatment outcome.

13. The coding scheme for scale A was as follows. A value of 1 indicates that the study had any statistically significant findings supporting a positive treatment effect, even if findings included results that were not significant or had negative or backfire findings. A value of 0 indicates that the study had only nonsignificant findings. A value of –1 indicates that the study had only statistically significant negative or backfire findings or statistically significant negative findings with other nonsignificant results.

14. Scale B was created according to the following rules. A value of 2 indicates that the study had only or mostly statistically significant findings supporting a treatment effect (more than 50 percent) when including all results, even nonsignificant ones. A value of 1 indicates that the study had some statistically significant findings supporting a treatment effect (50 percent or less, counting both positive significant and nonsignificant results) even if the nonsignificant results outnumbered the positive statistically significant results. A value of 0 indicates that no statistically significant findings were reported. A value of –1 indicates that the study evidenced statistically significant backfire effects (even if non-

significant results were present) but no statistically significant results supporting the effectiveness of treatment.

References

Bailey, Walter C. 1966. Correctional Outcome: An Evaluation of 100 Reports. *Journal of Criminal Law, Criminology and Police Science* 57:153-60.

Boruch, Robert F., Anthony Petrosino, and Iain Chalmers. 1999. The Campbell Collaboration: A Proposal for Systematic, Multi-National, and Continuous Reviews of Evidence. Background paper for the meeting at University College–London, School of Public Policy, July.

Boruch, Robert F., Brook Snyder, and Dorothy DeMoya. 2000. The Importance of Randomized Field Trials. *Crime & Delinquency* 46:156-80.

Burtless, Gary. 1995. The Case for Randomized Field Trials in Economic and Policy Research. *Journal of Economic Perspectives* 9:63-84.

Campbell, Donald P. and Robert F. Boruch. 1975. Making the Case for Randomized Assignment to Treatments by Considering the Alternatives: Six Ways in Which Quasi-Experimental Evaluations in Compensatory Education Tend to Underestimate Effects. In *Evaluation and Experiment: Some Critical Issues in Assessing Social Programs*, ed. Carl Bennett and Arthur Lumsdaine. New York: Academic Press.

Chalmers, Iain and Douglas G. Altman. 1995. *Systematic Reviews*. London: British Medical Journal Press.

Clarke, Ronald V. and Derek B. Cornish. 1972. *The Control Trial in Institutional Research: Paradigm or Pitfall for Penal Evaluators?* London: HMSO.

Cox, Stephen M., William S. Davidson, and Timothy S. Bynum. 1995. A Meta-Analytic Assessment of Delinquency-

Related Outcomes of Alternative Education Programs. *Crime & Delinquency* 41:219-34.

Cullen, Francis T. and Paul Gendreau. 2000. Assessing Correctional Rehabilitation: Policy, Practice, and Prospects. In *Policies, Processes, and Decisions of the Criminal Justice System: Criminal Justice 3*, ed. Julie Horney. Washington, DC: U.S. Department of Justice, National Institute of Justice.

Davies, Huw T. O., Sandra Nutley, and Peter C. Smith. 2000. *What Works: Evidence-Based Policy and Practice in Public Services*. London: Policy Press.

Davies, Philip. 1999. What Is Evidence-Based Education? *British Journal of Educational Studies* 47:108-21.

Eck, John. 2001. Learning from Experience in Problem Oriented Policing and Crime Prevention: The Positive Functions of Weak Evaluations and the Negative Functions of Strong Ones. Unpublished manuscript.

Egger, Matthias and G. Davey Smith. 1998. Bias in Location and Selection of Studies. *British Medical Journal* 316:61-66.

Farrington, David P. 1983. Randomized Experiments in Crime and Justice. In *Crime and Justice: An Annual Review of Research*, ed. Norval Morris and Michael Tonry. Chicago: University of Chicago Press.

———. 2000. Standards for Inclusion of Studies in Systematic Reviews. Discussion paper for the Campbell Collaboration Crime and Justice Coordinating Group.

Farrington, David P. and Anthony Petrosino. 2001. The Campbell Collaboration Crime and Justice Group. *Annals of the American Academy of Political and Social Science* 578:35-49.

Feder, Lynette and Robert F. Boruch. 2000. The Need for Experiments in Criminal Justice Settings. *Crime & Delinquency* 46:291-94.

Feder, Lynette, Annette Jolin, and William Feyerherm. 2000. Lessons from Two Randomized Experiments in Criminal Justice Settings. *Crime & Delinquency* 46:380-400.

Friedlander, Daniel and Philip K. Robins. 2001. Evaluating Program Evaluations: New Evidence on Commonly Used Non-Experimental Methods. *American Economic Review* 85:923-37.

Hedges, Larry V. 2000. Using Converging Evidence in Policy Formation: The Case of Class Size Research. *Evaluation and Research in Education* 14:193-205.

Heinsman, Donna T. and William R. Shadish. 1996. Assignment Methods in Experimentation: When Do Nonrandomized Experiments Approximate Answers from Randomized Experiments? *Psychological Methods* 1:154-69.

Kunz, Regina and Andy Oxman. 1998. The Unpredictability Paradox: Review of Empirical Comparisons of Randomized and Non-Randomized Clinical Trials. *British Medical Journal* 317:1185-90.

LaLonde, Robert J. 1986. Evaluating the Econometric Evaluations of Training Programs with Experimental Data. *American Economic Review* 76:604-20.

Lipsey, Mark W. and David B. Wilson. 1993. The Efficacy of Psychological, Educational, and Behavioral Treatment: Confirmation from Meta-Analysis. *American Psychologist* 48:1181-209.

Lipton, Douglas S., Robert M. Martinson, and Judith Wilks. 1975. *The Effectiveness of Correctional Treatment: A Survey of Treatment Evaluation Studies*. New York: Praeger.

Logan, Charles H. 1972. Evaluation Research in Crime and Delinquency—A Reappraisal. *Journal of Criminal Law, Criminology and Police Science* 63:378-87.

MacKenzie, Doris L. 2000. Evidence-based Corrections: Identifying What Works. *Crime & Delinquency* 46:457-71.

MacKenzie, Doris L. and Laura J. Hickman. 1998. *What Works in Corrections* (Report submitted to the State of Washington Legislature Joint Audit and Review Committee). College Park: University of Maryland.

Martinson, Robert. 1974. What Works? Questions and Answers About Prison Reform. *Public Interest* 35:22-54.

Millenson, Michael L. 1997. *Demanding Medical Excellence: Doctors and Accountability in the Information Age.* Chicago: University of Chicago Press.

Nutley, Sandra and Huw T. O. Davies. 1999. The Fall and Rise of Evidence in Criminal Justice. *Public Money & Management* 19:47-54.

Pawson, Ray and Nick Tilley. 1997. *Realistic Evaluation.* London: Sage.

Petrosino, Anthony, Carolyn Petrosino, and John Buehler. 2001. Pilot Test: The Effects of Scared Straight and Other Juvenile Awareness Programs on Delinquency. Unpublished manuscript.

Poyner, Barry. 1993. What Works in Crime Prevention: An Overview of Evaluations. In *Crime Prevention Studies.* Vol. 1, ed. Ronald V. Clarke. Monsey, NY: Criminal Justice Press.

Shadish, William R. and Kevin Ragsdale. 1996. Random Versus Nonrandom Assignment in Controlled Experiments: Do You Get the Same Answer? *Journal of Consulting and Clinical Psychology* 64:1290-305.

Sherman, Lawrence W. 1998. *Evidence-Based Policing.* In *Ideas in American Policing.* Washington, DC: Police Foundation.

Sherman, Lawrence W., Denise C. Gottfredson, Doris Layton MacKenzie, John E. Eck, Peter Reuter, and Shawn D. Bushway. 1997. *Preventing Crime: What Works, What Doesn't, What's Promising.* Washington, DC: U.S. Department of Justice, National Institute of Justice.

Visher, Christy A. and David Weisburd. 1998. Identifying What Works: Recent Trends in Crime Prevention. *Crime, Law and Social Change* 28:223-42.

Weisburd, David. 1997. *Reorienting Crime Prevention Research and Policy: From the Causes of Criminality to the Context of Crime* (Research Report NIJ 16504). Washington, DC: U.S. Department of Justice, National Institute of Justice.

Whitehead, John T. and Steven P. Lab. 1989. A Meta-Analysis of Juvenile Correctional Treatment. *Journal of Research in Crime and Delinquency* 26:276-95.

Wilkinson, Leland and Task Force on Statistical Inference. 1999. Statistical Methods in Psychology Journals: Guidelines and Explanations. *American Psychologist* 54:594-604.

Wilson, David B., Catherine A. Gallagher, Doris L. MacKenzie. 2000. A Meta-Analysis of Corrections-Based Education, Vocation, and Work Programs for Adult Offenders. *Journal of Research in Crime and Delinquency* 37:347-68.

Wilson, David B., Denise C. Gottfredson, and Stacy S. Najaka. In Press. School-Based Prevention of Problem Behaviors: A Meta-Analysis. *Journal of Quantitative Criminology.*

Zuger, Abigail. 1997. New Way of Doctoring: By the Book. *New York Times,* 16 Dec.

ANNALS, *AAPSS*, **578**, November 2001

Meta-Analytic Methods
for Criminology

By DAVID B. WILSON

ABSTRACT: Meta-analysis was designed to synthesize empirical relationships across studies, such as the effects of a specific crime prevention intervention on criminal offending behavior. Meta-analysis focuses on the size and direction of effects across studies, examining the consistency of effects and the relationship between study features and observed effects. The findings from meta-analysis not only reveal robust empirical relationships but also identify existing weaknesses in the knowledge base. Furthermore, meta-analytic results can easily be translated into summary statistics useful for informing public policy regarding effective crime prevention efforts.

David B. Wilson is an assistant professor of the administration of justice at George Mason University. His research interests include program evaluation research methodology, meta-analysis, crime and general problem behavior prevention programs, and juvenile delinquency intervention effectiveness.

NOTE: This work was supported by the Jerry Lee Foundation.

71

I MAGINE you are given the task of synthesizing what is currently known about the effectiveness of correctional boot camps for reducing future criminal behavior among juvenile and adult offenders. An exhaustive search for all relevant evaluations of boot camp programs compared with more traditional forms of punishment and rehabilitation identifies 29 unique studies. The findings from these studies range from large positive to large negative statistically significant effects. To complicate matters, the studies vary in the evaluation methods used, including the definition of recidivism (for example, rearrest, reconviction, and reinstitutionalization), offender populations, and program characteristics. How will you meaningfully make sense of this array of information?

The statistical methods of meta-analysis were designed specifically to address this situation. Meta-analysis represents a statistical and systematic approach to reviewing research findings across multiple independent studies. As such, meta-analyses are systematic reviews (Petrosino et al. 2001 [this issue]). However, not all criminological intervention research literatures can be successfully meta-analyzed, and thus not all systematic reviews will use the statistical methods of meta-analysis.

The basic idea behind meta-analysis dates back almost 100 years and is simple. Karl Pearson, the developer of the Pearson product-moment correlation coefficient, synthesized the findings from multiple studies of the effectiveness of inoculation for typhoid fever (Pearson 1904). His method involved computing the correlation between inoculation and mortality within each study and then averaging the correlations across studies, producing a composite correlation. By today's standards, this was a meta-analysis, although the term was not introduced until the 1970s (Glass 1976).

The logical framework of meta-analysis is based on the assumption that the averaging of findings across studies will produce a more valid estimate of the effect of interest than that of any individual study. Typically, the finding from any individual study is imprecise due to sampling error. Thus some studies of a specific phenomenon, such as the effectiveness of correctional boot camps, will overestimate and others will underestimate the size of the true effect. Instability in observed effects due to sampling error is an assumption at the core of statistical inference testing, such as a t test between an intervention and comparison condition. Averaging across studies is analogous to averaging across individuals within a single study or averaging across multiple test items.

For a collection of pure replications, the logic behind meta-analysis is indisputable if one accepts the logic and assumptions of the standard statistical practices of the social and medical sciences. Meta-analysis as it is applied in criminology and the other social sciences extends this logic to collections of studies that are conceptual replications, that is, studies that examine the same relationship of interest but differ from one another in other respects, such as the research design or elements of the intervention.

Conceptual replications are assumed to be estimating the same fundamental relationship, despite differences in methodology and other substantive features. This variability in study features can be viewed as a strength, however, because a synthesis of conceptual replications can show that a relationship is observed across a range of methodological and substantive variability. Unlike sampling error, however, errors in estimates of the relationship of interest that arise from poor study design will not necessarily cancel out as a result of aggregation. Therefore the meta-analyst must carefully assess the influence of methodological variation on observed effects (Wilson and Lipsey, in press).

WHY META-ANALYSIS?

Meta-analysis is not the only method of synthesizing or reviewing results across studies. Other approaches include the narrative and vote-count review. The narrative review relies on a researcher's ability to digest the array of findings across studies and arrive at a pronouncement regarding the evidence for or against a hypothesis using some unknown and unknowable (that is, subjective) mental calculus.

The vote-count method imposes discipline on this process by tallying the number of studies with statistically significant findings in favor of the hypothesis and the number contrary to the hypothesis (null findings). This approach is appealing, for

it is objective and systematic, yet simple. Furthermore it upholds the long-standing tradition in the social sciences of allowing the statistical significance test to be the arbiter of the validity of a scientific hypothesis.

The intuitive appeal of the vote count obscures its weaknesses. First, the vote count fails to account for the differential precision of the studies being reviewed. Larger studies, all else being equal, provide more precise estimates of the relationship of interest and thus should be given greater weight in a review.

Second, the vote count fails to recognize the fundamental asymmetry of the statistical significance test. A statistically significant finding is a strong conclusion, whereas a statistically nonsignificant (null) finding is a weak conclusion. In the vote-count review, null findings are typically interpreted as evidence that the relationship of interest does not exist (for example, the intervention is not effective). This is an incorrect interpretation. Failure to reject a null hypothesis is not support for the null, merely suspended judgment. Enough null findings in the same direction are evidence that the null is false. This possibility was recognized by Fisher (1944), a strong proponent of significance testing.

Third, the vote count ignores the size of the observed effects. By focusing on statistical significance, and not the size and direction of the effect, a study with a small but statistically significant effect would be viewed as evidence favoring the hypothesis, and a study with a large nonsignificant effect would be viewed as evidence against the hypothesis. Both studies provide evidence that the relationship is nonzero, although the strength of that evidence is weak in one of the studies. The benefits of a null hypothesis statistical significance test for interpreting a finding from an individual study do not translate into benefits when evaluating a collection of related studies.

Furthermore a counterintuitive feature of the vote-count method is that the likelihood of arriving at an incorrect conclusion increases as the number of studies on a topic increases, if the typical statistical power of the studies in that area is low. This is a common situation in criminology. For example, Lipsey and colleagues (1985) estimated that the typical power of evaluations of juvenile delinquency interventions was less than .50. A vote-count review of that literature is sure to yield misleading conclusions.

Meta-analysis avoids the pitfalls of the vote-count method by focusing on the size and direction of effects across studies, not whether the individual effects were statistically significant. The latter largely depends on the sample size of the study. Furthermore focusing on the size and direction of the effect makes better use of the data available in the primary studies, providing a mechanism for analyzing differences across studies and drawing inferences about the likely size of the true population effect of interest. The statistical methods of meta-analysis allow for an assessment of both the consistency of findings across studies and the relationship of study features with variability in effects.

As a method, meta-analysis includes all of the essential features of a systematic review (see Petrosino et al. 2001), including an exhaustive search for all relevant studies (published or not), explicit inclusion and exclusion criteria, and a coding protocol for extracting data from the studies. The distinctive feature of meta-analysis is the application of statistical techniques to the analysis of the study findings, where study findings are encoded on a common metric. The section below presents an overview of the analytic methods of meta-analysis. Several articles in this issue (MacKenzie, Wilson, and Kider 2001 [this issue]; Lipsey, Chapman, and Landenberger 2001 [this issue]) provide examples of meta-analytic methods. This article concludes with a discussion of the strengths and weaknesses of meta-analysis and guidance on when not to use meta-analysis.

A FRAMEWORK FOR META-ANALYSIS

A defining feature of meta-analysis is the effect size, that is, any index of the effect of interest that is comparable across studies. The effect size might index the effects of a treatment group relative to a comparison group or the relationship between two observed variables, such as gender and mathematical achievement or attachment to parents and delinquent behavior. In the analysis of meta-analytic data, the effect size is the dependent variable.

The need for an effect size places restrictions on what research can be meta-analyzed. The collection of studies of interest to the reviewer must examine the same basic relationship, even if at a broad level of abstraction. At the broad end of the continuum would be a group of studies examining the effects of school-based prevention programs on delinquent behavior. At the narrow end of the continuum would be a set of replications of a study on the effects of the drug DepoProvea on the perpetration of sexual offenses. The research designs of a collection of studies would all need to be sufficiently similar such that a comparable effect size could be computed from each. Thus most meta-analyses of intervention studies will stipulate that eligible studies use a comparison group design.

The specific effect size index used in a given meta-analysis will depend on the nature of the research being synthesized. Commonly used effect size indices for intervention research are the standardized mean difference, odds ratio, and correlation coefficient. The standardized mean difference–type effect size is well suited to two group comparison studies (for example, a treatment versus a comparison condition) with continuous or dichotomous dependent measures. The odds ratio is well suited to these same research domains with the exception that the dependent measures must be dichotomous, such as whether the participants recidivated within 12 months of leaving the program. The correlation coefficient can be applied to the broadest range of research designs, including all designs for which standardized mean difference and odds ratio effect sizes can be computed. Because of this, it

has been argued that the correlation coefficient is the ideal effect size (Rosenthal 1991). However, the standardized mean difference and odds ratio effect sizes have distinct statistical advantages over the correlation coefficient for intervention research and are more natural indices of program effects.

Standardized mean difference

The standardized mean difference, d, represents the effect of an intervention as the difference between the intervention and comparison group means on the dependent variable of interest, standardized by the pooled within-groups standard deviation. Thus findings based on different operationalizations of the dependent variable of interest (for example, delinquency) are standardized to a common metric: standard deviation units for the population. An advantage of d is that it can be computed from a wide range of statistical data, including means and standard deviations, t tests, F tests, correlation coefficients, and 2×2 contingency tables (see Lipsey and Wilson 2001). Although conceptualized as the difference between two groups on a continuous dependent variable, d can also be computed from dichotomous data.

Odds ratio

The odds ratio, o, represents the effect of an intervention as the odds of a favorable (or unfavorable) outcome for the intervention group relative to the comparison group. It is used when the outcome is measured dichotomously, such as is common in medicine and criminology. The odds ratio is easy to compute from either the raw frequencies of a 2×2 contingency table or the proportions of successes or failures in each condition. As a ratio of two odds, a value of 1 indicates an equal likelihood of a successful outcome, whereas values between 1 and 0 indicate a negative effect and values greater than 1 indicate a positive effect. Unlike the correlation coefficient, the odds ratio is unaffected by differential base rates (the marginal distribution) for the outcome across studies (see Farrington and Loeber 2000), thus eliminating a potential source of effect variability across studies.

Correlation coefficient

The correlation coefficient is a widely used and widely understood statistic within the social sciences. It can be used to represent the relationship between two dichotomous variables, a dichotomous and a continuous variable, and two continuous variables. The correlation coefficient has a distinct disadvantage, however, when one or both of the variables on which it is based are dichotomous (Farrington and Loeber 2000). For example, the correlation coefficient is restricted to less than +1 in absolute value if the percentage of participants in the intervention and comparison conditions is not split fifty-fifty. Thus it is recommended that it only be used for meta-analyses of correlational research and that meta-analyses of intervention studies use either the standardized mean difference, the odds ratio, or a more specialized effect size (for a dis-

cussion of other alternatives, see Lipsey and Wilson 2001).

ANALYSIS OF
META-ANALYTIC DATA

A typical meta-analysis extracts one or more effect sizes per study and codes a variety of study characteristics to represent the important substantive and methodological differences across studies. Before analysis of the data, statistical transformations and adjustments may need to be applied to the effect size. If multiple effect sizes were extracted per study, then a method of including only a single effect size per study (or sample within a study) per analysis will need to be adopted. The analysis of effect size data typically examines the central tendency of the effect size distribution and the consistency of effects across studies. Additional analyses test for the ability of study features to explain inconsistencies in effects across studies. Meta-analytic methods for performing these analyses are summarized below.

*Transformations
and adjustments*

There are standard adjustments and transformations that are routinely applied to effect sizes, and optional adjustments may be applied depending on the purpose of the meta-analysis. For example, Hedges (1982; Hedges and Olkin 1985) showed that the standardized mean difference effect size is positively biased when based on a small sample; that is, it is too large in absolute value, and the bias increases as sample size decreases. The size of bias is very modest for all but very small sample sizes, but the adjustment is easy to perform and routinely done when using d as the effect size index (for formulas, see the appendix).

When using the odds ratio, one encounters a complication that is also easily rectified. The odds ratio is asymmetric, with negative relationships represented as values between 0 and 1 and positive relationships represented as values between 1 and infinity. This complicates analysis. Fortunately, the natural logarithm of the odds ratio is symmetric about 0 with a well-defined standard error. The importance of the latter is discussed below. Thus, for purposes of analysis, the odds ratio is transformed into the logged odds ratio. Results can be transformed back into odds ratios for purposes of interpretation using the antilogarithm.

Similarly the correlation coefficient has a distributional shape that is less than ideal for purposes of computing averages. Furthermore the standard error is asymmetric, particularly as the correlation approaches −1 or +1. This is easily solved by applying Fisher's Z_r transformation, which normalizes the correlation and results in a standard error that is remarkably simple. As with the odds ratio, final results can be transformed back into correlation coefficients for interpretative purposes.

Hunter and Schmidt (1990) proposed adjusting effect sizes for measurement unreliability and invalidity, range restriction, and artificial dichotomization. These adjustments, however, depend on information that is rarely reported for outcome measures in crime and justice evaluation studies, such as reliability and validity coefficients. The logic of these adjustments is to estimate what would have been observed under more ideal research conditions. These adjustments, while common in meta-analyses of measurement generalizability studies, are rarely used in meta-analyses of intervention research. If they are used, it is recommended that a sensitivity analysis be performed to assess the effect the adjustments have on the results.

Statistical independence among effect sizes

A complication with effect size data is the often numerous effect sizes of interest available from each study. Effect sizes that are based on the same sample of individuals (or other units of analysis, such as city blocks and so forth) are statistically dependent, that is, correlated with each other. Meta-analytic analysis assumes that each data point (effect size in this case) is statistically independent of all other data points.[1] Thus we can include only one effect size per sample in any given analysis. An independent set of effect sizes can be obtained through several strategies. First, each major outcome construct of interest can, and should, be analyzed separately. For example, effect sizes representing employment success should be analyzed separately from those representing criminal behavior. Second, multiple effect sizes within each outcome construct can be averaged to produce one effect size per study or sample within a study. Alternatively, a meta-analyst may choose a single effect size based on an explicit criterion. That is, the meta-analyst may prefer rearrest data over reinstitutionalization data if the former are available. Finally, the meta-analyst may randomly select among those effect sizes that are of interest to a given analysis. Note that several analyses can be performed, each with a different set of independent effect sizes.

The inverse variance weight

An additional complication of meta-analytic data is the differential precision in effect sizes across studies. Effect sizes based on large samples, all other things being equal, are more precise than effect sizes based on small samples. A simple solution to this problem would be to weight each effect size by its sample size. Hedges (1982) showed, however, that the optimal weight is based on the variance (squared standard error) of each effect size. This is intuitively appealing as well, for the standard error is a statistical expression of the precision of parameter, such as an effect size. The smaller the standard error, the more precise is the effect size. Thus, in all meta-analytic analyses, weights are computed from the inverse of the squared standard error of the effect size. This is called the inverse variance weight method. Equations for the inverse variance weight for each of the three effect size indices discussed above are presented in the appendix.

The mean effect size and related statistics

A starting point for the analysis of effect size data is the computation of the overall mean effect size, computed as a weighted mean, weighting by the inverse variance weight. A z test can be performed to assess whether the mean effect size is statistically greater than (or less than) 0, and a confidence interval can be constructed around the mean effect size. Both statistics rely on the standard error of the mean effect size, computed from the sum of the weights. Thus both the precision and number of the individual effect sizes influence the precision of the mean effect size. (For equations, see the appendix.)

The mean effect size is meaningful only if the effects are consistent across studies, that is, statistically homogeneous. If the effects are highly heterogeneous, then a single overall mean effect size does not adequately represent the effects observed by the collection of studies. In meta-analysis, consistency in effects is assessed with the homogeneity statistic Q. A statistically significant Q indicates that the observed variability in effect sizes exceeds statistical expectations regarding the variability that would be observed across pure replications, that is, if the collection of studies were indeed estimating a common population effect size. A statistically nonsignificant Q suggests that the variability in effects across studies is no greater than expected due to sampling error.

A heterogeneous distribution (a significant Q) is often the desired outcome of a homogeneity analysis. Heterogeneity justifies the exploration of the relationship between study features and effects, an important aspect of meta-analysis. The analytic approaches available to the meta-analyst for examining between study effects are an analysis of mean effect sizes by a categorical study feature, analogous to a one-way ANOVA, and a meta-analytic regression analysis approach. Both approaches rely on inverse variance weighting, and both can be implemented under the assumptions of a fixed- or random-effects model. The assumptions of these models will be discussed below.

*Categorical analysis
of effect sizes: The
analog to the ANOVA*

The analog to the ANOVA-type analysis is used to examine the relationship between a single categorical variable, such as treatment type or research method, and effect size. There may be as few as two categories, in which case the analysis is conceptually similar to a t test, or many categories. A separate mean effect size and associated statistics, such as a z test and confidence interval, are computed for each category of the variable of interest. To test whether the mean effect sizes differ across categories, a Q between groups is calculated (see the appendix). Although this statistic is distributed as a chi-square, it is interpreted in the same fashion as an F from a one-way ANOVA. A significant Q between groups indicates that the variability in the mean effect sizes across categories is greater than expected due to sampling error. Thus the category is related to effect size. Examination of confidence intervals provides evidence of the source of the important difference(s).

As with the overall distribution, the residual distribution of effects within categories may be homogeneous or heterogeneous. This is tested with the Q within statistic (see the appendix). A homogeneous Q within indicates that the categorical variable explained the excess variability detected by the overall homogeneity test. In this case, the categorical variable provides an explanation for the variability in effects across studies. Alternatively, additional sources of variability in effects exist if the Q within is significant.

The computation of the analog to the ANOVA can be tedious. Macros that work with existing statistical software packages exist for performing this analysis (for example, Lipsey and Wilson 2001; Wang and Bushman 1998). BioStat (2000) has created a meta-analysis program that among other features performs the analog to the ANOVA analysis.

*Meta-analytic
regression analysis*

The analog to the ANOVA is limited to a single categorical variable. A more flexible and general analytic strategy for assessing the relationship between study features and effect size is regression analysis. Regression analysis can incorporate multiple independent variables (study features) in a single analysis, including continuous variables and categorical variables (via dummy coding). The differences between ordinary least squares regression and meta-analytic regression are the weighting by the inverse variance and a modification to the standard error of the regression coefficients, necessitating the use of specialized software (for example, Lipsey and Wilson 2001; Wang and Bushman 1998). As with the analog to the ANOVA, two Q values are calculated as part of meta-analytic regression: a Q for the model and a Q for the residual or error variance. The former is a test of the predictive ability of the study features in explaining between-studies variability in effects. The regression model accounts for significant variability in the effect size distribution if the Q for the model is significant. As with the Q within for the analog to the ANOVA, a significant Q for the error variance indicates that excess variability remains in the effects across studies after accounting for the variability explained by the regression model. That is, the residual distribution in effect sizes is heterogeneous.

Recognizing the correlational nature of the above analyses of the relationship between study features and effect size is critical. Study features are often correlated with one another and, as such, a moderating relationship may be the result of confounded between-studies features. For example, the mean effect size for treatment type A may be higher than the mean effect size for treatment type B. The studies examining treatment type B, however, may have used a less sensitive measure of the outcome construct, thus confounding treatment type with characteristics of the dependent variable. Multivariate analyses can help assess the interrelationships between study features, but these analyses cannot account for unmeasured study characteristics.

Fixed and random effects models

The statistical model presented above assumes that the collection of effect sizes being analyzed is estimating a common population effect size. In statistical terms, this is a fixed-effects model. Stated differently, a fixed-effects model assumes that each effect size differs from the true population effect size solely due to subject-level sampling error. Each observed effect size is viewed as an imperfect estimate of the true, single population effect for the intervention of interest. This provides the theoretical basis for incorporating the standard error of the effect size (an estimate of subject-level sampling error) into the analysis as the inverse variance weight.

This assumption is restrictive and likely to be untenable in many syntheses of criminological intervention research where studies of a common research hypothesis differ on many dimensions, some of which are likely to be related to effect size. Thus each effect size has variability (that is, instability) due to subject-level sampling error and study-level variability. The random-effects model assumes that at least some portion of the study-level variability is unexplained by the study features included in the statistical models of effect size. These study differences may simply be unmeasured, or they may be unmeasurable. In both cases, each effect size is assumed to estimate a true population effect size for that study, and the collection of true population effect sizes represents a random distribution of effects. In statistical terms, this is a random-effects model.

Methods for estimating random-effects models in meta-analysis are well developed. The basic method involves modifying the definition of the inverse variance weight such that it incorporates both the subject- and study-level estimates of instability. The inverse variance weight is thus based on both the standard error of the effect size and an estimate of the variability in the distribution of population effects. The latter is computed from the observed distribution of effects. Random-effects models are more conservative than fixed-effects models. Confidence intervals will be larger, and regression coefficients that were statistically significant under a fixed-effects model may no longer be significant under a random-effects model. It is recommended that meta-analyses of criminological literatures use a random-effects model of analysis unless a clear justification to do otherwise exists.

Sensitivity analysis

A final analytic issue is the sensitivity of the results to unusual study effects and decisions made by the meta-analyst. First, it is wise to examine the influence of outliers in the distribution of effect sizes and the distribution of inverse variance weights. A modest effect size outlier with a large weight can drive an analysis. Rerunning an important analysis with and without highly influential studies can help verify that the observed result is not solely a function of a single unusual study. Second, the method of selecting one

effect size per study for any given analysis may also affect the meta-analytic findings. For example, in the boot camp systematic review by Mac-Kenzie, Wilson, and Kider (2001), the analyses were performed on a single effect size selected from each study based on a set of decision rules. A sensitivity analysis showed that using a composite of all recidivism effect sizes produced the same results, bolstering the authors' confidence in the findings. Third, if the meta-analysis has included methodologically weak studies, analyses examining the relationship between method features and observed effects are essential.

Illustration: Cognitive-behavioral programs for sex offenders

To illustrate the methods outlined above, I have selected a subset of studies included in a meta-analysis of sex offender programs (Gallagher, Wilson, and MacKenzie no date). Presented below are the programs based on cognitive-behavioral principles. Studies were included if they used a comparison group design and the comparison received either no treatment or non-sex-offender-specific treatment. Studies also had to report a measure of sex offense recidivism at some point following termination of the program.

A total of 13 studies met the eligibility criteria for this meta-analysis. The recidivism data were dichotomous and as such, the odds ratio was selected as the effect size index. The odds ratio and 95 percent confidence interval for these 13 studies are presented in Figure 1. Visual inspection of these odds ratios shows a distinct

FIGURE 1
ODDS RATIO AND 95 PERCENT CONFIDENCE INTERVAL FOR EACH OF
THE 13 COGNITIVE-BEHAVIORAL SEX OFFENDER EVALUATION STUDIES

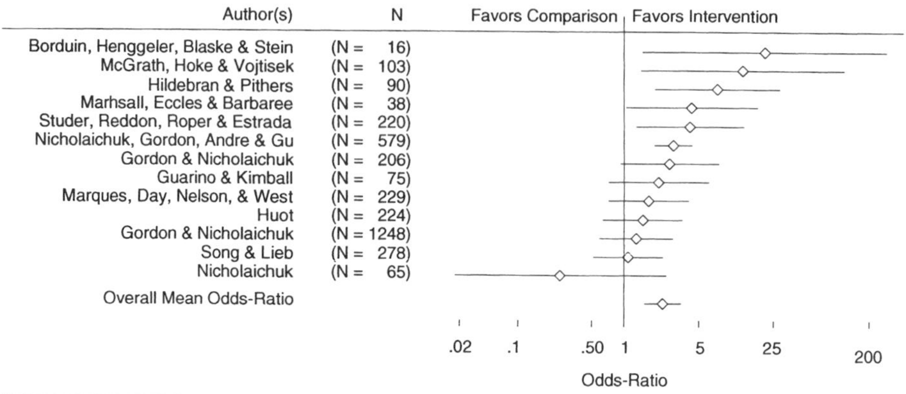

NOTE: Sources of programs are available from the author.

positive trend, with 12 of the 13 studies observing lower recidivism rates (and hence odds ratios greater than 1) for the sex offender treatment condition than the comparison condition. The sole study with a negative effect (an odds ratio between 0 and 1) had a large confidence interval that extended well into the positive range and was from a study of poor methodological quality.

The weighted mean odds ratio for this collection of 13 studies was 2.33, and the 95 percent confidence interval was 1.57 to 3.42. The z test indicates that this odds ratio was statistically significant at conventional levels, $z = 4.26, p < .001$. This collection of studies supports the conclusion that cognitive-behavioral programs for sex offenders reduce the risk of a sexual reoffense. The homogeneity statistic was significant, indicating that the findings are not consistent across studies and may be related to study features, $Q = 21.99$, $df = 12, p < .05$.

This collection of studies differed in many ways, both in the research methods used and the specifics of the sex offender treatment program. Many of these 13 studies evaluated a cognitive-behavioral approach called relapse prevention. Relapse prevention programs may be more (or less) effective than other cognitive-behavioral programs. To explore this, the mean effect size for relapse prevention and other cognitive-behavioral programs was calculated (2.41 and 1.73, respectively). Also calculated were the Q between and Q within. The Q between was $0.87, p > .05$, indicating that the observed difference between these two means was not statistically significant. The Q within was statistically significant, $Q_{WITHIN} = 21.12, df = 11, p = .03$, indicating that significant variability across groups remained after accounting for treatment type.

A regression analysis was performed to test whether the differential lengths of follow-up across studies and the different definitions of recidivism could account for the heterogeneity. The regression coefficient for whether the recidivism was measured at least five years posttreatment was statistically significant and positive, B = 1.58, p = .01, suggesting that studies with longer follow-up periods observed larger differences in the rates of sexual offending between the treated and nontreated groups. The effects of sex offender programs may increase over time, or the length of follow-up was related to an unmeasured program characteristic that led to greater effectiveness. The regression coefficient for whether the recidivism measure was an indicator of arrest or reconviction was also statistically significant, B = 1.25, p = .04, suggesting that arrest may be a more sensitive measure of the program effects. Significant variability in the effect size distribution was accounted for by this regression model, Q_{MODEL} = 7.05, df = 3, p = .03. Furthermore the Q associated with the residual variability in effect sizes was not statistically significant, $Q_{RESIDUAL}$ = 14.9, df = 10, p = .13, indicating that the residual variability in effects is not greater than would be expected due to sampling error.

INTERPRETATION OF META-ANALYTIC FINDINGS

A researcher who finds a statistically significant effect is presented with the difficult task of deciding whether the effect is meaningful from a practical or clinical perspective. That is, is the effect "significant" in the everyday meaning of that word? Meta-analysts are confronted with the same problem. What is the practical significance of an observed mean effect size? A common approach to addressing this problem is the translation of the effect size into a success rate differential for the intervention and comparison conditions, such as using the binomial effect size display (Rosenthal and Rubin 1983). For example, a standardized mean difference effect size of .40 is equivalent to a success rate differential of 20 percent (that is, 40 percent recidivism in the intervention condition and 60 percent recidivism in the comparison condition). If the audience for the meta-analysis is not familiar with standardized mean difference effect sizes, then the success rate differential provides a useful method of understanding the practical significance of the observed findings.

The odds ratio has a natural interpretation without transformation: the odds ratio is the odds of a successful outcome in the treated condition relative to the comparison condition. Thinking about odds is, however, odd for all but the more mathematically inclined. As with the standardized mean difference, a mean odds ratio can be translated into percentages of successes (or failures). This translation requires "fixing" the failure rate for one of the conditions. For example, if we assume a 50 percent recidivism rate for the comparison condition, then an odds ratio of 1.5 translates into a recidivism rate of 40 percent in the treatment condition.

Presenting the results of a meta-analysis of odds ratios as percentages provides a means of assessing the magnitude of the observed program effects.

ADVANTAGES AND DISADVANTAGES OF META-ANALYSIS

Meta-analysis has several distinct advantages over alternative forms of reviewing empirical research. As a systematic method of review, meta-analysis is replicable by independent researchers. The methods are explicit and open to the scrutiny of other scholars, who may question the inclusion and exclusion criteria and critique the variables used to examine between-studies differences. This can lead to productive debates and competing analyses of the meta-analytic data. In addition, meta-analysis makes efficient use of the information contained in the primary studies. Focusing on the direction and magnitude of the findings across studies using a common statistical benchmark allows for the exploration of relationships between study features of effects that would not otherwise be observable. The statistical methods of meta-analysis help guard against interpreting the dispersion in results as meaningful when it can just as easily be explained as sampling error. Finally, meta-analysis can handle a much larger number of studies than could effectively be summarized with alternative methods. There is no theoretical limit to the number of studies that can be incorporated into a single meta-analysis, yet as a method it can also be applied to a small number of similar studies.

As a practitioner of meta-analysis, I see few justified disadvantages to the use of meta-analysis. This does not mean that meta-analysis does not have its disadvantages. On the practical side, meta-analysis is far more time-consuming than traditional forms of review and requires a moderate level of statistical sophistication. Meta-analysis also simplifies the findings of the individual studies, often representing each study as a single effect size and a small set of descriptor variables. Complex patterns of effects often found in individual studies do not lend themselves to synthesis, such as the results from individual growth-curve modeling. To accommodate this, a reviewer may wish to augment a meta-analytic review with narrative descriptions of important studies and interesting study-level findings obscured in the meta-analytic synthesis. Finally, the methods of meta-analysis cannot overcome weaknesses in the primary studies. If the research base that examines the hypothesis of interest is methodologically weak, then the findings from the meta-analysis will also be weak. In these situations, meta-analysis creates a solid foundation for the next generation of studies by clearly identifying the weaknesses of the current knowledge base on a given issue.

WHEN NOT TO DO META-ANALYSIS

Meta-analysis is the preferred method of systematically reviewing a collection of empirical studies examining a common research hypothesis. However, meta-analysis is not appropriate for the synthesis of all empirical research literatures. First, meta-analysis cannot be used when a common effect size index cannot be computed across the studies of interest. For example, the appropriate effect size for area studies (that is, studies that have a geographic area as the unit of analysis) is currently being discussed among members of the Campbell Collaboration. Second, the research designs across a collection of studies examining the relationship of interest may be too disparate for meaningful synthesis. For example, studies with different units of analysis cannot be readily meta-analyzed unless sufficient data are presented to compute an effect size at a common level of analysis. Studies with fundamentally different research designs, such as one-group longitudinal studies and comparison group studies also should not be combined in the same meta-analysis. Third, the research question for a meta-analysis may involve a multivariate relationship. Although methods have been developed for meta-analyzing multivariate research studies (for example, Becker 1992; Becker 1996; Premack and Hunter 1988), these methods have rarely been applied and are still not well developed. It is unlikely that the more elaborate research designs will ever easily lend themselves to synthesis. Thus some research questions addressed by primary studies are not easily meta-analyzed. Finally, meta-analysis does not address broad theoretical issues that may be important to a debate regarding the value of various crime prevention efforts. Meta-analysis is designed to synthesize the evidence regarding the strength of a relationship across distinct research studies. This is a very specific task that may be imbedded in a larger scholarly endeavor.

CONCLUSIONS

Systematic reviews approach the task of summarizing findings of a collection of research studies as a research task. As a method of systematic reviewing, meta-analysis takes this a step further by quantifying the direction and magnitude of the findings of interest across studies and uses specialized statistical methods to analyze the relationship between findings and study features. Properly executed, meta-analysis provides a firm foundation for future research. That is, empirical relationships that are well established and areas that are underresearched or that have equivocal findings are identified through the meta-analytic process. In addition, meta-analysis provides a defensible strategy for summarizing crime prevention and intervention efforts for informing public policy. Although the methods are technical, the findings can be translated into summary statistics readily understandable by non–social science researchers.

APPENDIX
EQUATIONS FOR THE CALCULATION OF EFFECT
SIZES AND META-ANALYTIC SUMMARY STATISTICS

No.	Equation	Notes

Common effect size indices

(1) $d = \dfrac{\overline{X}_1 - \overline{X}_2}{s_{pooled}}$ — Standardized mean difference effect size; X_1 is the mean of the intervention condition; X_2 is the mean of the comparison condition; and s_{pooled} is the pooled within-groups standard deviation

(2) $o = \dfrac{ad}{bc}$ — Odds ratio effect size; a and c are the number of successful outcomes in the intervention and comparison conditions, and b and d are the number of failures in the intervention and comparison conditions (based on a 2×2 contingency table)

(3) $r = r$ — Correlation coefficient effect size; r is the Pearson product-moment correlation coefficient between the two variables of interest

Common transformations of effect size

(4) $d' = \left[1 - \dfrac{3}{4N - 9}\right] d$ — Small sample size bias correction; d is the standardized mean difference effect size and N is the total sample size

(5) $lor = \log(o)$ — Log transformation of the odds ratio

(6) $z = .5\log\left(\dfrac{1 + r}{1 - r}\right)$ — Fisher's transformation of the correlation effect size

(7) $o = e^{lor}$ — Logged odds ratio (lor) transformed into an odds ratio (o); e is the constant 2.7183

(8) $r = \dfrac{e^{2z} - 1}{e^{2z} + 1}$ — Transforms the effect size z from equation 6 back into a correlation; e is the constant 2.7183

Fixed effects model inverse variance weights

(9) $v_d = \dfrac{n_1 + n_2}{n_1 n_2} + \dfrac{d'^2}{2(n_1 + n_2)}$ — The variance for the standardized mean difference; n_1 and n_2 are the sample sizes for the intervention and comparison conditions

(10) $v_{lor} = \dfrac{1}{a} + \dfrac{1}{b} + \dfrac{1}{c} + \dfrac{1}{d}$ — The variance for the logged odds ratio; a, b, c, and d are the cell frequencies of a 2×2 contingency table

(11) $v_z = \dfrac{1}{N - 3}$ — The variance for the Fisher's transformed correlation coefficient; N is the total sample size

(12) $w = \dfrac{1}{v}$ — The inverse variance weight; v is the inverse variance from equation 9, 10, or 11

Mean effect size and related statistics

(13) $\overline{ES} = \dfrac{\sum(ES \cdot w)}{\sum w}$ — Weighted mean effect size, where ES is the effect size index (equations 4, 5, or 6) and w is the inverse variance weight (equation 12)

APPENDIX Continued

No.	Equation	Notes
(14)	$se_{\overline{ES}} = \sqrt{\dfrac{1}{\sum w}}$	The standard error of the mean effect size
(15)	$z = \dfrac{\overline{ES}}{se_{\overline{ES}}}$	A z test; tests whether $\overline{ES}$ is statistically greater than or less than 0
(16)	$LowerCI = \overline{ES} - 1.96 se_{\overline{ES}}$	Lower bound of the 95 percent confidence interval
(17)	$UpperCI = \overline{ES} + 1.96 se_{\overline{ES}}$	Upper bound of the 95 percent confidence interval

Homogeneity test Q

(18)	$Q = \sum (\overline{ES}^{\,2} \cdot w) - \dfrac{\left(\sum (\overline{ES} \cdot w) \right)^2}{\sum w}$	Homogeneity test Q; distributed as a chi-square, degrees of freedom equals the number of effect sizes less 1

Random effects variance component and weight

(19)	$V_\theta = \dfrac{Q - (k-1)}{\sum w - \dfrac{\sum w^2}{\sum w}}$	The random effects variance component; the random effects variance component has a more complex form when used as part of the analog to the ANOVA or regression models
(20)	$w = \dfrac{1}{v + v_\theta}$	The random effects inverse variance weight, where v is defined as in equations 9 through 11

Analog to the ANOVA

(21)	$Q_j = \sum (\overline{ES}_j^{\,2} \cdot w_j) - \dfrac{\left(\sum (\overline{ES}_j \cdot w_j) \right)^2}{\sum w_j}$	Q between groups; where j is 1 to the number of categories for the independent variable; distributed as a chi-square with $j-1$ degrees of freedom
(22)	$Q_W = Q - Q_B$	Q within groups; where Q is the overall homogeneity statistics defined in equation 18 and Q_B is defined in equation 21; distributed as a chi-square with the number of effect sizes minus the number of categories in the independent variable as the degrees of freedom

Meta-analytic regression analysis

(23)	Use specialized software	For example, SAS, SPSS, or Stata macros by Lipsey and Wilson (2001); SAS macros by Wang and Bushman (1998)

Note

1. Methods have been developed for handling dependent effect sizes in a single analysis, but these methods are beyond the scope of this article. (For details, see Gleser and Olkin 1994; Kalaian and Raudenbush 1996.)

References

Becker, Betsy J. 1992. Models of Science Achievement: Forces Affecting Performance in School Science. In *Meta-analysis for Explanation: A Casebook*, ed. Thomas D. Cook, Harris Cooper, David S. Cordray, Heidi Hartmann, Larry V. Hedges, Richard J. Light, Thomas A. Louis, and Frederick Mosteller. New York: Russell Sage.

Becker, G. 1996. The Meta-Aanalysis of Factor Analyses: An Illustration Based on the Cumulation of Correlation Matrices. *Psychological Methods* 1:341-53.

BioStat. 2000. *Comprehensive Meta-Analysis* (Software Program, Version 1.0.9). Englewood, NJ: BioStat. Available: www.metaanalysis.com.

Farrington, David P. and Rolf Loeber. 2000. Some Benefits of Dichotomization in Psychiatric and Criminological Research. *Criminal Behaviour and Mental Health* 10:100-122.

Fisher, Ronald A. 1944. *Statistical Methods for Research Workers*. 9th ed. London: Oliver and Boyd.

Gallagher, Catherine A., David B. Wilson, and Doris Layton MacKenzie. N.d. A Meta-Analysis of the Effectiveness of Sexual Offender Treatment Programs. Unpublished manuscript, University of Maryland at College Park.

Glass, Gene V. 1976. Primary, Secondary and Meta-Analysis of Research. *Educational Researcher* 5:3-8.

Gleser, Leon J. and Ingram Olkin. 1994. Stochastically Dependent Effect Sizes. In *The Handbook of Research Synthesis*, ed. Harris Cooper and Larry V. Hedges. New York: Russell Sage.

Hedges, Larry V. 1982. Estimating Effect Size from a Series of Independent Experiments. *Psychological Bulletin* 92: 490-99.

Hedges, Larry V. and Ingram Olkin. 1985. *Statistical Methods for Meta-Analysis*. Orlando, FL: Academic Press.

Hunter, John E. and Frank L. Schmidt. 1990. *Methods of Meta-Analysis: Correcting Error and Bias in Research Findings*. Newbury Park, CA: Sage.

Kalaian, H. A. and Stephen W. Raudenbush. 1996. A Multivariate Mixed Linear Model For Meta-Analysis. *Psychological Methods* 1:227-35.

Lipsey, Mark W., Gabrielle L. Chapman, and Nana A. Landenberger. 2001. Cognitive-Behavioral Programs for Offenders. *Annals of the American Academy of Political and Social Science* 578:144-157.

Lipsey, Mark W., Scott Crosse, J. Dunkle, J. Pollard, and G. Stobart. 1985. Evaluation: The State of the Art and the Sorry State of the Science. *New Directions for Program Evaluation* 27:7-28.

Lipsey, Mark W. and David B. Wilson. 2001. *Practical Meta-Analysis*. Thousand Oaks, CA: Sage.

MacKenzie, Doris Layton, David B. Wilson, and Suzanne B. Kider. 2001. Effects of Correctional Boot Camps on Offending. *Annals of the American Academy of Political and Social Science* 578:126-143.

Pearson, Karl. 1904. Report on Certain Enteric Fever Inoculation Statistics. *British Medical Journal* 3:1243-46. Quoted in Morton Hunt, *How Science Takes Stock: The Story of Meta-Analysis* (New York: Russell Sage, 1997).

Petrosino, Anthony, Robert F. Boruch, Haluk Soydan, Lorna Duggan, and Julio Sanchez-Meca. 2001. Meeting the Challenges of Evidence-Based Policy: The Campbell Collaboration.

Annals of the American Academy of Political and Social Science 578:14-34.

Premack, Steven L. and John E. Hunter. 1988. Individual Unionization Decisions. *Psychological Bulletin* 103: 223-34.

Rosenthal, Robert. 1991. *Meta-Analytic Procedures for Social Research. Applied Social Research Methods Series.* Vol. 6. Newbury Park, CA: Sage.

Rosenthal, Robert and Donald B. Rubin. 1983. A Simple, General Purpose Display of Magnitude of Experimental Effect. *Journal of Educational Psychology* 74:166-69.

Wang, Morgan C. and Brad J. Bushman. 1998. *Integrating Results Through Meta-Analytic Review Using SAS Software.* Cary, NC: SAS Institute.

Wilson, David B. and Mark W. Lipsey. In press. The Role of Method in Treatment Effect Estimates: Evidence from Psychological, Behavioral, and Educational Treatment Intervention Meta-Analyses. *Psychological Methods.*

ANNALS, *AAPSS*, **578**, November 2001

Early Parent Training to Prevent Disruptive Behavior Problems and Delinquency in Children

By ODETTE BERNAZZANI, CATHERINE CÔTÉ, and RICHARD E. TREMBLAY

ABSTRACT: Early forms of disruptive behaviors in children often leading to juvenile delinquency are associated with poor parenting skills. Thus early intervention programs targeting parenting skills may have an important impact on disruptive behaviors in children. The objective of this review was to assess the impact of early parenting and home visitation programs on behavior problems and delinquency in children. Selected trials were identified using electronic databases and relevant reviews. The following selection criteria were used: (1) the intervention involved the provision of parent training to families with a child under age 3, and (2) the design was a randomized or quasi-experimental trial. Overall, of the seven trials identified, only three reported some beneficial effects on disruptive behavior or delinquency. Due to the limited number of adequately designed studies, caution is recommended in the interpretation of available results. Numerous well-designed early prevention experiments specifically targeting disruptive behaviors and delinquency should be initiated.

Odette Bernazzani, M.D., Ph.D., is an associate professor in the Department of Psychiatry, University of Montreal. Her funded research concerns the intergenerational transmission of emotional problems related to childhood neglect and abuse.

Catherine Côté is a Ph.D. student in the Department of Psychology, University of Montreal. She has been awarded a research scholarship from the St-Justine Hospital Research Center and the Fonds pour la Formation de Chercheurs et l'Aide à la Recherche (FCAR) agency.

Richard E. Tremblay, Ph.D., FRSC, is a professor in the Departments of Psychiatry and Psychology, University of Montreal. He has recently received the Canada Research Chair in Child Development. He has published more than 200 papers in the field of child development.

NOTE: We thank the following agencies for financial support: Canadian Institute for Advanced Research, FCAR, Fonds de la Recherche en Santé de Québec, Molson Foundation, Social Sciences and Humanities Research Council of Canada, and St-Justine Hospital Research Centre.

DISRUPTIVE behavior can be defined as an array of behavior problems including opposition to adults, hyperactivity, stealing, lying, truancy, extreme noncompliance, aggression, physical cruelty to people and animals, and destructive and sexually coercive behaviors (American Psychiatric Association 1994; Quay and Hogan 1999a). Oppositional Defiant Disorder, Conduct Disorder, and Attention Deficit Hyperactivity Disorder are the diagnostic categories most often used in the psychiatric field to refer to children presenting severe disruptive behavior patterns. Although epidemiological studies in this area face important measurement problems and are limited by sample size (Lahey et al. 1999), it has been suggested that the three forms of disruptive behaviors account for up to two-thirds of all childhood and adolescent psychiatric disorders (Quay and Hogan 1999a). Most children manifest disruptive behaviors during early childhood and show a gradual decline in frequency with age (Broidy, Nagin, and Tremblay 1999; Lahey et al. 1999; Nagin and Tremblay 1999; Tremblay 2000; McCord, Widom, and Crowell 2001). The term "delinquent behavior" refers to disruptive behaviors sanctioned by the law. Age of the child who performs a disruptive behavior is generally a key factor in deciding whether the behavior is, or is not, sanctioned by the law (McCord, Widom, and Crowell 2001).

Longitudinal studies have shown that there are long-term consequences of disruptive behavior disorders for the individual as well as his or her family, friends, community, and even the following generation (White et al. 1990; Farrington 1995; Fergusson and Horwood 1998; Serbin et al. 1998; Frick and Loney 1999; Loeber 2001; Côté et al. in press). Prevention appears a worthy goal as treatment programs have shown a modest impact (Chamberlain 1999; Kavale, Forness, and Walker 1999). The developmental trajectories of disruptive behaviors are a major reason to argue for very early prevention. There is good evidence that chronic disruptive behavior leading to serious delinquency appears during early childhood (Moffitt et al. 1996; Broidy, Nagin, and Tremblay 1999; Nagin and Tremblay 1999). There is also evidence to suggest that children with disruptive behavior problems become increasingly resistant to change with age despite treatment efforts (Kazdin 1985; Frick and Loney 1999; Tremblay 2000). All these considerations underscore the need for early preventive programs targeting high-risk families.

During the past 40 years, parenting programs have been offered in a variety of settings and to a variety of families. Many of these programs have targeted families with school-age disruptive children (Patterson 1982; Webster-Stratton, Kolpacoff, and Hollinsworth 1988; Kazdin, Siegel, and Bass 1992; Tremblay et al. 1995; Hawkins et al. 1999). Parenting interventions as early as pregnancy have recently been stimulated by the evidence of reduced delinquent behavior in adolescents of poorly educated mothers who received a home visitation program during pregnancy and the first two years following birth (Olds et al. 1998). These home visitation programs aim at a wide range of outcomes including maternal physical and psychosocial health, parenting skills, and children's psychosocial development and physical health. The long-term impact on delinquency of intensive home visitation during a period of more than two years supports the hypothesis that quality of family environment during the early years is a key to delinquency prevention (Patterson, Reid, and Dishion 1992; Yoshikawa 1994; McCord, Widom, and Crowell 2001; Nagin and Tremblay 2001). Early parenting interventions generally postulate that quality of parent-child relations will facilitate learning of control over impulsive, oppositional, and aggressive behavior, thus reducing disruptive behavior and its long-term negative impact on social integration.

This review aims to address whether early parenting and home visitation programs are effective in preventing behavior problems and delinquency in children.

CRITERIA FOR CONSIDERING STUDIES FOR THIS REVIEW

Types of studies

Only studies employing random assignment or quasi-experimental (preintervention and postintervention assessments and adequate control groups) designs were included. Studies lacking control groups were excluded as they cannot help differentiate intervention

effects from other effects including developmental effects.

Types of participants

The review was limited to families with a child under age 3 at the start of the intervention to ensure that the interventions were provided early in the child's life. However, no limits were set concerning the child's age at the end of the intervention. In addition, selected interventions could target either the general population (universal intervention) or a high-risk group (selective intervention).

Types of intervention

Studies were eligible for this review when parent training or support was a major component of the intervention, although not necessarily the only one.

Types of outcomes

The original aim of the review was to assess the impact of the interventions on the children's delinquent behavior. However, since we found only one study assessing delinquency, we used a broader scope in our review and selected studies with outcome measures of disruptive behaviors. These assessments included self-reported delinquency; self-, parent-, or teacher-rated measures of disruptive behavior; and observer-rated assessments of disruptive behavior in the classroom.

SEARCH STRATEGY FOR IDENTIFICATION OF STUDIES

Our starting point for searching through the literature was two previous reviews. The first (Mrazek and Brown 1999) reviewed psychosocial interventions during the preschool years that were designed to enhance child development according to a wide variety of outcomes. The second review (Tremblay, LeMarquand, and Vitaro 1999) focused on programs targeting families of preadolescents for the prevention of disruptive behavior.

To identify additional relevant trials potentially overlooked by, or published since, these reviews, two major electronic databases were searched: PsychINFO and MEDLINE (1967 to 2001). These specific databases were the most relevant considering the topic of our review. A wide search strategy was used to ensure that relevant studies were not missed. Hence the search terms excluded study design and reflected a wide age group. Our selection criteria regarding study design and age of participants were applied later during the systematic review of the abstracts yielded by the search. The search terms used were "parent training" and "childhood" or "pre-school" and "delinquency" or "conduct disorder" or "antisocial behavior" or "aggression" or "physical aggression" or "behavior problems." Finally, two other major sources of information were searched, the *Cochrane Library* and the *Future of Children* publications, as well as all the potentially relevant review articles identified during the search (Gomby et al. 1993; Yoshikawa 1995; Vitaro, De Civita, and Pagani 1996; Culross 1999; Gomby, Culross, and Behrman 1999; Barlow and Coren 2001).

METHOD OF THE REVIEW

Data collection, quality assessment, and data analysis

Titles and abstracts of studies identified through our searches were reviewed to determine whether they met inclusion criteria. Trials were selected for methodological quality using the criteria suggested by Mrazek and Brown (1999). These authors have extensively reviewed outcomes in psychosocial prevention and early intervention in young children. They have developed an instrument called the Threats to Trial Integrity Score (TTIS) that allows one to measure the quality of the design of a controlled trial, whether it be randomized or not. This scale assesses the potential threat regarding 10 dimensions of quality design on a 4-point scale including *null or minimal risk* (N or 0), *low risk* (L or 1), *moderate risk* (M or 2), and *high risk* (H or 3). Scores for each of the 10 dimensions are combined in a weighted fashion to obtain a global score (for additional information, see Mrazek and Brown 1999). The authors then categorized this ordinal scale into a five-level Trial Quality Grade. Each trial was classified as a 1- to 5-star design. The 5-star designs were the highest-scoring trials based on TTIS score (about 5 percent). The 4-star designs were among the top quarter of trials; the 3-star designs were in the second quartile, and so forth. Mrazek and Brown suggested concentrating on trials with 5-star and 4-star designs as they are clearly well-designed studies with sufficient design integrity. Mrazek and Brown identified 165 prevention studies with preschool children, but only 34 met the 4- or 5-star classification. Of the 34 studies, a total of 6 trials met our inclusion criteria. Three additional trials were identified in Tremblay, LeMarquand, and Vitaro (1999), but they were not kept in our review as they did not meet the 4-star design criteria of Mrazek and Brown.

The PsychINFO search yielded 151 new abstracts, none of which were included in the review. Most of them were excluded because they targeted older children. Others were excluded for methodological reasons, mostly because of the absence of a control group. Searching the *Cochrane Library* and the *Future of Children* publications generated an additional four reviews that provided information about one trial that had not already been identified and met our criteria.

Thus seven trials met our criteria. The data were summarized using effect sizes but were not combined in a meta-analysis due to the small number of studies and the presence of substantial heterogeneity among them.

RESULTS

Sample characteristics

All seven trials were randomized controlled experiments (see Table 1). All but two were conducted in the United States; one was done in Australia and another in Bermuda. Two interventions targeted the general population (universal preventive interventions) while the remaining five were selective preventive

interventions (that is, they targeted high-risk groups, mostly socially disadvantaged families or, in one study, premature babies). Boys and girls were included in all studies. Two studies targeted minority groups: African Americans and Mexican Americans. The latter study was the only one that did not attempt to obtain a representative population sample due to major recruitment challenges. While it can be argued that nearly all studies tried to involve families, in practice, most studies intervened mainly with mothers.

In total, 7917 families were randomized to receive parent training or to be in a control group. One study had more than 4000 participants involving 21 sites, two had more than 1000 participants, three had more than 300, and one had 125. Attrition rates varied greatly from one study to another, ranging from 20 to 67 percent. Sample numbers relevant to our review varied from 117 to more than 2000 (exact number was not available for St-Pierre and Layzer 1999).

Intervention characteristics

Four interventions began when the child was 12 months old or younger (see Table 2). All four continued beyond age 2, up to age 3, 5, or 6. Two trials began during the prenatal period, and both continued up to 2 years. Finally, one trial began when children were 24 months old and ended when they were about 4 years. Overall duration of interventions ranged from more than 2 to 6 years. Length of follow-up ranged from immediate end of intervention to 13

TABLE 1
SAMPLE CHARACTERISTICS OF STUDIES INCLUDED IN THE REVIEW

Study	Target Population	Country	Final N^a
Cullen (1976)	Universal	Australia	246
Johnson and Breckenridge (1982) Johnson and Walker (1987)	Low-income Mexican American families Selective	United States	139
Kitzman et al. (1997)	Pregnant women with at least two of the following characteristics: unmarried, less than 12 years of education, unemployed Most participants were African American Selective	United States	743
McCarton et al. (1997)	Low-birth-weight premature infants Selective	United States	874
Olds et al. (1986, 1998)	Women who were young (younger than 19 years), unmarried, or of low socioeconomic status Selective	United States	323
Scarr and McCartney (1988)	All families with a 2-year-old child in a Bermudian parish Universal	Bermuda	117
St-Pierre and Layzer (1999)	Families with incomes below the poverty level Selective	United States	More than 2,000 (exact number not available)

NOTES: Universal = a universal preventive intervention: an intervention that targets the general population. Selective = a selective preventive intervention: an intervention that targets high-risk groups.
  a. Sample number related to outcomes examined in this review.

years following the end. The longest follow-up was for the Elmira project (Olds et al. 1998). Nearly all studies (six) involved intensive home visitation. Half of these had additional intervention components, either participation in a child development center or participation in parent groups. One study involved a clinic-based interview conducted with mothers by a general practitioner. In all but one study (Scarr and McCartney 1988), control groups were offered a nonintensive follow-up including screening procedures, pediatric surveillance, free transportation, or annual contact by the secretary of the study.

Outcome characteristics

Overall, results concerning the effectiveness of parent training in the prevention of behavior problems in children were mixed (see Table 3). Four studies reported no evidence of effectiveness, two reported beneficial effects, and one study reported mainly beneficial effects with some harmful effects. Of the studies with

TABLE 2
INTERVENTION CHARACTERISTICS OF STUDIES INCLUDED IN THE REVIEW

Study	Average Age at Start of Intervention	Intervention Period (child's age)	Type of Intervention
Cullen (1976)	3 months	Up to 6 years	Clinic-based interview with general practitioner
Johnson and Breckenridge (1982) Johnson and Walker (1987)	12 months	1 to 3 years	Home visits, family workshops, and child development center
Kitzman et al. (1997)	Gestational age: 16.5 weeks	Prenatal to 2 years	Home visits
McCarton et al. (1997)	7 weeks	Up to 3 years	Home visits, parent groups, child development center
Olds et al. (1986, 1998)	Gestational age: 25 weeks	Prenatal to 2 years	Home visits
Scarr and McCartney (1988)	24 months	2 to 4 years	Home visits
St-Pierre and Layzer (1999)	Not available	Younger than 1 year to 5 years	Home visits, child development center

significant results, which provided sufficient data to calculate an effect size, the treatment effect ranged from 0.25 to 1.05 (calculations from Mrazek and Brown 1999). All of the studies, with the exception of one (Scarr and McCartney 1988), included mothers' reports of disruptive behavior. Two studies also included teachers' or schools' reports (Johnson and Walker 1987; Olds et al. 1998), and one study used self-reported delinquency (Olds et al. 1998). Only two of the seven trials were designed to target specifically behavior problems, the Houston Parent-Child Development Center Program (Johnson and Breckenridge 1982; Johnson and Walker 1987) and the Brusselton study (Cullen 1976). Most studies looked at behavior problems among a wide range of other outcomes, for example,

cognitive development and physical health. The child's age at evaluation varied greatly from one study to the other, ranging from 2 to 15 years. Only two studies reported differential effects according to gender, but both girls and boys benefited from the interventions.

Only one study (Olds et al. 1998) evaluated the effectiveness of home visitation and parent training on delinquent behaviors. Although not initially designed with the aim of preventing delinquency, the Elmira project reported beneficial effects with respect to children's delinquent behavior 13 years after the end of the intervention (age 15). However, the beneficial effect of the intervention concerned a subgroup of children of poor, young, and unmarried women only ($n = 68$). The intervention was an intensive nurse home-visiting

TABLE 3
OUTCOME FINDINGS OF THE STUDIES INCLUDED IN THE REVIEW

Study	Outcome	Effect Size[a]	p Value	Direction of Outcome
Cullen (1976)	At age 6			
	Mother's report			Beneficial
	Talked loudly	< -0.25	< 0.05	T
	Hit or struck others	< -0.25	< 0.05	T
		< -0.35	< 0.05	G
	Exaggerated/told lies	< -0.35	< 0.05	G
				Harmful
	Late for school	> 0.42	< 0.001	T
		> 0.48	< 0.01	B
Johnson and	At age 5.3			
Breckenridge	Mother's report			Beneficial
(1982)	Behavior assessment			
Johnson and	Destructive	-1.05	< 0.01	B
Walker (1987)	High activity	-0.55	< 0.05	B
	At age 5.5			
	Teacher's report			Beneficial
	Classroom Behavior Inventory			
	Hostility Scale	-0.46	0.01	T
		-0.66	0.01	B
	Behavior problems			
	Disrupts	$-0.42, -0.53$	0.019, 0.038	T, B
	Obstinate	$-0.48, -0.61$	0.007, 0.018	T, B
	Restless	$-0.47, -0.70$	0.008, 0.007	T, B
	Fights	$-0.46, -0.68$	0.01, 0.008	T, B
	Impulsive	$-0.58, -0.54$	0.025, 0.03	B, G
Kitzman et al.	At age 2			
(1997)	Mother's report			
	Child Behavior Checklist			ns
McCarton et al.	At age 8			
(1997)	Mother's report			
	Child Behavior Checklist			ns
	Behavior Profile			ns
Olds et al.	At age 15			
(1986, 1998)	Child's report			Beneficial[b]
	Running away	NA[c]	0.003	Beneficial
	Arrests	NA	0.03	Beneficial
	Convictions, probation			
	violations	NA	< 0.001	Beneficial
	Number of sex partners	NA	0.003	Beneficial
	Days having consumed			
	alcohol	NA	0.03	Beneficial
	Minor antisocial acts			ns
	Major delinquent acts			ns
	Externalizing problems			ns
	Acting out problems			ns

(continued)

TABLE 3 Continued

Study	Outcome	Effect Size[a]	p Value	Direction of Outcome
	Incidence of times stopped by police			ns
	Alcohol impairment			ns
	Days using drugs			ns
	Parent's report			
	Similar scales			ns
	School's report			
	Incidence of short- or long-term school suspensions			ns
Scarr and McCartney (1988)	At age 45 months Blind examiner			
	Childhood Personality Scale			ns
	Infant Behavior Record			ns
St-Pierre and Layzer (1999)	At ages 3, 4, and 5 Mother's report			
	Child Behavior Checklist			ns
	Total score			
	Externalizing score			
	Internalizing score			

NOTES: T = total sample. B = boys. G = girls. ns = not significant.

a. Effect size calculations are taken from Mrazek and Brown (1999). They can be either negative or positive, and their interpretation depends on the way the outcome measure is coded.

b. The beneficial outcomes concerned only the subgroup of children of poor unmarried women.

c. Insufficient data were provided to calculate an effect size.

program that started early during the pregnancy of high-risk women and continued during the 2 years after birth. The nurses promoted several aspects of maternal functioning and well-being including competent care of the children. The nurses completed an average of 9 visits during pregnancy and 23 visits from birth to the child's second year (Olds et al. 1997).

DISCUSSION

A very limited number of well-designed studies including both early interventions and outcomes related to disruptive behaviors were available for this review. In addition, overall results were mixed: four studies reported no evidence of effectiveness, two reported beneficial effects, and one reported mainly beneficial effects with some harmful effects. The latter effects, however, concerned one specific item only: late for school. Studies varied greatly from one another on various aspects, including outcome measures, child's age at evaluation, the nature and duration of the intervention, and sample size. Studies reporting beneficial effects showed no specific patterns allowing distinction from the other studies. In this context, it is impossible to make a definitive statement as to whether early parent training and support is effective in preventing disruptive behaviors in children and delinquency during adolescence. Thus caution is suggested in the interpretation of the existing studies.

Similar caution has already been expressed with regard to home visiting programs, which provide an important amount of parent training. Some authors have argued that home visits are a necessary but insufficient component of programs seeking to help families and young children (Weiss 1993). More recently, a major review of six home visiting models that were being, or had been, implemented nationally in the United States concluded that results regarding the effectiveness of home visiting for a wide range of outcomes were quite modest, at the most (Gomby, Culross, and Behrman 1999).

Several factors can contribute to these overall disappointing results (for an excellent review of these factors, see Gomby, Culross, and Behrman 1999; St-Pierre and Layzer, 1999). The heterogeneity in the definition of parent training and the absence of evidence regarding which components of parent training are most effective appear most relevant to our own review. The three trials reporting beneficial results varied greatly with regard to the nature of the intervention. The Elmira project in New York State (Olds et al. 1998), an intensive nurse home-visitation program that emphasized parental development and was provided during the first 2 years of the child's life, had a significant effect on children of poor, young, and unmarried women. Several aspects of maternal functioning were promoted in addition to the competent care of the child, including maternal personal development and positive health behaviors. In addition, an important focus was put on the involvement of other family members and people in the social network.

On the other hand, the Brusselton project in Australia (Cullen 1976) was significantly different in nature and intensity. Only 20- to 30-minute counseling sessions were provided by the same general practitioner to all mothers living in a rural community. Four sessions were provided during the first 2 years of life, followed by two sessions per year for the next 4 years. Hence, although significantly less intensive, the duration of the Brusselton intervention was 3 times longer than the duration of the Elmira intervention. The progress of the child formed the basis of each interview in the Brusselton trial. Mothers were encouraged to accept themselves as they were and to reflect on, and eventually modify, their child-rearing practices. Finally, the third study, showing beneficial effects on disruptive behaviors—the Houston, Texas, project (Johnson and Breckenridge 1982)—targeted low-income Mexican American families and combined several intervention components that emphasized parenting skills: home visits, family workshops, and the participation in a child development center. Fathers were strongly encouraged to participate. This heterogeneity in the small number of studies showing beneficial effects underscores the fact that little information is available to guide intervention programs when they choose to target parent education. As St-Pierre and Layzer (1999) pointed out, the field of parent education targeting young families seems to suffer from a lack of evidence about which intervention components are most important, which parents are more likely to benefit from the intervention, how long it should last, and whether parent training should be combined with other intervention types.

It is of interest to note that the Brusselton and Houston studies were the only two initially designed to prevent behavior disorders, and both reported beneficial effects. This, perhaps, highlights the relevance of developing specific models for the prevention of behavior problems rather than using general models to improve a wide range of maternal and child outcomes. In their review of major American home-visiting programs targeting broad outcomes, Gomby, Culross, and Behrman (1999) advocated a more modest view of the potential of home-visiting programs. In addition, they strongly recommended the use of new models to improve the overall effectiveness of home-visiting programs. We believe this recommendation is especially relevant for interventions targeting the prevention of children's disruptive behavior problems and delinquency. Without any doubt, many additional studies are required in order to identify the characteristics of early parent training and support programs that can prevent the development of disruptive behavior disorders and delinquency.

CONCLUSIONS

Caution is suggested in the interpretation of findings of research on the effectiveness of early parent training for the prevention of disruptive behavior problems in children and juvenile delinquency due to three important considerations: (1) there is a limited number of adequately designed studies; (2) results of the well-designed studies available are mixed and, where positive, often modest in magnitude; and (3) very few studies (two of seven) were specifically designed to prevent disruptive behaviors in children. Since there is good evidence from longitudinal studies that disruptive behavior starts during the preschool years and often leads to juvenile delinquency, there is clearly a need for numerous trials testing different types of early interventions specifically designed for the prevention of disruptive behavior problems and juvenile delinquency.

References

American Psychiatric Association. 1994. *Diagnostic and Statistical Manual of Mental Disorders.* 4th ed. Washington, DC: Author.

Barlow, Jane and Esther Coren. 2001. Parent-Training for Improving Maternal Psychosocial Health. *The Cochrane Library* [online] 2.

Broidy, Lisa, Daniel Nagin, and Richard E. Tremblay. 1999. The Linkage of Trajectories of Childhood Externalizing Behaviors to Later Violent and Nonviolent Delinquency. Paper presented at the biennial meeting of the Society for Research in Child Development, Albuquerque, NM, Apr.

Chamberlain, Patricia. 1999. Residential Care for Children and Adolescents with Oppositional Defiant Disorder and Conduct Disorder. In *Handbook of Disruptive Behavior Disorders*, ed. Herbert C. Quay and Anne E. Hogan. New York: Kluwer Academic/Plenum.

Côté, Sylvana, Mark Zoccolillo, Richard E. Tremblay, Daniel Nagin, and Frank Vitaro. In press. Predicting Girls' Conduct Disorder in Adolescence from Childhood Trajectories of Disruptive Behaviors. *Journal of the American Academy of Child and Adolescent Psychiatry*.

Cullen, Kevin J. 1976. A Six-Year Controlled Trial of Prevention of Children's Behavior Disorders. *Journal of Pediatrics* 88:662-66.

Culross, Patti L. 1999. Summary of Home Visiting Program Evaluation Outcomes. *Future of Children* 9:195-223.

Farrington, David P. 1995. The Development of Offending and Antisocial Behavior from Childhood: Key Findings from the Cambridge Study in Delinquent Development. *Journal of Child Psychology and Psychiatry* 36:929-64.

Fergusson, David M. and L. John Horwood. 1998. Early Conduct Problems and Later Life Opportunities. *Journal of Child Psychology and Psychiatry* 39:1097-108.

Frick, Paul J. and Bryan R. Loney. 1999. Outcomes of Children and Adolescents with Oppositional Defiant Disorder and Conduct Disorder. In *Handbook of Disruptive Behavior Disorders*, ed. Herbert C. Quay and Anne E. Hogan. New York: Kluwer Academic/Plenum.

Gomby, Deanna S., Patti L. Culross, and Richard E. Behrman. 1999. Home Visiting: Recent Program Evaluations—Analysis and Recommendations. *Future of Children* 9:4-26.

Gomby, Deanna S., Carol S. Larson, Eugene M. Lewit, and Richard E. Behrman. 1993. Home Visiting: Analysis and Recommendations. *Future of Children* 3:6-22.

Hawkins, J. David, Richard F. Catalano, Richard Kosterman, Robert Abbott, and Karl G. Hill. 1999. Preventing Adolescent Health-Risk Behaviors by Strengthening Protection During Childhood. *Archives of Pediatrics and Adolescent Medicine* 153:226-34.

Johnson, Dale L. and James N. Breckenridge. 1982. The Houston Parent-Child Development Center and the Primary Prevention of Behavior Problems in Young Children. *American Journal of Community Psychology* 10:305-16.

Johnson, Dale L. and Todd T. Walker. 1987. Primary Prevention of Behavior Problems in Mexican-American Children. *American Journal of Community Psychology* 15:375-95.

Kavale, Kenneth. A., Steven R. Forness, and Hill M. Walker. 1999. Interventions for Oppositional Defiant Disorder and Conduct Disorder in the Schools. In *Handbook of Disruptive Behavior Disorders*, ed. Herbert C. Quay and Anne E. Hogan. New York: Kluwer Academic/Plenum.

Kazdin, Alan E. 1985. *Treatment of Antisocial Behavior in Children and Adolescents*. Homewood, IL: Dorsey.

Kazdin, Allan E., Todd C. Siegel, and Debra Bass. 1992. Cognitive Problem-Solving Skills Training and Parent Management Training in the Treatment of Antisocial Behavior in Children. *Journal of Consulting and Clinical Psychology* 60:733-47.

Kitzman, Harriet, David L. Olds, Charles R. Henderson, Carole Hanks, Robert Cole, Robert Tatelbaum, Kenneth M. McConnochie, Kimberly Sidora, Dennis W. Luckey, David Shaver, Kay Engelhardt, David James, and Kathryn Barnard. 1997. Effect of Prenatal and Infancy Home Visitation by Nurses on Pregnancy Outcomes, Childhood Injuries and Repeated

Childbearing. *Journal of the American Medical Association* 278:644-52.

Lahey, Benjamin B., Terri L. Miller, Rachel A. Gordon, and Anne W. Riley. 1999. Developmental Epidemiology of the Disruptive Behavior Disorders. In *Handbook of Disruptive Behavior Disorders*, ed. Herbert C. Quay and Anne E. Hogan. New York: Kluwer Academic/Plenum.

Loeber, Rolf. 2001. Developmental Aspects of Juvenile Homicide. Paper presented at the biennial meeting of the Society for Research in Child Development, Minneapolis, MN, Apr.

McCarton, Cecilia M., Jeanne Brooks-Gunn, Ina F. Wallace, Charles R. Bauer, Forrest C. Bennet, Judy C. Bernbaum, Sue Broyles, Patrick H. Casey, Marie C. McCormick, David T. Scott, Jon Tyson, James Tonascia, and Curtis L. Meinert. 1997. Results at Age 8 Years of Early Intervention for Low-Birth-Weight Premature Infants: The Infant Health and Development Program. *Journal of the American Medical Association* 277:126-32.

McCord, Joan, Cathy Spatz Widom, and Nancy E. Crowell. 2001. *Juvenile Crime, Juvenile Justice*. Washington, DC: National Academy Press.

Moffitt, Terrie E., Avshalom Caspi, Nigel Dickson, Phil S. Silva, and Warren Stanton. 1996. Childhood-onset Versus Adolescent-Onset Antisocial Conduct Problems in Males: Natural History from Ages 3 to 18 Years. *Development & Psychopathology* 8:399-424.

Mrazek, Patricia J. and C. Henricks Brown. 1999. *An Evidenced-Based Literature Review Regarding Outcomes in Psychosocial Prevention and Early Intervention in Young Children*. Toronto, Canada: Invest in Kids Foundation.

Nagin, Daniel and Richard E. Tremblay. 1999. Trajectories of Boys' Physical Aggression, Opposition, and Hyperactivity on the Path to Physically Violent and Non-Violent Juvenile Delinquency. *Child Development* 70:1181-96.

———. 2001. Parental and Early Childhood Predictors of Persistent Physical Aggression in Boys from Kindergarten to High School. *Archives of General Psychiatry* 58:389-94.

Olds, David L., Charles R. Henderson, Robert Chamberlin, and Robert Tatelbaum. 1986. Preventing Child Abuse and Neglect: A Randomized Trial of Nurse Home Visitation. *Pediatrics* 78:65-78.

Olds, David L., Charles R. Henderson, Robert Cole, John Eckenrode, Harriet Kitzman, Dennis Luckey, Lisa Pettitt, Kimberly Sidora, Pamela Morris, and Jane Powers. 1998. Long-Term Effects of Nurse Home Visitation on Children's Criminal and Antisocial Behavior: 15-year Follow-Up of a Randomized Controlled Trial. *Journal of the American Medical Association* 280:1238-44.

Olds, David L., Harriet Kitzman, Robert Cole, and JoAnn Robinson. 1997. Theoretical and Empirical Foundations of a Program of Home Visitation for Pregnant Women and Parents of Young Children. *Journal of Community Psychology* 25:9-25.

Patterson, Gerald R. 1982. *Coercive Family Process*. Eugene, OR: Castalia.

Patterson, Gerald R., John B. Reid, and Thomas J. Dishion. 1992. *Antisocial Boys*. Eugene, OR: Castalia.

Quay, Herbert C. and Anne E. Hogan. 1999a. Preface. In *Handbook of Disruptive Behavior Disorders*, ed. Herbert C. Quay and Anne E. Hogan. New York: Kluwer Academic/Plenum.

———, eds. 1999b. *Handbook of Disruptive Behavior Disorders*. New York: Kluwer Academic/Plenum.

St-Pierre, Robert G. and Jean I. Layzer. 1999. Using Home Visits for Multiple Purposes: The Comprehensive Child

Development Program. *Future of Children* 9:134-51.

Scarr, Sandra and Kathleen McCartney. 1988. Far from Home: An Experimental Evaluation of the Mother-Child Home Program in Bermuda. *Child Development* 59:531-43.

Serbin, Lisa A., Jessica M. Cooperman, Patrica L. Peters, Pascale M. Lehoux, Dale M. Stack, and Alex E. Schwartzman. 1998. Intergenerational Transfer of Psychosocial Risk in Women with Childhood Histories of Aggression, Withdrawal, or Aggression and Withdrawal. *Developmental Psychology* 34:1246-62.

Tremblay, Richard E. 2000. The Development of Aggressive Behaviour During Childhood: What Have We Learned in the Past Century? *International Journal of Behavioral Development* 24:129-41.

Tremblay, Richard E., Linda Kurtz, Louise C. Mâsse, Frank Vitaro, and Robert O. Pihl. 1995. A Bimodal Preventive Intervention for Disruptive Kindergarten Boys: Its Impact Through Mid-Adolescence. *Journal of Consulting and Clinical Psychology* 63:560-68.

Tremblay, Richard E., David LeMarquand, and Frank Vitaro. 1999. The Prevention of Oppositional Defiant Disorder and Conduct Disorder. In *Handbook of Disruptive Behavior Disorders*, ed. Herbert C. Quay and Anne E. Hogan. New York: Kluwer Academic/ Plenum.

Vitaro, Frank, Mirella De Civita, and Linda Pagani. 1996. The Impact of Research-Based Prevention Programs on Children's Disruptive Behavior. *Exceptionality Education Canada* 5:105-35.

Webster-Stratton, Carolyn, Mary Kolpacoff, and Terri Hollinsworth. 1988. Self-Administered Videotape Therapy for Families with Conduct-problem Children: Comparison with Two Cost-Effective Treatments and a Control Group. *Journal of Consulting and Clinical Psychology* 56:558-66.

Weiss, Heather B. 1993. Home Visits: Necessary but Not Sufficient. *Future of Children* 3:113-28.

White, Jennifer L., Terrie E. Moffitt, Felton Earls, Lee Robins, and Phil A. Silva. 1990. How Early Can We Tell? Predictors of Childhood Conduct Disorder and Adolescent Delinquency. *Criminology* 28:507-33.

Yoshikawa, Hirokazu. 1994. Prevention as Cumulative Protection: Effects of Early Family Support and Education on Chronic Delinquency and Its Risks. *Psychological Bulletin* 115:28-54.

———. 1995. Long-Term Effects of Early Childhood Programs on Social Outcomes and Delinquency. *Future of Children* 5:51-75.

ANNALS, *AAPSS*, **578**, November 2001

The Effects of Hot Spots Policing on Crime

By ANTHONY A. BRAGA

ABSTRACT: In recent years, researchers have argued that police actions should be focused on high-risk crime places rather than spread thinly across the urban landscape. This review examines the available evaluation evidence on the effects of concentrating police enforcement efforts on crime hot spots. Five randomized experiments and four nonequivalent control group quasi-experiments were identified. The findings of these evaluations suggest that focused police actions can prevent crime and disorder in crime hot spots. These studies also suggest that focused police actions at specific locations do not necessarily result in crime displacement. Unintended crime prevention benefits were also associated with the hot spots policing programs. Although these evaluations reveal that these programs work in preventing crime, additional research is needed to unravel other important policy-relevant issues such as community reaction to focused police enforcement efforts.

Anthony A. Braga is a senior research associate in the Program in Criminal Justice Policy and Management of the Malcolm Wiener Center for Social Policy at Harvard University's John F. Kennedy School of Government and a visiting fellow at the U.S. National Institute of Justice.

NOTE: The author would like to thank Phyllis Schultze at Rutgers University's Criminal Justice Library for her valuable assistance in completing this review.

P LACE-ORIENTED crime prevention strategies have begun to occupy a central role in police crime prevention research and policy (Eck and Weisburd 1995). This idea developed from the hot spots of crime perspective, which suggests that crime does not occur evenly across urban landscapes; rather, it is concentrated in relatively small places that generate more than half of all criminal events (Pierce, Spaar, and Briggs 1988; Sherman, Gartin, and Buerger 1989; Weisburd, Maher, and Sherman 1992). Even within the most crime-ridden neighborhoods, crime clusters at a few discrete locations, and other areas are relatively crime free (Sherman, Gartin, and Buerger 1989). A number of researchers have argued that many crime problems could be reduced more efficiently if police officers focused their attention on these deviant places (Sherman 1995; Weisburd 1997). Three complementary perspectives on crime theoretically support these observations on the uneven distribution of deviance: rational choice, routine activities, and environmental criminology (Cornish and Clarke 1986; Cohen and Felson 1979; Brantingham and Brantingham 1991). By preventing victims and offenders from converging in space and time, police can reduce crime. A growing body of research evidence suggests that focused police interventions, such as directed patrols, proactive arrests, and problem solving, can produce significant crime prevention gains at high-crime hot spots (Sherman 1997).

These new perspectives on the ability of the police to prevent crime contrast with conventional social science views that the police make only minimal contributions to crime prevention relative to more powerful social institutions like the family and labor markets (as discussed in Sherman 1997). A number of well-known empirical studies on basic police crime control strategies—random patrol, rapid response, and criminal investigation—support the assertion that police can do little to prevent crime (Kelling et al. 1974; Spelman and Brown 1984; Greenwood, Chaiken, and Petersilia 1977). However, based on new research evidence, many crime prevention scholars suggest the ability of the police to prevent crime may have more to do with how well they are focused on specific crime risk factors rather than how well they randomly patrol large areas, rapidly respond to calls for service, and make large numbers of reactive arrests (Sherman 1997; Clarke 1992; Goldstein 1990; Wilson and Kelling 1982). As such, police should focus their actions on the places, times, and people who pose the highest risks to public safety rather than dilute their crime prevention potency by spreading them thinly across the urban landscape. This review examines the available evaluation evidence on one type of risk-focused policing to prevent crime: concentrating police enforcement efforts in high-risk places where crime is concentrated, or hot spots policing.

SYSTEMATIC REVIEW OF
HOT SPOTS POLICING STUDIES

This study reviews and synthesizes existing published and non-published empirical evidence on the effects of focused police enforcement interventions at crime hot spots and provides a systematic assessment of the preventive value of these programs. In keeping with the conventions established by the systematic reviews methods literature, the stages of this review and the criteria used to select eligible studies are described below.

Types of studies

This review was limited to studies that used a no-treatment control group design involving before and after measures. In eligible studies, the no-treatment control group experienced routine police interventions (that is, regular levels of random patrol, ad hoc investigations, and the like). Crime places that received the focused police interventions were compared to places that experienced routine levels of traditional police service. The comparison group study designs had to be either experimental or quasi-experimental (nonrandomized) (Campbell and Stanley 1966; Cook and Campbell 1979).

Types of areas

To be included in this review, the focus of police interventions in the evaluations had to be crime hot spots or crime places. As John Eck (1997) suggested,

a place is a very small area reserved for a narrow range of functions, often controlled by a single owner, and separated from the surrounding area. . . . Examples of places include stores, homes, apartment buildings, street corners, subway stations, and airports. (7.1)

All studies where police interventions were focused on places smaller than a neighborhood, community, or police beat were considered. The units of analysis in eligible studies did not have to be hot spots or high-activity crime places. However, the police interventions had to be specifically targeted at hot spots within these larger area units.

Types of interventions

The interventions used to control crime hot spots were limited to police enforcement efforts. Suitable police enforcement efforts included traditional tactics such as directed patrol and heightened levels of traffic enforcement as well as alternative strategies such as aggressive disorder enforcement and problem-oriented policing (POP) interventions with limited situational responses and limited engagement of the public. To be considered for this review, POP initiatives had to engage primarily traditional policing tactics such as law enforcement actions, informal counseling and cautioning, and referrals to other agencies.[1] POP programs that involved multiple interventions implemented by other stakeholders, such as community members, business owners, or residential managers, were not considered.

Types of outcome measures

Eligible studies had to measure the effects of the police intervention on officially recorded levels of crime at the places. Appropriate measures of crime could include crime incident reports, citizen emergency calls for service, or arrest data. Other outcomes measures such as surveys, interviews, and systematic observations of physical and social changes at places used by eligible studies were included in the assessment of program effectiveness. Particular attention was paid to studies that measured crime displacement effects and diffusion of crime control benefit effects. The value of policing strategies focused on specific locations has been questioned by the threat of crime displacement. That is, efforts aimed at reducing specific crime at a place will simply cause criminal activity to move elsewhere, be committed in another way, or even be manifested as another type of crime, thus negating any crime control gains (Reppetto 1976). More recently, academics have observed that crime prevention programs may result in the complete opposite of displacement—that crime control benefits were greater than expected and "spill over" into places beyond the target areas (Clarke and Weisburd 1994). The quality of the methodologies used to measure displacement and diffusion effects, as well as the types of displacement examined, was assessed.

Search strategies for
identification of studies

All published and unpublished studies, including those not written in the English language, were considered for this review. To identify studies meeting the criteria of this review, the following four search strategies were used:

1. Searches of online databases (see below);
2. Searches of narrative and empirical reviews of literature that examine the effectiveness of police interventions on crime hot spots;
3. Searches of bibliographies of police crime prevention efforts and place-oriented crime prevention programs; and
4. Contacts with leading researchers.

The following 10 databases were searched:

1. Criminal Justice Periodical Index;
2. Sociological Abstracts;
3. Social Science Abstracts;
4. Arts and Humanities Search;
5. Criminal Justice Abstracts;
6. National Criminal Justice Reference Service Abstracts;
7. Educational Resources Information Clearinghouse;
8. Legal Resource Index;
9. Dissertation Abstracts; and
10. Government Publications Office Monthly Catalog.

The following terms were used to search the 10 databases listed above:

1. Hot spot;
2. Crime place;
3. Crime clusters;
4. Crime displacement;
5. Place-oriented interventions;
6. High crime areas;
7. High crime locations; and
8. Targeted policing.

In addition, two existing registers of randomized controlled trials were consulted. These included (1) the *Registry of Randomized Experiments in Criminal Sanctions, 1950-1983* (Weisburd, Sherman, and Petrosino 1990), and (2) the *Social, Psychological, Educational, and Criminological Trials Register*, or *SPECTR*, being developed by the U.K. Cochrane Centre and the University of Pennsylvania (Petrosino et al. in press).

Selection of studies

The four search strategies led to the identification of 588 distinct abstracts. The text of each abstract was screened carefully to identify potentially eligible studies, per the criteria described above. The screening process yielded 43 distinct abstracts that identified 18 potentially eligible evaluation studies.[2] The full-text reports, journal articles, and books for these 43 abstracts were acquired and carefully assessed to determine whether the interventions involved focused police enforcement efforts at crime hot spots and whether the studies used randomized experimental or nonrandomized quasi-experimental designs. Of the 18 studies, 9 were excluded from this review because the focused policing interventions were applied uniformly across areas much larger than specific high-crime locations (see, for example, Caulkins, Larson, and Rich 1993; Novak et al. 1999)[3] and/or the treatment was not composed of primarily police-initiated enforcement tactics (see, for example, Green Mazerolle, Price, and Roehl 2000; Eck and Wartell 1996). The nine studies included in this review were the following:

1. Minneapolis Repeat Call Address Policing (RECAP) Program (Sherman, Buerger, and Gartin 1989);
2. Minneapolis Hot Spots Patrol Program (Sherman and Weisburd 1995);
3. Jersey City Drug Markets Analysis Program (DMAP) (Weisburd and Green 1995);
4. Jersey City POP at Violent Places Project (Braga et al. 1999);
5. St. Louis POP in Three Drug Market Locations Study (Hope 1994);
6. Kansas City Crack House Police Raids Program (Sherman and Rogan 1995a);
7. Kansas City Gun Project (Sherman and Rogan 1995b);
8. Houston Targeted Beat Program (Caeti 1999); and
9. Beenleigh Calls for Service Project (Criminal Justice Commission 1998).

Characteristics related to the methodological quality of the nine selected studies were extracted from the full-text journal articles and reports. These characteristics included the definition criteria used to identify crime hot spots, the quality of analytic methods to evaluate program outcomes, the measurement of displacement, any violation of randomization procedures, case attrition from the study, and any subversion of the experiment by participants. When appropriate and possible, the role of these methodological factors on the observed empirical results was noted. Since there were only nine studies selected, this review was conducted as a structured qualitative exercise; no quantitative analyses were conducted.

Characteristics of selected studies

The nine evaluations were conducted in five large cities in the United States and one suburb in Australia. Research teams involving either Lawrence W. Sherman or David L. Weisburd conducted six of the nine evaluations. The treatments used to prevent crime at hot spots fell into three broad categories: enforcement POP interventions, directed and aggressive patrol programs, and police crackdowns and raids (see Table 1). The effects of POP initiatives comprising mostly traditional tactics with limited situational responses were evaluated in the Minneapolis RECAP Program, Jersey City POP at Violent Places Study, St. Louis POP at Drug Market Locations Study, and Beenleigh Calls for Service Project (Buerger 1994, 6-7; Braga et al. 1999, 554; Criminal Justice Commission 1998, 28). The evaluation of the Houston Targeted Beat Program examined the effects of three types of treatments applied in different target areas; these interventions included high-visibility patrol, zero tolerance disorder policing, and enforcement POP (Caeti 1999, 246-50). The Kansas City Gun Project examined the gun violence prevention effects of proactive patrol and intensive enforcement of firearms laws via safety frisks during traffic stops, plain view searches and seizures, and searches incident to arrests on other charges (Sherman and Rogan 1995b, 681). The Minneapolis Hot Spots Patrol Program

evaluated the effects of increased levels of preventive patrol on crime (Sherman and Weisburd 1995, 634). The Jersey City DMAP and the Kansas City Crack House Police Raids Program evaluated the effects of well-planned crackdowns on street-level drug markets and court authorized raids on crack houses, respectively (Weisburd and Green 1995, 718; Sherman and Rogan 1995a, 766-67).

Five of the selected studies used randomized experimental designs, and four used nonequivalent control group quasi-experimental designs. All randomized experiments and one quasi-experiment, the St. Louis POP study, used crime hot spots as the unit of analysis. The remaining three quasi-experiments evaluated the aggregate beat-level effects of focused police interventions at hot spots within targeted beats. With the exception of the Minneapolis RECAP experiment, the experimental designs used more sophisticated methodologies to identify crime hot spots. The Minneapolis Hot Spots Patrol, Jersey City DMAP, and Jersey City POP at Violent Places experiments used the most sophisticated methods to identify hot spots. In general, the research teams defined hot spot areas by mapping official police call data to identify high volume street address clusters and intersection areas, ensured that these locations had stable numbers of calls over time, and considered qualitative indicators such as police and researcher observations to define hot spot boundaries (Sherman and Weisburd 1995, 630-32; Weisburd and Green 1995, 713-15; Braga et al.

TABLE 1
HOT SPOTS POLICING EXPERIMENTS AND QUASI-EXPERIMENTS

Study	Treatment	Hot Spot Definition	Research Design[a]
Minneapolis (MN) RECAP Program (Sherman, Buerger, and Gartin 1989)	POP interventions comprising mostly traditional enforcement tactics with some situational responses One-year intervention period Integrity of treatment threatened by large caseloads that outstripped the resources the RECAP unit could bring to bear	Addresses ranked by frequency of citizen calls for service divided into commercial and residential lists; the top 250 commercial and top 250 residential addresses were included in the experiment	Randomized experiment; control and treatment groups were each randomly allocated 125 commercial and 125 residential addresses Differences in the number of calls to each address from a baseline year to the experimental year were compared between RECAP and control groups
Minneapolis (MN) Hot Spots Patrol Program (Sherman and Weisburd 1995)	Uniformed police patrol; experimental group, on average, experienced twice as much patrol presence One-year intervention period Breakdown in the treatment noted during the summer months	One-hundred-ten hot spots comprising address clusters that experienced high volumes of citizen calls for service, had stable numbers of calls for over 2 years, and were visually proximate	Randomized experiment; control and treatment groups were each randomly allocated 55 hot spots within statistical blocks Differences of differences between citizen calls in baseline and experimental years, comparing control and experimental groups
Jersey City (NJ) DMAP (Weisburd and Green 1995)	Well-planned crackdowns followed by preventive patrol to maintain crime control gains Fifteen-month intervention period Slow progress at treatment places caused intervention time period to be extended by 3 months	Fifty-six drug hot spot areas identified based on ranking intersection areas with high levels of drug-related calls and narcotics arrests, types of drugs sold, police perceptions of drug areas, and offender movement patterns	Randomized experiment; control and treatment groups were each randomly allocated 28 drug hot spots within statistical blocks Differences of differences between citizen calls during 7-month pretest and posttest periods, comparing control and experimental groups

TABLE 1 Continued

Study	Treatment	Hot Spot Definition	Research Design[a]
Jersey City (NJ) POP at Violent Places Project (Braga et al. 1999)	POP interventions comprising mostly aggressive disorder enforcement tactics with some situational responses Sixteen-month intervention period Initial slow progress at places caused by resistance of officers to implement intervention	Twenty-four violent crime places identified based on ranking intersection areas with high levels of assault and robbery calls and incidents as well as police and researcher perceptions of violent areas	Randomized experiment; 24 places were matched into like pairs based on simple quantitative and qualitative analyses; control and treatment groups were each randomly allocated 12 places within matched pairs Differences of differences between a number of indicators during 6-month pretest and posttest periods, comparing control and experimental groups
St. Louis (MO) POP in Three Drug Market Locations Study (Hope 1994)	POP interventions comprising mostly traditional enforcement tactics with some situational responses Nine-month intervention period No threats to the integrity of the treatment reported	Subjective selection of POP efforts made at three hot spot locations comprising specific addresses associated with street-level drug sales	Quasi-experiment with nonequivalent control group; changes in citizen calls at hot spot addresses location were compared to changes in calls at other addresses on the block as well as other blocks in surrounding areas Simple trend analyses including 12-month preintervention and 6-month postintervention periods
Kansas City (MO) Crack House Police Raids Program (Sherman and Rogan 1995a)	Court-authorized raids on crack houses conducted by uniformed police officers Intervention period was the day of the raid All but seven cases received randomly assigned treatment as assigned No threats to the integrity of the treatment reported	Two hundred seven blocks with at least five calls for service in the 30 days preceding an undercover drug buy; sample was restricted to raids on the inside of residences where a drug buy was made that was eligible for a search warrant	Randomized experiment; raids were randomly allocated to 104 blocks and were conducted at 98 of those sites; the other 109 blocks did not receive raids Differences of differences analytic design; prepost time periods were 30 days before and after raid for experimental blocks and 30 days before and after controlled buy at treatment block for control blocks

(continued)

TABLE 1 Continued

Study	Treatment	Hot Spot Definition	Research Design[a]
Kansas City (MO) Gun Project (Sherman and Rogan 1995b)	Intensive enforcement of laws against illegally carrying concealed firearms via safety frisks during traffic stops, plain view, and searches incident to arrest on other charges Twenty-nine–week intervention period No threats to the integrity of the treatment reported; two phases of patrols reported due to shifts in grant funding	Eight-by-ten-block target beat selected by federal officials for Weed and Seed grant Enforcement actions targeted at hot spots in beat identified by computer analyses	Quasi-experiment with nonequivalent control group; target beat matched to a control beat with nearly identical levels of drive-by shootings Difference of means comparing weekly gun crimes between intervention period and 29-week pretest period Time series analyses of weekly gun crimes for 52-week before-after period Analysis of variance models with one extra pre year and post year to examine changes in homicides and drive-by shootings for both patrol phases
Houston (TX) Targeted Beat Program (Caeti 1999)	Patrol initiative designed to reduce index crimes in seven beats Three beats used high-visibility patrol at hot spots Three beats used zero tolerance policing at hot spots One beat used a POP approach comprising mostly traditional tactics to control hot spots Two-year intervention period Three high-visibility patrol beats managed by one substation Experienced police resistance to the program	Seven highest crime beats were selected for this program Enforcement actions targeted at hot spots in beats identified by computer analyses	Quasi-experiment with nonequivalent control groups; target beats were matched to noncontiguous comparison beats through cluster analysis and correlations of census data Difference of means in reported crime were used to evaluate program effects for 3-year preintervention and 2-year intervention period

TABLE 1 Continued

Study	Treatment	Hot Spot Definition	Research Design[a]
Beenleigh (Australia) Calls for Service Project (Criminal Justice Commission 1998)	POP interventions comprising mostly traditional enforcement tactics with some situational responses Six-month intervention period No threats to the integrity of the treatment reported	Two groups of 10 addresses that experienced the highest volume of calls during separate 6-month periods	Quasi-experiment with nonequivalent control group: Beenleigh, a lower-income suburb with a population of 40,000, was matched to similar Brown Plains suburb Simple time series analyses of total monthly calls for service in 5-month pretest, 6-month intervention, and 3-month posttest periods Nineteen pre-post, no control case studies

a. The control group in each study received routine levels of traditional police enforcement tactics.

1999, 549-50). The Kansas City Crack House Raid experiment focused on blocks that had at least five calls for service in the month preceding an undercover drug buy made on the inside of a residence (Sherman and Rogan 1995a, 767). The remaining studies used less refined methods. Simple ranking procedures to identify high-volume addresses based on numbers of citizen calls for service were used to define specific locations for focused police interventions in the Minneapolis RECAP experiment (Sherman, Buerger, and Gartin 1989, 4-5) and the Beenleigh quasi-experiment (Criminal Justice Commission 1998, 9). In the Kansas City Gun quasi-experiment (Sherman and Rogan 1995b, 678) and the Houston Targeted Beat quasi-experiment (Caeti 1999, 248-50), simple computer analyses of call and incident data were used to focus police interventions within larger targeted areas. The high-activity addresses evaluated in the St. Louis POP quasi-experiment were subjectively selected after a researcher searched for candidate cases within the St. Louis Police Department (Hope 1994, 10).

Effects of hot spots policing programs on crime and disorder

Noteworthy crime reductions were reported in seven of the nine selected studies (see Table 2). The strongest crime control gains were reported in the Jersey City POP at Violent Places experiment and the Kansas City Gun Project quasi-experiment. In the Jersey City POP experiment, the enforcement POP strategy resulted in statistically significant reductions in total calls for service and total crime incidents, as well as varying reductions in all subcategories of crime types, in the treatment violent crime hot spots relative to controls (Braga et al. 1999, 562-63). Analyses of systematic observation data collected during the pretest and posttest periods revealed that social disorder was alleviated at 10 of 11 treatment places relative to controls (Braga et al. 1999, 564).[4] Nonexperimental systematic observation data collected pretest and posttest at treatment places suggested that physical disorder was alleviated at 10 of 11 treatment places (Braga et al. 1999, 564).[5] Pretest and posttest interviews with key community members suggested that community perceptions of places improved at 7 of 12 treatment places (Braga 1997, 235-36). Proactive patrols focused on firearm recoveries in the Kansas City quasi-experiment resulted in a statistically significant 65 percent increase in gun seizures and a statistically significant 49 percent decrease in gun crimes in the target beat area; gun seizures and gun crimes in the comparison beat area did not significantly change (Sherman and Rogan 1995b, 684). A separate nonequivalent control group quasi-experiment examined community reaction to the Kansas City intervention and found that the community strongly supported the intensive patrols and perceived an improvement in the quality of life in the treatment neighborhood (Shaw 1995).

The Minneapolis Hot Spots Patrol experiment revealed that roughly doubling the level of patrol in crime hot spots resulted in modest, but significant, reductions in total calls for service, ranging from 6 percent to 13 percent, in treatment places relative to control places (Sherman and Weisburd 1995, 643). Moreover, systematic observations of the hot spots suggested that disorder was only half as prevalent in treatment hot spots as compared to control hot spots (Sherman and Weisburd 1995, 643). The Jersey City DMAP experiment suggested that well-planned crackdowns followed by patrol maintenance resulted in significant reductions in disorder calls for service at the treatment drug hot spots relative to controls (Weisburd and Green 1995, 723-26). Similarly, the St. Louis POP quasi-experiment found that the enforcement POP strategy was associated with varying degrees of reductions in total calls for service at all three high-activity drug locations; these reductions were greater than any reductions observed in other blocks and intersections in the surrounding areas (Hope 1994, 17, 21, 26). The Kansas City Crack House Raid experiment reported modest decreases in citizen calls for service and crime offenses at treatment blocks relative to controls that decayed within two weeks of the raids (Sherman and Rogan 1995a, 770-76).

The results of the Houston Targeted Beat quasi-experiment must be interpreted with caution. The key analytic measures of effectiveness were comparisons of pretest and posttest differences (as measured by t tests) in reported crime incidents at treatment beats relative to control beats (Caeti 1999, 319-22). However, the research did not examine the differences of differences between

TABLE 2
RESULTS OF HOT SPOTS POLICING EVALUATIONS

Study	Crime Outcomes	Other Outcomes	Displacement/ Diffusion
Minneapolis (MN) RECAP Program (Sherman, Buerger, and Gartin 1989)	No statistically significant differences in the prevalence of citizen calls for service	None	Not measured
Minneapolis (MN) Hot Spots Patrol Program (Sherman and Weisburd 1995)	Modest, but statistically significant, reductions in total crime calls for service ranging from 6 percent to 13 percent	Systematic observations of crime and disorder were half as prevalent in experimental as in control hot spots	Not measured
Jersey City (NJ) DMAP (Weisburd and Green 1995)	Statistically significant reductions in disorder calls for service in treatment drug markets relative to control drug markets	None	Examined displacement and diffusion effects in two-block catchment areas surrounding the treatment and control drug places and replicated the drug market identification process Little evidence of displacement; analyses suggest modest diffusion of benefits

(continued)

treatment and control areas. As such, the quasi-experimental analyses did not directly measure whether observed changes in treatment beats were significantly different from observed changes in control beats. Reported significant reductions in treatment beats relative to nonsignificant decreases and any increases in reported crime can be interpreted with some confidence. However, conclusions that the

TABLE 2 Continued

Study	Crime Outcomes	Other Outcomes	Displacement/ Diffusion
Jersey City (NJ) POP at Violent Places Project (Braga et al. 1999)	Statistically significant reductions in total calls for service and total crime incidents All crime categories experienced varying reductions; statistically significant reductions in street fight calls, property calls, narcotics calls, robbery incidents, and property crime incidents	Observation data revealed that social disorder was alleviated at 10 of 11 treatment places relative to control places Nonexperimental observation data revealed that physical disorder was alleviated at 10 of 11 treatment places Nonexperimental interviews with key community members in target locations suggest no noteworthy improvements in citizen perceptions of places	Examined displacement and diffusion effects in two-block catchment areas surrounding the treatment and control drug places Little evidence of immediate spatial displacement or diffusion
St. Louis (MO) POP in Three Drug Market Locations Study (Hope 1994)	All three drug locations experienced varying reductions in total calls Regression analysis suggests that reductions on blocks where drug locations were located were greater than other blocks and intersections in surrounding areas	None	Compared trends in calls at targeted addresses to trends in calls at other addresses on same block Location 1—significant displacement into surrounding addresses; location 2—no displacement or diffusion; location 3—no displacement or diffusion

TABLE 2 Continued

Study	Crime Outcomes	Other Outcomes	Displacement/ Diffusion
Kansas City (MO) Crack House Police Raids Program (Sherman and Rogan 1995a)	Modest decreases in citizen calls and offense reports that decayed in 2 weeks	None	Not measured
Kansas City (MO) Gun Project (Sherman and Rogan 1995b)	Sixty-five-percent increase in guns seized by the police; 49-percent decrease in gun crimes	Separate pre-post quasi-experiment surveying citizen opinions of the Kansas City Gun Project suggests citizens were aware of the project, generally supported the intensive approach, and perceived an improvement in the quality of life in treatment neighborhood	Displacement tests using pre-post difference in means and Auto Regressive Integrated Moving Average time series analyses were conducted in seven contiguous beats No significant displacement into specific beats; two beats showed significant reductions in gun crimes
Houston (TX) Targeted Beat Program (Caeti 1999)	Aggregated experimental beats experienced significant reductions in auto theft, total part 1 index crimes, and total part 1 suppressible (robbery, burglary, auto theft) index crimes relative to aggregate control beats Three zero-tolerance beats experienced mixed results; certain reported crimes decreased in particular beats Three high-visibility beats experienced reductions in a wide variety of index crimes Problem-solving beat experienced no significant decrease relative to control beat	None	Simple pre-post analyses of reported crimes in beats contiguous to treatment beats No evidence of significant displacement; contiguous beats surrounding three target areas (problem-solving beat, two zero-tolerance beats) experienced possible diffusion of benefits in particular reported crimes

(continued)

TABLE 2 Continued

Study	Crime Outcomes	Other Outcomes	Displacement/ Diffusion
Beenleigh (Australia) Calls for Service Project (Criminal Justice Commission 1998)	No noteworthy differences in total number of calls between Beenleigh and Brown Plains areas Noteworthy reductions in calls reported by nonexperimental pre-post impact assessments in 16 of the 19 case studies	None	Not measured

program did not work in treatment beats with reported significant crime reductions relative to control beats with significant crime reductions were not justified. It is completely possible that the observed significant reductions in the treatment beats were significantly greater than the significant reductions in control beats.

Given these caveats, the Houston Targeted Beat quasi-experiment suggests that the aggregated treatment beats experienced significant reductions in auto theft, total part 1 index crimes, and total part 1 patrol-suppressible crimes (robbery, burglary, and auto theft) relative to aggregated control beats. The three treatment beats where zero-tolerance aggressive disorder policing was used to control hot spots experienced mixed reductions in part 1 crimes relative to control beats; the three treatment beats where high-visibility directed patrol was used to control hot spots experienced reductions in a wide variety of part 1 crimes relative to control beats; the one treatment beat where an enforcement POP strategy

was implemented to control hot spots did not experience noteworthy decreases relative to a control beat. The limits of the analytic framework preclude conclusions that certain types of policing strategies may be more effective in preventing crime in hot spots. Nevertheless, the results of this study can be broadly taken to support the position that focused police enforcement efforts can be effective in reducing crime at hot spots.

The Beenleigh Calls for Service quasi-experiment found no noteworthy differences in the total number of calls in the town of Beenleigh relative to the matched town of Brown Plains (Criminal Justice Commission 1998, 25). However, simple nonexperimental pre-post comparisons found noteworthy reductions in total citizen calls for service in 16 of 19 case studies included in the report. The research team concluded that the POP strategy enjoyed some success in reducing calls for service at the targeted locations, but due to the small scale of the project and limitations of the research design, these crime prevention gains were not large enough to be detected at the aggregate town level (Criminal Justice Commission 1998, 28).

The Minneapolis RECAP experiment showed no statistically significant differences in the prevalence of citizen calls for service at addresses that received the POP treatment as compared to control addresses (Sherman, Buerger, and Gartin 1989, 21). These results were probably due to the assignment of too many cases to the RECAP unit, thus outstripping the amount of resources and attention the police officers provided to each address (Buerger 1993). Moreover, the simple randomization procedure led to the placing of some of the highest-event addresses into the treatment group; this led to high variability between the treatment and control groups and low statistical power. Although the overall findings suggest that the RECAP program was not effective in preventing crime, a case study analysis revealed that several addresses experienced dramatic reductions in total calls for service (Buerger 1992).

Beyond the RECAP experiment, only three other studies reported potential threats to the internal validity of the research designs. The Jersey City DMAP experiment (Weisburd and Green 1995, 721) and Jersey City POP at Violent Places experiment (Braga 1997, 107-42) reported instances where the treatments were threatened by subversion by the participants. The officers charged with preventing crime at the treatment hot spots were resistant to participating in the programs, and

this resulted in low levels of treatment during the early months of both experiments. In the Jersey City DMAP experiment, this situation was remedied by providing a detailed crackdown schedule to the narcotics squad commander and extending the experiment from 12 to 15 months. This problem was remedied in the Jersey City POP experiment by changing the leadership of the POP unit, developing an implementation accountability system, and providing additional training in the POP approach as well as through other smaller adjustments.

The patrol treatment in the Minneapolis Hot Spots experiment (Sherman and Weisburd 1995, 638-39) was disrupted during summer months due to a peak in the overall calls for service received by the Minneapolis Police Department and a shortage of officers due to vacations; this situation was further complicated by changes in the computerized calls for service system implemented in the fall. The changes in the calls for service system and the disappearance of differences in patrol dosage between treatment and control hot spots during summer months were addressed by conducting separate outcome analyses using different intervention time periods; there were no substantive differences in the outcomes of the experiment across the different time periods. Of course, these implementation problems are not unique to these experiments; many well-known criminal justice field experiments have experienced and successfully dealt with methodological difficulties.[6]

*Displacement and
    diffusion effects*

Five studies examined whether focused police efforts were associated with crime displacement or diffusion of crime control benefits (see Table 2). Prior to a discussion of the research findings, it must be noted that it is very difficult to detect displacement effects because the potential manifestations of displacement are quite diverse. As Barr and Pease (1990) suggested,

if, in truth, displacement is complete, some displaced crime will fall outside the areas and types of crime being studied or be so dispersed as to be masked by background variation. . . . No research study, however massive, is likely to resolve the issue. (293)

Diffusion effects are likely to be as difficult to assess. All five studies were limited to examining immediate spatial displacement and diffusion effects, that is, whether focused police efforts in targeted areas resulted in crime's moving around the corner or whether these proximate areas experienced unintended crime control benefits.

None of the five studies reported substantial immediate spatial displacement of crime into areas surrounding the targeted locations. Four studies suggested possible diffusion effects associated with the focused police interventions. The two Jersey City experiments used the most sophisticated methodologies to measure immediate spatial displacement and diffusion effects. In both experiments, the research teams examined the differences of differences in citizen calls for service in two-block catchment areas surrounding treatment and control hot spot areas. The Jersey City POP at Violent Places experiment found little evidence of displacement in the catchment areas and reported significant decreases in total calls for service and disorder calls for service in the catchment areas.[7] The Jersey City DMAP experiment found significant decreases in public morals calls for service and narcotics calls for service in treatment catchment areas relative to controls. The Jersey City DMAP experiment also replicated the drug market identification process and found six new drug hot spots within two blocks of the treatment locations. This result suggests that some modest displacement may have occurred, but it could not be determined whether these new drug hot spots were the result of experimental squad actions or control squad actions or if they would have developed naturally without any enforcement efforts (Weisburd and Green 1995, 730-31).

The Kansas City Gun quasi-experiment used before and after difference of means tests and Auto Regressive Integrated Moving Average time series analyses to examine whether gun crimes were displaced into seven beats contiguous to the target beat. None of the contiguous beats showed significant increases in gun crime, and two of the contiguous beats reported significant decreases in gun crimes. The Houston Targeted Beat quasi-experiment examined displacement and diffusion effects by conducting simple pre-post comparisons of reported part 1 index crimes in beats contiguous to the treatment beats. The analyses revealed no overall evidence of displacement, and contiguous beats surrounding three targeted beats (one POP beat and two zero tolerance beats) experienced possible diffusion effects as several types of reported index crimes decreased notably. The St. Louis POP at Drug Locations quasi-experiment assessed displacement effects by comparing trends in calls for service at targeted addresses to nontargeted addresses on the same block. Significant increases in calls for service at nontargeted addresses on the same block were reported in only one of the three analyses. The primary cause of the observed displacement was a shift in drug sales from a targeted apartment building to a similar nontargeted apartment building on the same block.

CONCLUSION

The results of this systematic review support the assertion that focusing police efforts at high-activity crime places can be used to good effect in preventing crime. Seven of nine experimental and quasi-experimental evaluations reported noteworthy crime and disorder reductions. Methodological problems in the research and evaluation designs probably accounted for the lack of crime prevention gains in the Minneapolis RECAP and Beenleigh studies. This review also supports the growing body of research evidence that suggests that focused crime

prevention efforts do not inevitably lead to the displacement of crime problems (Clarke and Weisburd 1994; Hesseling 1994; Eck 1993); rather, when displacement was measured, it was quite limited, and often, unintended crime prevention benefits were associated with the hot spots policing programs.

Unfortunately, the results of this review provide criminal justice policy makers and practitioners with little insight on what types of policing strategies are most preferable in controlling crime hot spots. Clearly, the enforcement-oriented strategies reviewed here work in preventing crime. We do not know, however, which enforcement strategies are more effective in preventing crime and under what circumstances certain strategies are more appropriate. This review also offers little insight on the effectiveness of enforcement tactics relative to other broader-based community problem-solving policing programs (see, for example, Skogan and Hartnett 1997). This small body of evaluation research does not unravel the important question of whether enforcement-oriented programs result in long-term crime reductions in hot spot areas. Research suggests that a variety of situational factors cause crime to cluster at particular places (Eck and Weisburd 1995). Proactive patrols, raids, and crackdowns do not specifically address the site features and facilities that cause specific locations to generate high volumes of crime. With the exception of the POP programs with limited situational interventions, the place-oriented interventions in this review consisted of uniform tactics applied across heterogeneous places. Perhaps a greater focus on changing these criminogenic situational characteristics would result in longer-lasting crime reductions at crime places.

Beyond thinking about the relative crime prevention value of these programs, we need to know more about community reaction to increased levels of police enforcement action. The results of the Kansas City Gun quasi-experiment suggest that residents of communities suffering from high rates of gun violence welcome intensive police efforts against guns (Shaw 1995). However, some observers question the fairness and intrusiveness of such approaches and caution that street searches, especially of young men and minorities, look like police harassment (Moore 1980; Kleck 1991). In New York City, although the gun-oriented policing strategies of the New York Police Department (NYPD) have been credited with a decrease in gun homicides (see, for example, Fagan, Zimring, and Kim 1998), the aggressive policing tactics of the NYPD have been criticized as resulting in increased citizen complaints about police misconduct and abuse of force (Greene 1999). We need to know more about the appropriate ways to implement increased enforcement programs in a manner that will not undermine the legitimacy of the police in the communities they serve. Future evaluations of hot spots policing initiatives that engage enforcement tactics need to focus closely on the reaction of the community to these programs.

Notes

1. For a discussion of "enforcement" and "situational" problem-oriented policing strategies, see Eck (1992).

2. There were multiple distinct abstracts identifying the same study. For example, a doctoral dissertation leading to a journal article would generate two distinct abstracts describing the same evaluation.

3. A replication of the Kansas City Gun Project was not included in this review because the interventions tested did not focus specifically on hot spots within the targeted beats (McGarrell and Chermak 2000).

4. One case was excluded from these analyses because the observational data were inappropriately collected (Braga et al. 1999, 564).

5. One case was excluded from these analyses because it did not have any physical disorder in the pretest and posttest periods (Braga et al. 1999, 564).

6. The landmark Kansas City Preventive Patrol Experiment had to be stopped and restarted three times before it was implemented properly; the patrol officers did not respect the boundaries of the treatment and control areas (Kelling et al. 1974). Likewise, the design of the Minneapolis Spouse Abuse Experiment was modified to a quasi-experiment when randomization could not be achieved because officers chose to arrest certain offenders on a nonrandom basis (Berk, Smyth, and Sherman 1988).

7. Property crime incidents increased significantly while property crime calls for service did not significantly change in the treatments catchment areas relative to controls. The research team viewed this result as an artifact of the experiment rather than a substantive finding (Braga et al. 1999, 567-69).

References

Barr, Robert and Ken Pease. 1990. Crime Placement, Displacement, and Deflection. In *Crime and Justice: A Review of Research*. Vol. 12, ed. Michael Tonry and Norval Morris. Chicago: University of Chicago Press.

Berk, Richard, Gordon Smyth, and Lawrence W. Sherman. 1988. When Random Assignment Fails: Some Lessons from the Minneapolis Spouse Abuse Experiment. *Journal of Quantitative Criminology* 4:209-23.

Braga, Anthony A. 1997. Solving Violent Crime Problems: An Evaluation of the Jersey City Police Department's Pilot Program to Control Violent Places. Ph.D. diss., Rutgers University, NJ.

Braga, Anthony A., David L. Weisburd, Elin Waring, Lorraine Green Mazerolle, William Spelman, and Francis Gajewski. 1999. Problem-Oriented Policing in Violent Crime Places: A Randomized Controlled Experiment. *Criminology* 37:541-80.

Brantingham, Paul and Patricia Brantingham, eds. 1991. *Environmental Criminology*. 2nd ed. Prospect Heights, IL: Waveland Press.

Buerger, Michael, ed. 1992. *The Crime Prevention Casebook: Securing High Crime Locations*. Washington, DC: Crime Control Institute.

————. 1993. Convincing the Recalcitrant: Reexamining the Minneapolis RECAP Experiment. Ph.D. diss., Rutgers University, NJ.

————. 1994. The Problems of Problem Solving: Resistance, Interdependencies, and Conflicting Interests. *American Journal of Police* 13:1-36.

Caeti, Tory. 1999. Houston's Targeted Beat Program: A Quasi-Experimental Test of Police Patrol Strategies. Ph.D. diss., Sam Houston State University, TX.

Campbell, Donald T. and Julian Stanley. 1966. *Experimental and Quasi-Experimental Designs for Research*. Chicago: Rand McNally.

Caulkins, Jonathan P., Richard C. Larson, and Thomas F. Rich. 1993. Geography's Impact on the Success of Focused Local Drug Enforcement Operations. *Socio-Economic Planning Sciences* 27:119-30.

Clarke, Ronald V., ed. 1992. *Situational Crime Prevention: Successful Case Studies*. Albany, NY: Harrow and Heston.

Clarke, Ronald V. and David L. Weisburd. 1994. Diffusion of Crime Control Benefits: Observations on the Reverse of Displacement. In *Crime Prevention Studies*. Vol. 2, ed. Ronald V. Clarke. Monsey, NY: Criminal Justice Press.

Cohen, Lawrence E. and Marcus Felson. 1979. Social Change and Crime Rate Trends: A Routine Activity Approach. *American Sociological Review* 44:588-605.

Cook, Thomas D. and Donald T. Campbell. 1979. *Quasi-Experimentation: Design and Analysis Issues for Field Settings*. Boston: Houghton Mifflin.

Cornish, Derek and Ronald V. Clarke, eds. 1986. *The Reasoning Criminal: Rational Choice Perspectives on Offending*. New York: Springer-Verlag.

Criminal Justice Commission. 1998. *Beenleigh Calls for Service Project: Evaluation Report*. Brisbane, Australia: Author.

Eck, John E. 1992. Alternative Futures for Policing. In *Police Innovation and Control of the Police*, ed. David L. Weisburd and Craig Uchida. New York: Springer-Verlag.

————. 1993. The Threat of Crime Displacement. *Criminal Justice Abstracts* 25:527-46.

————. 1997. Preventing Crime at Places. In *Preventing Crime: What Works, What Doesn't, What's Promising*, ed. Lawrence W. Sherman, Denise C. Gottfredson, Doris Layton MacKenzie, John E. Eck, Peter Reuter, and Shawn D. Bushway. Washington, DC: U.S. Department of Justice, National Institute of Justice.

Eck, John E. and Julie Wartell. 1996. *Reducing Crime and Drug Dealing by Improving Place Management: A Randomized Experiment* (Final report to the San Diego Police Department). Washington, DC: Crime Control Institute.

Eck, John E. and David L. Weisburd. 1995. Crime Places in Crime Theory. In *Crime and Place*, ed. John E. Eck and David L. Weisburd. Monsey, NY: Criminal Justice Press.

Fagan, Jeffrey, Franklin E. Zimring, and June Kim. 1998. Declining Homicide in New York City: A Tale of Two Trends. *Journal of Criminal Law and Criminology* 88:1277-324.

Goldstein, Herman. 1990. *Problem-Oriented Policing*. Philadelphia: Temple University Press.

Green Mazerolle, Lorraine, James F. Price, and Jan Roehl. 2000. Civil Remedies and Drug Control: A Randomized Field Trial in Oakland, California. *Evaluation Review* 24:212-41.

Greene, Judith A. 1999. Zero Tolerance: A Case Study of Police Practices and Policies in New York City. *Crime & Delinquency* 45:171-81.

Greenwood, Peter, Jan Chaiken, and Joan Petersilia. 1977. *The Investigation Process*. Lexington, MA: Lexington Books.

Hesseling, Rene. 1994. Displacement: A Review of the Empirical Literature. In *Crime Prevention Studies*. Vol. 3, ed. Ronald V. Clarke. Monsey, NY: Criminal Justice Press.

Hope, Timothy. 1994. Problem-Oriented Policing and Drug Market Locations: Three Case Studies. In *Crime Prevention Studies*. Vol. 2, ed. Ronald V. Clarke. Monsey, NY: Criminal Justice Press.

Kelling, George, Anthony Pate, Duane Dickman, and Charles Brown. 1974. *The Kansas City Preventive Patrol Experiment: A Technical Report*. Washington, DC: Police Foundation.

Kleck, Gary. 1991. *Point Blank: Guns and Violence in America*. New York: Aldine de Gruyter.

McGarrell, Edmund and Steven Chermak. 2000. *Targeting Firearms Violence Through Directed Police Patrol*. Washington, DC: Brookings Institution.

Moore, Mark H. 1980. The Police and Weapons Offenses. *Annals of the American Academy of Political and Social Science* 452:22-32.

Novak, Kenneth J., Jennifer Hartman, Alexander Holsinger, and Michael Turner. 1999. The Effects of Aggressive Policing of Disorder on Serious Crime. *Policing: An International Journal of Police Strategies and Management* 22:171-90.

Petrosino, Anthony, Robert Boruch, Cath Rounding, Steve McDonald, and Iain Chalmers. In press. Assembling a Social, Psychological, Educational, and Criminological Trials Register (SPECTR). *Evaluation Research in Education*.

Pierce, Glenn L., Susan Spaar, and LeBaron Briggs. 1988. *The Character of Police Work: Strategic and Tactical Implications*. Boston: Northeastern University, Center for Applied Social Research.

Reppetto, Thomas. 1976. Crime Prevention and the Displacement Phenomenon. *Crime & Delinquency* 22:166-77.

Shaw, James. 1995. Community Policing Against Guns: Public Opinion of the Kansas City Gun Experiment. *Justice Quarterly* 12:695-710.

Sherman, Lawrence W. 1995. The Police. In *Crime*, ed. James Q. Wilson and Joan Petersilia. San Francisco: ICS Press.

———. 1997. Policing for Crime Prevention. In *Preventing Crime: What Works, What Doesn't, What's Promising*, ed. Lawrence W. Sherman, Denise C. Gottfredson, Doris Layton MacKenzie, John E. Eck, Peter Reuter, and Shawn D. Bushway. Washington, DC: U.S. Department of Justice, National Institute of Justice.

Sherman, Lawrence W., Michael Buerger, and Patrick Gartin. 1989. *Repeat Call Address Policing: The Minneapolis*

RECAP Experiment (Final report to the National Institute of Justice). Washington, DC: Crime Control Institute.

Sherman, Lawrence W., Patrick Gartin, and Michael Buerger. 1989. Hot Spots of Predatory Crime: Routine Activities and the Criminology of Place. *Criminology* 27:27-56.

Sherman, Lawrence W. and Dennis Rogan. 1995a. Deterrent Effects of Police Raids on Crack Houses: A Randomized Controlled Experiment. *Justice Quarterly* 12:755-82.

———. 1995b. Effects of Gun Seizures on Gun Violence: "Hot Spots" Patrol in Kansas City. *Justice Quarterly* 12:673-94.

Sherman, Lawrence W. and David L. Weisburd. 1995. General Deterrent Effects of Police Patrol in Crime "Hot Spots": A Randomized, Controlled Trial. *Justice Quarterly* 12:625-48.

Skogan, Wesley G. and Susan M. Hartnett. 1997. *Community Policing, Chicago Style*. New York: Oxford University Press.

Spelman, William and Dale Brown. 1984. *Calling the Police: Citizen Reporting of Serious Crime*. Washington, DC: Government Printing Office.

Weisburd, David L. 1997. *Reorienting Criminal Justice Research and Policy: From the Causes of Criminality to the Context of Crime*. Washington, DC: U.S. Department of Justice, National Institute of Justice.

Weisburd, David L. and Lorraine Green. 1995. Policing Drug Hot Spots: The Jersey City Drug Market Analysis Experiment. *Justice Quarterly* 12:711-36.

Weisburd, David L., Lisa Maher, and Lawrence W. Sherman. 1992. Contrasting Crime General and Crime Specific Theory: The Case of Hot Spots of Crime. *Advances in Criminological Theory* 4:45-69.

Weisburd, David L., Lawrence W. Sherman, and Anthony J. Petrosino. 1990. *Registry of Randomized Experiments in Criminal Sanctions, 1950-1983*. Los Altos, CA: Sociometrics Corporation, Data Holdings of the National Institute of Justice.

Wilson, James Q. and George Kelling. 1982. Broken Windows: The Police and Neighborhood Safety. *Atlantic Monthly* Mar.:29-38.

ANNALS, *AAPSS*, **578**, November 2001

Effects of Correctional Boot Camps on Offending

By DORIS LAYTON MacKENZIE, DAVID B. WILSON,
and SUZANNE B. KIDER

ABSTRACT: A systematic review incorporating meta-analytic techniques of correctional boot camps studies was conducted. An intensive search identified 771 documents of which 144 were deemed potentially relevant, located, and evaluated for eligibility. In 37 documents, 29 studies were judged eligible for inclusion in the systematic review. The 29 studies resulted in 44 samples providing the primary unit of analysis. Quasi-experimental and experimental studies evaluated a residential program with a militaristic environment and compared the recidivism of participants to a comparison group receiving another correctional sanction. In 9 studies, boot camp participants had lower recidivism than did comparison groups; in 8, comparison groups had lower recidivism; and in the remaining studies, no significant differences were found. A meta-analysis found no overall significant differences in recidivism between boot camp participants and comparison samples. Further analyses indicated the results cannot be explained by differences in study methodology, offender characteristics, or boot camp program components.

Doris Layton MacKenzie is the director of the Evaluation Research Group and a professor in the Department of Criminology and Criminal Justice, University of Maryland. Her research interests include evaluation of correctional programs, correctional alternatives, correctional boot camps, self-report criminal activities, and offender behavior.

David B. Wilson is an assistant professor of the administration of justice at George Mason University. His research interests include program evaluation research methodology, meta-analysis, crime and general problem behavior prevention programs, and juvenile delinquency intervention effectiveness.

Suzanne B. Kider is a master's student in the Department of Criminology and Criminal Justice at the University of Maryland. Her main research interests include corrections and probation and parole reentry.

CORRECTIONAL boot camps, also called shock or intensive incarceration, are short-term incarceration programs modeled after basic training in the military (MacKenzie and Parent 1992; MacKenzie and Hebert 1996). Participants are required to follow a rigorous daily schedule of activities including drill and ceremony and physical training. They rise early each morning and are kept busy most of the day. Correctional officers are given military titles, and participants are required to use these titles when addressing staff. Staff and inmates are required to wear uniforms. Punishment for misbehavior is immediate and swift and usually involves some type of physical activity like push-ups. Frequently, groups of inmates enter the boot camps as squads or platoons. There is often an elaborate intake ceremony where inmates are immediately required to follow the rules, respond to staff in an appropriate way, stand at attention, and have their heads shaved. Many programs have graduation ceremonies for those who successfully complete the program. Frequently, family members and others from the outside public attend the graduation ceremonies.

While there are some basic similarities among the correctional boot camps, the programs differ greatly in other aspects (MacKenzie and Hebert 1996). For example, the camps differ in the amount of focus given to the physical training and hard labor aspects of the program versus therapeutic programming such as academic education, drug treatment, or cognitive skills. Some camps emphasize the therapeutic programming, while others focus on discipline and rigorous physical training. Programs also differ in whether they are designed to be alternatives to probation or to prison. In some jurisdictions judges sentence participants to the camps; in others, participants are identified by department of corrections personnel from those serving terms of incarceration. Another difference among programs is whether the residential phase is followed by an aftercare or reentry program designed to assist the participants with adjustment to the community.

Correctional boot camps were first opened in adult correctional systems in the United States in 1983, in Georgia and Oklahoma. Since that time they have rapidly grown, first within adult correctional systems and later in juvenile corrections. Today, correctional boot camps exist in federal, state, and local juvenile and adult jurisdictions in the United States. Juvenile boot camps developed later than the adult camps. However, during the 1990s camps for juveniles rapidly developed, and by 2000, 70 juvenile camps had been opened in the United States (see the Koch Crime Institute Web site at www.kci.org). The camps for adjudicated juveniles differ somewhat from the adult camps. In juvenile camps, less emphasis is placed on hard labor, and as required by law, the camps offer academic education. Juvenile camps are also apt to provide more therapeutic components. However, in many other aspects the juvenile camps are similar to adult camps with rigorous intake procedures, shaved heads, drill and ceremony, physical training, immediate physical punishment for misbehavior (for example, push-ups), and graduation ceremonies.

Despite their continuing popularity, correctional boot camps remain controversial. Primarily, the debate involves questions about the impact of the camps on the adjustment and behavior of participants while they are in residence and after they are released. According to advocates, the atmosphere of the camps is conducive to positive growth and change (Clark and Aziz 1996; MacKenzie and Hebert 1996). In contrast, critics argue that many of the components of the camps are in direct opposition to the type of relationships and supportive conditions that are needed for quality therapeutic programming (Andrews et al. 1990; Gendreau, Little, and Goggin 1996; Morash and Rucker 1990; Sechrest 1989).

Research examining the effectiveness of the correctional boot camps has focused on various potential impacts of the camps. Some have examined whether the camps change participants' attitudes, attachments to the community, or impulsivity (MacKenzie et al. 2001; MacKenzie and Shaw 1990; MacKenzie and Souryal 1995). Others have examined the impact of the camps on the need for prison bed space (MacKenzie and Piquero 1994; MacKenzie and Parent 1991). However, the research receiving the most interest appears to be that examining the impact of the camps on recidivism (MacKenzie 1997).

According to a survey of state correctional officials, the major goals of the camps are to deter future crime, protect the public, rehabilitate the offenders, reduce costs, and lower recidivism (Gowdy 1996). Thus, except for reducing the costs of corrections, all of the major goals are associated in some way with reducing the criminal activities of participants. Sufficient time has now elapsed since the beginning of these camps so that a body of research examining the impact of the camps on the recidivism of participants has been produced. This systematic review is designed to examine this research in order to draw conclusions regarding what is currently known about the effectiveness of correctional boot camps in reducing recidivism.

METHOD

Search strategy and eligibility criteria

The scope of this review was experimental and quasi-experimental evaluations that examined boot camp and boot camp–like programs for juvenile and adult offenders. To be eligible to be included in the review a study had to (1) examine a residential program that incorporated a militaristic environment (the programs were called by various names such as boot camp, shock incarceration, and intensive incarceration); (2) include a comparison group that received either community supervision (for example, probation) or incarceration in an alternative facility such as jail, prison, or juvenile residential facility; (3) include participants who were convicted or adjudicated; and (4) report a postprogram measure of criminal behavior, such as arrest or conviction (the measure may be based on official records or self-report and may be reported on a dichotomous or continuous scale). The comparison group in a quasi-experimental design had to be selected to be reasonably similar to the experimental group; thus any study that compared the experimental group to a general national or state sample was eliminated from the study. Furthermore the study eligibility criteria eliminated quasi-experimental designs that only compared program dropouts to program completers.

The strategies used to identify all studies, published or otherwise, that met these criteria included a keyword search of computerized databases and contact with authors working in this area. The following databases were searched: Criminal Justice Periodical Index, Dissertation Abstracts Online, Government Publications Office Monthly Catalog, Government Publications Reference File, National Criminal Justice Reference Service, PsychINFO, Sociological Abstracts, Social SciSearch, and U.S. Political Science Documents. The keywords used were "boot camp(s)," "intensive incarceration," and "shock incarceration." Several of the searched databases indexed unpublished works. This identified 771 unique documents. Review of the titles and abstracts suggested that 152 might meet the above criteria or were relevant review articles that might contain additional references. Of these 152, 144 were obtained and evaluated for eligibility, resulting in 29 eligible studies reported in 37 documents (see references). The majority of these studies were state or federal technical reports ($n = 22$). Only 9 of these studies were published in peer-reviewed journals. One study was conducted in Canada, and another study was conducted in England. The remaining studies evaluated boot camp programs in the United States.

*Data collection
and analysis*

The coding protocol developed for the synthesis allowed for the coding of multiple samples from a single study (distinct evaluations reported in a single report, different cohorts or data reported for males and females separately). This resulted in 44 distinct samples, and these samples represent the primary unit of analysis for this systematic review. The coding protocol also allowed for the coding of multiple indicators of criminal involvement, such as arrest, conviction, and technical violation, measured at multiple time points following release from the program. A copy of the coding protocol can be obtained from the authors. All studies were double coded, and any discrepancies in the coding between the two coders were resolved.

The protocol captured aspects of the research design, including methodological quality, characteristics of the boot camp program, comparison group condition, study participants, outcome measures, and direction and magnitude of the observed effects. The primary effect of interest was recidivism or a return to criminal activity on the part of the offender after leaving the program. Recidivism data were reported dichoto-mously across all studies and were based on official records, generally reflected as arrest, reconviction, or reinstitutionalization. As such, the natural index of effectiveness is the odds ratio (see Fleiss, 1994) and was the index of effect (see below). The mean odds ratio and homogeneity of effects across studies was computed using the inverse variance weight method. A random-effects model was assumed, and the random-effects variance component was estimated using the methods outlined by Dersimonian and Laird (1986) and Raudenbush (1994). The computa-tions were performed using macros written by the second author that are available for use with SAS, SPSS, and Stata (Lipsey and Wilson 2001).

A total of 155 recidivism effect sizes were extracted from the stud-ies. Recidivism effects that reflected technical violations only were excluded from the analyses reported below, reducing the set of effect sizes to 142. The recidivism effects were examined in two ways. First, multi-ple recidivism effects from a single study and sample were averaged prior to analysis, producing a set of 44 recidivism effect sizes for the analysis. The second set of analyses used arrest as the measure of recidi-vism if it was available; if not, reconvictions were used as the mea-sure, and if neither of these was available, reinstitutionalizations were used. The results from the two methods of measuring recidivism were compared and did not yield any substantive differences in the results. Therefore, results based on the second method of measuring

recidivism are reported in the follow-ing analyses.

RESULTS

The distribution of recidivism effects across the 44 boot camp ver-sus comparison group samples is shown in Figure 1. Each row of this forest plot represents a distinct sam-ple, identified by the label in the left column. The recidivism odds ratio (effect size) is represented by the small diamonds, and the line spans the 95 percent confidence interval around the odds ratio. The samples are sorted with the largest positive effect at the top and the smallest neg-ative effect (odds ratios between 1 and 0) on the bottom. At the very bot-tom of the plot is the overall random-effects mean odds ratio.

The effects across these studies ranged from large reductions to large increases in the risk of recidivating for the boot camp participants rela-tive to the comparison groups. The overall mean odds ratio was 1.02 (95 percent confidence interval of 0.90 to 1.17), indicating an almost equal odds of recidivating between the boot camp and comparison groups, on average. Thus there appears to be no relationship between program par-ticipation (boot camp or comparison) and recidivism. The equivalent recid-ivism rates for the average boot camp and comparison group, given this overall odds ratio, would be 49.4 per-cent for the boot camp and 50 percent for the comparison condition. This is a small difference by most any stan-dard. Thus, overall, the evidence sug-gests that boot camps do not reduce the risk of recidivism relative to

FIGURE 1

**A FOREST PLOT SHOWING THE RECIDIVISM ODDS RATIOS AND
95 PERCENT CONFIDENCE INTERVAL FOR EACH STUDY AND
SAMPLE AND THE OVERALL MEAN ODDS RATIO**

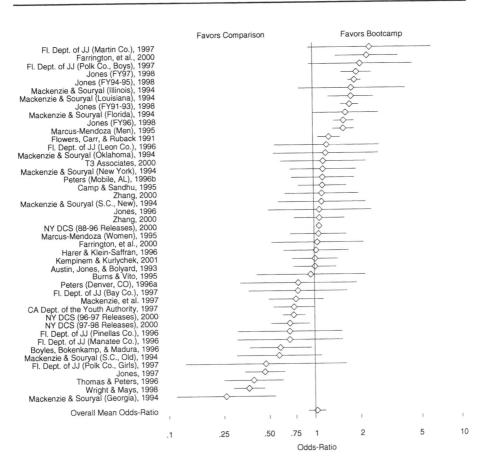

other existing criminal justice system forms of punishment and rehabilitation. From the forest plot, it is also evident that 9 studies observed a statistically significant positive benefit of boot camps, whereas 8 studies observed a statistically significant positive benefit of the comparison condition. The remaining 27 studies found no significant differences between the boot camp samples and the comparisons.

The distribution of odds ratios was highly heterogeneous, $Q = 464.6$, $df = 43$, $p < .0001$, suggesting the presence of moderators of the effects, either methodological or substantive, such as the nature of the boot camp program and comparison conditions and the types of offenders served.

TABLE 1
CROSS-TABULATION OF QUALITATIVE METHODOLOGICAL
QUALITY SCORE AND OTHER METHOD DESCRIPTORS ($N = 44$)

Method Variable	Qualitative Methodological Quality Score		
	4 ($n = 19$)	3 ($n = 17$)	2 ($n = 8$)
Randomly assigned participants to conditions			
Yes	4 (21)	1 (6)	0 (0)
No	15 (79)	16 (94)	8(100)
Used group-level matching**			
Yes	14 (74)	5 (29)	1 (13)
No	5 (26)	12 (71)	7 (87)
Prospective research design**			
Yes	17 (89)	9 (53)	6 (75)
No	2 (11)	8 (47)	2 (25)
Used statistical controls in analyses**			
Yes	13 (68)	3 (18)	1 (13)
No	6 (32)	14 (82)	7 (87)
Boot camp dropouts in analysis**			
Yes	9 (47)	9 (53)	0 (0)
No	10 (53)	8 (47)	8(100)
Overall attrition apparent			
Yes	3 (16)	2 (12)	1 (12)
No	16 (84)	15 (88)	7 (88)
Differential attrition apparent			
Yes	3 (16)	3 (18)	2 (25)
No	16 (84)	14 (82)	6 (75)

NOTE: Percentages are in parentheses.
**$p < .05$, based on a chi-square test.

Possible moderating effects are explored below.

Methodological characteristics of the studies

Any conclusion regarding the effectiveness (or ineffectiveness, as the data suggest) of boot camps relative to more traditional correctional approaches in reducing the risk of recidivism is valid only if the methodological quality of this collection of studies is sufficiently high. Table 1 displays the frequency of studies with various methodological characteristics by our qualitative methodological rating scale. This scale was developed by Sherman and colleagues (1997) and has five levels of methodological rigor. The lowest level of methodological quality was excluded from this synthesis and reflects studies without a comparison group. The highest level of methodological rigor (level 5) represents randomized designs that are not compromised through attrition or other common problems in carrying out a randomized evaluation study.

As can be seen in Table 1, none of the five randomized evaluations included in this synthesis were granted a method quality score of 5. This was generally because the studies had high attrition or excluded program dropouts from the recidivism analysis, creating a potential threat from selection bias. Thus there were no evaluations of the effectiveness of boot camps that were free from methodological blemishes. That said, however, many of the studies (19 of 44, or 43 percent) were judged to be methodologically solid (method score of 4). These studies were generally the higher-quality quasi-experimental designs that either carefully selected the comparison group so as to maximize similarity with the boot camp group (for example, selecting boot camp eligible offenders and matching the groups on demographic characteristics) or used statistical controls in the analysis of recidivism effects. Only 8 of the 44 evaluations (18 percent) were judged to be of poor methodological quality.

To assess the robustness of the general finding of no effect, a separate mean odds ratio was computed for each category of the different methodological variables (see Table 2). The mean effect size was slightly lower for the studies judged to be of overall higher methodological quality, although the trend was statistically nonsignificant. Studies that used a prospective research design had observed larger positive effects (although not significantly different from a null odds ratio of 1) than did retrospective designs. That is, while the mean odds ratio of prospective and retrospective designs are significantly different from each other, neither design produces an odds ratio that suggests that the experimental and control samples are significantly

different from each other (for example, confidence interval includes 1). In contrast to studies that did not use statistical controls in the analysis of recidivism outcomes, studies that used controls observed smaller effects that were negative in direction. Once again, neither category differed significantly from the null hypothesis. All other methodological variables were unrelated to the observed odds ratios.

Offender characteristics across studies

There was generally little information regarding the characteristics of the offenders in the studies. For 11 of the 44 samples, the authors did not indicate the gender, although it is reasonable to assume that in these cases the samples were all male. Only 3 of the 44 samples were all female, and the mean odds ratio for these samples was 1.06 and statistically nonsignificant. This mean odds ratio is roughly the same as that for the overall sample. Four samples were mixed gender, although they were predominantly male (equal to or greater than 80 percent). Thus there are insufficient data to adequately explore whether boot camps are differentially effective for males and females, as some theorists have hypothesized (Morash and Rucker 1990).

All samples were successfully classified as either juvenile or adult. The adult samples were typically young adults and in some cases included at least a small percentage of juveniles who were adjudicated as adults. As shown in Table 3, the mean odds ratio for the studies evaluating

TABLE 2
MEAN ODDS RATIO AND 95 PERCENT CONFIDENCE
INTERVAL BY METHOD VARIABLES (N = 44)

Method Variable	Mean Odds Ratio	95 Percent Confidence Interval		k^a
		Lower	Upper	
Qualitative methodological quality score				
Random assignment, not degraded				0
High-quality quasi-experiment	0.92	0.73	1.15	19
Standard quasi-experiment	1.07	0.85	1.34	17
Poor-quality quasi-experiment	1.15	0.84	1.59	8
Randomly assigned participants to conditions				
Yes	0.75	0.48	1.17	5
No	1.06	0.91	1.24	39
Used group-level matching				
Yes	1.11	0.88	1.40	20
No	0.97	0.80	1.17	24
Prospective research design**				
Yes	1.13	0.95	1.34	32
No	0.83	0.65	1.06	12
Used statistical controls in analyses**				
Yes	0.85	0.68	1.07	17
No	1.14	0.96	1.37	27
Boot camp dropouts in analysis				
Yes	1.03	0.82	1.28	18
No	1.02	0.83	1.24	26
No overall attrition apparent				
Yes	1.06	0.91	1.24	39
No	0.72	0.46	1.14	5
No differential attrition apparent				
Yes	1.03	0.87	1.21	36
No	0.96	0.67	1.41	8

a. k = number of samples included in analysis.
**$p < .05$.

the effectiveness of juvenile boot camps was lower than that of the studies evaluating adult (often young adult) boot camps, although this difference was not statistically significant. This difference may reflect a difference in the typical comparison group for juveniles relative to adults. Traditional juvenile detention facilities are qualitatively different from adult prison or adult probation, the common comparison groups for the studies of adult boot camps.

Juvenile detention facilities are more likely, although not guaranteed, to have a greater emphasis on rehabilitation than their adult counterparts. Unfortunately, the availability of rehabilitative treatment within the comparison facilities was not reported by the primary studies.

The racial/ethnic makeup of the offender populations and the offender risk level were often unreported, with no information available for 9 of the 44 samples (20 percent).

TABLE 3
MEAN ODDS RATIO AND 95 PERCENT CONFIDENCE
INTERVAL BY OFFENDER CHARACTERISTICS (N = 44)

Offender Characteristic	Mean Odds Ratio	95 Percent Confidence Interval		k^a
		Lower	Upper	
Age group of offender				
Juvenile	0.88	0.68	1.14	16
Adult	1.09	0.92	1.30	28
Offender type				
Juveniles				
Nonviolent/nonperson crimes	0.92	0.61	1.38	4
Mixed (violent and nonviolent) crimes	0.85	0.65	1.11	12
Adults				
Nonviolent/nonperson crimes	1.17	0.92	1.50	13
Mixed (violent and nonviolent) crimes	1.01	0.79	1.31	15

a. k = number of samples included in analysis.

For an additional 8 samples, only the percentage of African Americans was reported. Thus roughly half of the samples had complete racial/ethnic makeup information. In general, African Americans were the predominant racial group, representing roughly 52 percent of the samples reporting this information. Caucasians represented 23 percent of the 24 samples, and Hispanics represented roughly 9 percent of the 21 samples reporting these data. The data did not lend themselves to an analysis of the relationship between racial/ethnic makeup of the samples and the observed odds ratios.

Programmatic differences across studies

Boot camps vary in the emphasis placed on rehabilitative treatment relative to physical exercise and military drill and ceremony. It has been speculated that the greater the emphasis on treatments, such as drug abuse counseling, vocational education, and aftercare transition assistance, the greater the likelihood that boot camps will have positive benefits relative to alternative correctional approaches, such as prison and probation. To assess this issue, we coded whether the evaluation report described the boot camp program as providing various rehabilitative programs listed in Table 4. Mean odd ratios were computed separately for juvenile and adult programs.

The only program characteristic that showed a strong relationship to the effectiveness of the boot camp programs was the presence of an aftercare treatment component for the adult programs. The 11 odds ratios for boot camps with an aftercare component versus comparison group contrasts had a mean of 1.46 with a 95 percent confidence interval that did not include 1, indicating a statistically significant positive effect. This evidence suggests that

TABLE 4

MEAN ODDS RATIO AND 95 PERCENT CONFIDENCE INTERVAL BY PROGRAM CHARACTERISTICS (JUVENILES n = 16, ADULTS n = 28)

Program Characteristic	Mean Odds Ratio	95 Percent Confidence Interval		k^a
		Lower	Upper	
Aftercare treatment component				
Juveniles				
Yes	0.88	0.70	1.12	14
No	0.79	0.44	1.43	2
Adults***				
Yes	1.46***	1.14	1.87	11
No	0.89	0.72	1.10	17
Academic education				
Juveniles				
Yes	0.88	0.68	1.14	16
No				0
Adults				
Yes	1.13	0.93	1.38	24
No	0.86	0.51	1.43	4
Vocational education				
Juveniles				
Yes	0.98	0.62	1.55	3
No	0.84	0.66	1.08	13
Adults*				
Yes	0.82	0.56	1.20	6
No	1.17*	0.97	1.43	22
Drug treatment				
Juveniles				
Yes	0.90	0.70	1.15	12
No	0.78	0.49	1.24	4
Adults				
Yes	1.08	0.88	1.33	22
No	1.12	0.73	1.72	6
Counseling (group and individual)				
Juveniles				
Yes	0.91	0.70	1.17	10
No	0.79	0.52	1.18	6
Adults				
Yes	1.17	0.95	1.44	21
No	0.85	0.58	1.26	7
Manual labor				
Juveniles				
Yes	1.03	0.73	1.44	7
No*	0.79	0.61	1.02	9
Adults				
Yes	1.07	0.88	1.31	24
No	1.22	0.73	2.04	4

a. k = number of samples included in analysis.
*$p \leq$ .10. ***$p \leq$ .01.

aftercare may be important in reducing the risk of recidivism, at least for adult samples.

A counterintuitive finding is the negative relationship between vocational education and odds ratio for the adult samples. Study samples with vocational education had a lower mean odds ratio than did those without. The number of boot camp programs with vocational education was small, however, raising the possibility that this relationship is confounded with other study differences.

Multivariate analysis of effect size and study characteristics

The simple univariate analyses of the relationships between odds ratios and study characteristics do not take into account the possible confounding of study features. To assess this possibility, a mixed-effects regression model (see Lipsey and Wilson 2001; Raudenbush 1994) was estimated, regressing the logged odds ratios onto study features. The basic model included the major methodological features, accounting for significant variability in odds ratios across studies, $R^2 = .28$, $Q = 16.19$, $df = 7$, $p = .02$. Significant variability remained, however, after accounting for methodological differences. Building on this basic methods model, separate regression analyses were run for each major program characteristic shown in Table 4. Because of the possibility of an interaction between program characteristics and offender age, these models were run separately for juveniles and adults. The finding of a positive benefit from aftercare for the adult offenders remained statistically significant

after adjusting for methods features. The counterintuitive finding regarding vocational education was not robust to method difference; that is, it was statistically nonsignificant once conditioned on method features. This reinforces our hunch that this finding was the result of a confounding of study features and not due to any negative effects of vocational education. No new significant study characteristics emerged in the multivariate analyses.

DISCUSSION AND CONCLUSION

In our overall meta-analysis of recidivism, we found no differences between the boot camp and comparison samples. Our analysis predicts that if the comparison sample's recidivism is estimated to be 50 percent, the boot camp sample's recidivism would be estimated to be 49.4 percent, or only 0.6 percent lower. When the individual studies were examined, no significant differences were found between the boot camp samples and the comparisons in the majority of the studies. In only 17 samples out of the total of 44, a significant difference between the experimental and control samples was found; approximately half favored the boot camp while the remaining favored the comparisons. Thus, by whatever criteria are used, there is no evidence that the boot camps reduce recidivism.

The results of this systematic review and meta-analysis will be disappointing for many people. Advocates of the programs expect them to successfully reduce the future

criminal activities of adults and juveniles. Critics argue that the programs are poorly conceived as therapeutic interventions, they will not
reduce recidivism, and they may
actually have the opposite effect by
increasing criminal activities. Our
results do not support either side of
this argument because we found no
differences in recidivism between the
44 boot camp samples and the comparisons. Correctional boot camps
are neither as good as the advocates
assert nor as bad as the critics
hypothesize.

An examination of the forest plot
of the individual studies (see Figure
1) and our analysis of the data demonstrated large differences in the
studies in terms of the effect of boot
camps. Some studies found boot
camp participants did better than
the comparisons, and others found
comparison samples did better. For
this reason, we explored whether the
differences among studies could be
attributed to the methods or design
of the studies or to characteristics of
the programs or individual participants. In our examination of the
methodological variables, we did not
find any evidence that differences in
the results of studies could be
explained by the study methodology.

Our examination of the offender
characteristics was disappointing
because very few studies reported
sufficient information to enable us to
code and analyze the possible impact
of these characteristics on study outcomes. Few studies even reported on
the gender of the samples. The only
variables we could examine were (1)
whether the studies focused on adult
offenders or adjudicated juveniles,

and (2) whether the participants
were limited to those convicted
or adjudicated for nonviolent/
nonperson crimes or mixed violent
and nonviolent crimes. Again we
found no evidence that differences in
these characteristics explained the
differences in the results.

We were able to code and analyze
the possible impact of six program
characteristics, including whether
the boot camps had aftercare, academic education, vocational education, drug treatment, counseling, or
manual labor components. It is
important to note that this information was limited to general information about the characteristics of the
programs. We assume the quality
and intensity of the programs differed greatly. From our knowledge of
the boot camps we know that some
programs consider Narcotics Anonymous or Alcoholics Anonymous meetings drug treatment, whereas others
provide a more intensive drug treatment experience using a Therapeutic
Community–type model. We did not
have enough information to code
such differences. Almost no information was given about what happened
to the comparison samples. The
potential impact of these differences
on recidivism cannot be overlooked.

When we examined the impact of
program characteristics, the only differences we found were for adult
studies and, after controlling for
methodological differences, the only
difference was for boot camps that
included an aftercare component. In
other words, whereas the odds ratios
differed for boot camps with and
without aftercare, in neither case did
the boot camp samples differ

significantly from the comparisons. While the recidivism of releasees from boot camps with aftercare differed from the recidivism of releasees from boot camps without aftercare, there were no significant differences in recidivism between boot camp releasees and comparisons for either type of boot camp (for example, with or without aftercare). Thus we were unable to identify any characteristic of the methods, offenders, or programs that would explain differences in results of the studies.

Why don't boot camps reduce recidivism when compared to other correctional alternatives? In our opinion, one possible reason boot camps are not any more or less effective than other alternatives is because they may offer no more therapy or treatment than the alternatives. That is, boot camps by themselves have little to offer as far as moving offenders away from criminal activities. Sufficient research currently exists to demonstrate that appropriate correctional treatment with particular characteristics can be effective in changing offenders (Andrews and Bonta 1998; Gendreau and Ross 1987; Lipsey 1992). Some boot camps incorporate this type of treatment and therapy into the regime of the camps, while others do not. Similarly, some comparison facilities or programs provide such treatment. Almost all studies compared offenders or juveniles in boot camps to others in correctional programs within the same jurisdictions. We hypothesize that there are similarities within jurisdictions such that boot camps with therapy and treatment will be located in

jurisdictions that also provide such treatment to those in the comparison programs within the jurisdiction. Thus, in terms of the type of treatment or therapy that has been shown to be effective, correctional programs within the same jurisdictions will be similar. The boot camps may only differ from other correctional programs in the same jurisdiction in the military aspects and not in therapy and treatment. It seems likely that the therapy and treatment are the important components in reducing recidivism. Therefore, since boot camps and other correctional programs provide similar therapy and treatment, the impact on recidivism will be similar.

The research demonstrates that there are no differences in recidivism when boot camp samples are compared to those who receive other correctional sanctions. In our opinion, this can be interpreted to show that a military atmosphere in a correctional setting is not effective in reducing recidivism. However, many questions remain. It would be particularly valuable to have more information about the characteristics of the participants, and the components of the programs, both for the boot camps and for the comparisons. From these studies, we were able to code very little of this information. We anticipate that programs with more treatment and therapy will be more successful in reducing recidivism. The question is whether this would explain some of the differences in results across studies. Future research would greatly benefit by increasing the amount of detailed information about the programs and the participants.

APPENDIX
SECONDARY SOURCES USED IN THE META-ANALYSIS

1. Burns and Vito (1995)

Burns, Jerald C. 1994. A Comparative Analysis of the Alabama Department of Corrections Boot Camp Program. Unpublished Ph.D. diss., University of Alabama, Tuscaloosa.

2. State of New York Department of Correctional Services (2000)

Courtright, Kevin E. 1991. An Overview and Evaluation of Shock Incarceration in New York State. Unpublished master's thesis, Mercyhurst College, Erie, PA.

3. Marcus-Mendoza (1995)

Holley, Philip D. and David E. Wright. 1995. Oklahoma's Regimented Inmate Discipline Program for Males: Its Impact on Recidivism. *Journal of the Oklahoma Criminal Justice Research Consortium* 2:58-70.

4. Kempinem and Kurlychek (2001)

Kempinem, Cynthia and Mark Motivans. 1998. Who Goes to Pennsylvania's Boot Camp? Paper presented at the meeting of the American Society of Criminology, Washington, DC, Nov.

5. Harer and Klein-Saffran (1996)

Klein-Saffran, Jody. 1991. Shock Incarceration, Bureau of Prisons Style. *Research Forum* 1:1-9.

6. MacKenzie and Souryal (1994)

MacKenzie, Doris L., Robert Brame, David McDowall, and Claire Souryal. 1995. Boot Camp Prisons and Recidivism in Eight States. *Criminology* 33:327-57.

MacKenzie, Doris Layton, James W. Shaw, and Voncile B. Gowdy. 1990. *Evaluation of Shock Incarceration in Louisiana, Executive Summary.* Washington, DC: U.S. Department of Justice, National Institute of Justice.

7. Peters (1996a), Peters (1996b), and Thomas and Peters (1996)

Peters, Michael, David Thomas, and Christopher Zamberlan. 1997. *Boot Camps for Juvenile Offenders: Program Summary.* Rockville, MD: U.S. Department of Justice, National Institute of Justice.

NOTE: Secondary sources are shown after the primary sources included in the reference list.

References

Andrews, Donald A. and James Bonta. 1998. *The Psychology of Criminal Conduct.* Cincinnati, OH: Anderson.

Andrews, Donald A., Ivan Zinger, Robert D. Hoge, James Bonta, Paul Gendreau, and Frances T. Cullen. 1990. Does Correctional Treatment Work? A Clinically Relevant and Psychologically Informed Meta-Analysis. *Criminology* 28:369-404.

*Austin, James, Michael Jones, and Melissa Bolyard. 1993. *Assessing the Impact of a County Operated Boot Camp: Evaluation of the Los Angeles County Regimented Inmate Diversion Program* (NCJRS document reproduction service no. 154401). San Francisco: National Council on Crime and Delinquency.

*References marked with an asterisk indicate studies included in the meta-analysis. (See appendix for secondary sources used in the meta-analysis showing primary resource.)

*Boyles, Cecilia E., Eric Bokenkamp, and William Madura. 1996. *Evaluation of the Colorado Juvenile Regimented Training Program*. Golden: Colorado Department of Human Services, Division of Youth Corrections.

*Burns, Jerald C. and Gennaro F. Vito. 1995. An Impact Analysis of the Alabama Boot Camp Program. *Federal Probation* 59:63-67.

*California Department of the Youth Authority. 1997. *LEAD: A Boot Camp and Intensive Parole Program; the Final Impact Evaluation* (Report to the California Legislature). Sacramento: Author.

*Camp, David A. and Harjit S. Sandhu. 1995. Evaluation of Female Offender Regimented Treatment Program (FORT). *Journal of the Oklahoma Criminal Justice Research Consortium* 2:50-57.

Clark, Cheryl L. and David W. Aziz. 1996. Shock Incarceration in New York State: Philosophy, Results, and Limitations. In *Correctional Boot Camps: A Tough Intermediate Sanction*, ed. Doris Layton MacKenzie and Eugene E. Hebert. Washington, DC: U.S. Department of Justice, National Institute of Justice.

Dersimonian, Rebecca and Nan Laird. 1986. Meta-Analysis in Clinical Trials. *Controlled Clinical Trials* 7:177-88.

*Farrington, David P., G. Hancock, M. Livingston, Kate Painter, and G. Towl. 2000. *Evaluation of Intensive Regimes for Young Offenders* (Home Office research findings). London: Home Office Research, Development and Statistics Directorate.

Fleiss, Joseph L. 1994. Measures of Effect Size for Categorical Data. In *The Handbook of Research Synthesis*, ed. Harris Cooper and Larry V. Hedges. New York: Russell Sage.

*Florida Department of Juvenile Justice. 1996a. *Leon County Sheriff's Department Boot Camp: A Follow-Up Study of the First Five Platoons*. Tallahassee: Florida Department of Juvenile Justice, Bureau of Data and Research.

*——. 1996b. *Manatee County Sheriff's Boot Camp: A Follow-Up Study of the First Four Platoons*. Tallahassee: Florida Department of Juvenile Justice, Bureau of Data and Research.

*——. 1996c. *Pinellas County Boot Camp: A Follow-Up Study of the First Five Platoons* (research rep. no. 33). Tallahassee: Florida Department of Juvenile Justice, Bureau of Data and Research.

*——. 1997a. *Bay County Sheriff's Office Boot Camp: A Follow-Up Study of the First Seven Platoons* (research rep. no. 44). Bay County: Florida Department of Juvenile Justice, Bureau of Data and Research.

*——. 1997b. *Martin County Sheriff's Office Boot Camp: A Follow-Up of the First Four Platoons* (research rep. no. 43). Martin County: Florida Department of Juvenile Justice, Bureau of Data and Research.

*——. 1997c. *Polk County Juvenile Boot Camp: A Follow-Up Study of the First Four Platoons*. Tallahassee: Florida Department of Juvenile Justice, Bureau of Data and Research.

*——. 1997d. *Polk County Juvenile Boot Camp—Female Program: A Follow-Up Study of the First Seven Platoons*. Polk County: Florida Department of Juvenile Justice, Bureau of Data and Research.

*Flowers, Gerald T., Timothy S. Carr, and R. Barry Ruback. 1991. *Special Alternative Incarceration Evaluation*. Atlanta: Georgia Department of Corrections.

Gendreau, Paul, Tracy Little, and Claire E. Goggin. 1996. A Meta-Analysis of the Predictors of Adult Offender Recidivism: What Works! *Criminology* 34:575-607.

Gendreau, Paul and Robert R. Ross. 1987. Revivication of Rehabilitation: Evidence from the 1980s. *Justice Quarterly* 4:349-408.

Gowdy, Voncile B. 1996. Historical Perspective. In *Correctional Boot Camps: A Tough Intermediate Sanction*, ed. Doris Layton MacKenzie and Eugene E. Hebert. Washington, DC: U.S. Department of Justice, National Institute of Justice.

*Harer, Miles D. and Jody Klein-Saffran. 1996. An Evaluation of the Federal Bureau of Prisons Lewisburg Intensive Confinement Center. Unpublished manuscript, Federal Bureau of Prisons, Research and Evaluation, Washington, DC.

*Jones, Mark. 1996. Do Boot Camp Graduates Make Better Probationers? *Journal of Crime and Justice* 19:1-14.

*———. 1997. Is Less Better? Boot Camp, Regular Probation and Rearrest in North Carolina. *American Journal of Criminal Justice* 21:147-61.

*Jones, Robert J. 1998. *Annual Report to the Governor and the General Assembly: Impact Incarceration Program*. Springfield: Illinois Department of Corrections.

*Kempinem, Cynthia A. and Megan C. Kurlychek. 2001. *Pennsylvania's Motivational Boot Camp* (2000 Report to the Legislature). Quehanna: Pennsylvania Commission on Sentencing.

Lipsey, Mark. 1992. Juvenile Delinquency Treatment: A Meta-Analytic Inquiry into the Variability of Effects. In *Meta-Analysis for Explanation: A Casebook*, ed. Thomas Cook, Harris Cooper, David S. Cordray, Heidi Hartmann, Larry V. Hedges, Richard J. Light, Thomas A. Louis, and Frederick Mosteller. New York: Russell Sage.

Lipsey, Mark W. and David B. Wilson. 2001. *Practical Meta-Analysis*. Thousand Oaks, CA: Sage.

MacKenzie, Doris L. 1997. Criminal Justice and Crime Prevention. In *Preventing Crime: What Works, What Doesn't, What's Promising*, ed. Lawrence W. Sherman, Denise C. Gottfredson, Doris Layton MacKenzie, John Eck, Peter Reuter, and Shawn Bushway. Washington, DC: U.S. Department of Justice, National Institute of Justice.

MacKenzie, Doris Layton and Eugene E. Hebert, eds. 1996. *Correctional Boot Camps: A Tough Intermediate Sanction*. Washington, DC: U.S. Department of Justice, National Institute of Justice.

MacKenzie, Doris Layton and Dale G. Parent. 1991. Shock Incarceration and Prison Crowding in Louisiana. *Journal of Criminal Justice* 19:225-37.

MacKenzie, Doris L. and Dale G. Parent. 1992. Boot Camp Prisons for Young Offenders. In *Smart Sentencing: The Emergence of Intermediate Sanctions*, ed. James M. Byrne, Arthur J. Lurigio, and Joan Petersilia. Newbury Park, CA: Sage.

MacKenzie, Doris Layton and Alex Piquero. 1994. The Impact of Shock Incarceration Programs on Prison Crowding. *Crime & Delinquency* 40:222-49.

MacKenzie, Doris Layton and James W. Shaw. 1990. Inmate Adjustment and Change During Shock Incarceration. *Justice Quarterly* 7:125-50.

*MacKenzie, Doris L. and Claire Souryal. 1994. *Multi-Site Evaluation of Shock Incarceration: Executive Summary*. Washington, DC: U.S. Department of Justice, National Institute of Justice.

———. 1995. Inmate Attitude Change During Incarceration: A Comparison of Boot Camp with Traditional Prison. *Justice Quarterly* 12:325-54.

*MacKenzie, Doris L., Claire Souryal, Miriam Sealock, and Mohammed Bin Kashem. 1997. *Outcome Study of the Sergeant Henry Johnson Youth Leadership Academy (YLA)*. Washington, DC: University of Maryland, U.S. Department of Justice, National Institute of Justice.

MacKenzie, Doris L., David B. Wilson, Gaylene S. Armstrong, and Angela R. Gover. 2001. The Impact of Boot Camps and Traditional Institutions on Juvenile Residents: Perception, Adjustment, and Change. *Journal of Research in Crime and Delinquency* 38:279-313.

*Marcus-Mendoza, Susan T. 1995. Preliminary Investigation of Oklahoma's Shock Incarceration Program. *Journal of the Oklahoma Criminal Justice Research Consortium* 2:44-49.

Morash, Merry and Lila Rucker. 1990. A Critical Look at the Idea of Boot Camp as a Correctional Reform. *Crime & Delinquency* 36:204-22.

*Peters, Michael. 1996a. *Evaluation of the Impact of Boot Camps for Juvenile Offenders: Denver Interim Report*. Fairfax, VA: U.S. Department of Justice, Office of Juvenile Justice and Delinquency Prevention.

*———. 1996b. *Evaluation of the Impact of Boot Camps for Juvenile Offenders: Mobile Interim Report*. Fairfax, VA: U.S. Department of Justice, Office of Juvenile Justice and Delinquency Prevention.

Raudenbush, Stephen W. 1994. Random Effects Models. In *The Handbook of Research Synthesis*, ed. Harris Cooper and Larry V. Hedges. New York: Russell Sage.

Sechrest, Dale D. 1989. Prison "Boot Camps" Do Not Measure Up. *Federal Probation* 53:15-20.

Sherman, Lawerence W., Denise C. Gottfredson, Doris Layton MacKenzie, John Eck, Peter Reuter, and Shawn Bushway. 1997. *Preventing Crime: What Works, What Doesn't, What's Promising*. Washington, DC: U.S. Department of Justice, National Institute of Justice.

*State of New York Department of Correctional Services, Division of Parole. 2000. *The Twelfth Annual Shock Legislative Report (Shock Incarceration and Shock Parole Supervision)*. Albany, NY: Division of Parole.

*Thomas, David and Michael Peters. 1996. *Evaluation of the Impact of Boot Camps for Juvenile Offenders: Cleveland Interim Report*. Fairfax, VA: U.S. Department of Justice, Office of Juvenile Justice and Delinquency Prevention.

*T3 Associates Training and Consulting. 2000. *Project Turnaround Outcome Evaluation. Final Report*. Ottawa, Canada: Author.

*Wright, Dionne T. and G. Larry Mays. 1998. Correctional Boot Camps, Attitudes, and Recidivism: The Oklahoma Experience. *Journal of Offender Rehabilitation* 28:71-87.

*Zhang, Sheldon X. 2000. *An Evaluation of the Los Angeles County Juvenile Drug Treatment Boot Camp (Final Report)*. Washington, DC: U.S. Department of Justice, National Institute of Justice.

ANNALS, *AAPSS*, **578**, November 2001

Cognitive-Behavioral Programs for Offenders

By MARK W. LIPSEY, GABRIELLE L. CHAPMAN,
and NANA A. LANDENBERGER

ABSTRACT: A systematic review using meta-analytic techniques was conducted with 14 studies selected to provide the best evidence on the effectiveness of cognitive-behavioral programs for reducing the reoffense recidivism of criminal offenders. The results indicated that, overall, cognitive-behavioral programs are effective, and the best of them are capable of producing sizable reductions in recidivism. Many of the available studies, however, investigate research-oriented demonstration programs; the effects found for routine practical programs were notably smaller. Moreover, the research coverage of both juvenile and adult programs in institutional and noninstitutional settings is uneven and leaves troublesome gaps in the evidence.

Mark W. Lipsey is a professor of public policy at Vanderbilt University and a codirector of the Center for Evaluation Research and Methodology at the Vanderbilt Institute for Public Policy Studies.

Gabrielle L. Chapman is the director of planning and research at the Tennessee Department of Correction and a doctoral candidate in sociology at Vanderbilt University.

Nana A. Landenberger is a doctoral candidate in clinical psychology at Vanderbilt University with several years' experience providing cognitive-behavioral treatment to adult offenders.

ONE of the notable characteristics of chronic offenders is distorted cognition—self-justificatory thinking, misinterpretation of social cues, deficient moral reasoning, schemas of dominance and entitlement, and the like (Beck 1999; Dodge 1993; Walters 1990; Walters and White 1989; Yochelson and Samenow 1976). Offenders with such distorted thinking may react to essentially benign situations as if they were threatening, for example, be predisposed to perceive comments others make about them as disrespectful or attacking. They may hold conceptualizations of themselves, others, and the world that justify antisocial behavior, for example, "nobody can be trusted," "everyone is against me," or "society doesn't give me a chance." Their behavior may be guided by dysfunctional assumptions and rules about how one should behave, for example, "you have to punish people for messing with you or they won't respect you," "you have to rebel against authority or they will break you." And they may have deficient cognitive skills for long-term planning, problem solving, and decision making that contribute to maladaptive and rigid behavior.

Cognitive-behavioral treatments (CBTs) for offenders are designed to correct these dysfunctional and criminogenic thinking patterns. They employ systematic training regimens aimed at creating cognitive restructuring and flexible cognitive skills such that offenders develop more adaptive patterns of reasoning and reacting in situations that trigger their criminal behavior. For instance, CBTs may train offenders to monitor their patterns of automatic thoughts to situations in which they tend to react with violence. Various techniques are rehearsed for assessing the validity of those thoughts and substituting accurate interpretations for biased ones. Often role-play or practice in real situations is used to help consolidate new ways of coping with situations that tend to prompt criminal behavior. CBTs may focus on managing anger, assuming personal responsibility for behavior (for example, challenging offenders' tendency to excuse their behavior by blaming the victim, society, or other circumstances beyond their control), taking a moral and empathetic perspective on interpersonal behavior (for example, victim impact awareness), solving problems, developing life skills, setting goals, or any combination of these themes. A relapse prevention component is also often included, which teaches offenders strategies for avoiding or deescalating the precursors to offending behavior (for example, high-risk situations, places, associates, or maladaptive coping responses).

Prototypical examples of CBT programs for offenders include the Reasoning and Rehabilitation program (Ross and Fabiano 1985), Moral Reconation Therapy (Little and Robinson 1986), and Aggression Replacement Training (Goldstein and Glick 1987). The Reasoning and Rehabilitation program is organized around a series of exercises (for example, critical thinking, social perspective taking) that focus on modifying the impulsive, egocentric, illogical and rigid thinking of the offenders and teaching them to stop and think before acting, to consider the consequences of their behaviour, to conceptualize alternative ways of responding to interpersonal problems and to consider the impact of their behaviour on other people, particularly their victims. (Ross, Fabiano, and Ewles 1988, 31)

Moral Reconation Therapy is based on Kohlberg's stages of moral development and uses a series of group and workbook exercises designed to raise the moral reasoning level of offenders stepwise through 16 graded moral and cognitive stages (Finn 1998). Aggression Replacement Training is structured around a curriculum comprising three components—"Skillstreaming," "Anger Control Training," and "Moral Education" (Goldstein and Glick 1994). Skillstreaming teaches 50 prosocial behaviors through modeling and role playing; Anger Control Training instructs offenders in self-control by having them record anger-arousing experiences, identify triggers and cues, and then apply anger control techniques; Moral Education exposes offenders to Kohlberg-type moral dilemmas in a discussion format aimed at advancing the level of moral reasoning.

THE EFFECTIVENESS OF CBT FOR OFFENDERS

Several reviews and meta-analyses have found that structured, directive, skill-oriented programs are generally more effective in reducing the subsequent reoffense rates of offenders than less-structured programs (for example, Andrews et al. 1990; Lipsey and Wilson 1998; Lösel and Köferl 1989; Palmer 1994; Redondo, Sanchez-Meca, and Garrido 1999). Cognitive-behavioral interventions appear to be especially effective among such programs. A recent meta-analysis of group-oriented cognitive behavioral programs for offenders examined 20 studies of varying levels of methodological quality and concluded that CBT was effective for reducing criminal behavior among offenders (Wilson, Allen, and MacKenzie 2000). Nearly all of the studies showed positive effects (though not necessarily statistically significant), and representative CBT programs were found to reduce recidivism by 20 percent to 30 percent compared to untreated control groups.

Wilson, Allen, and MacKenzie's (2000) meta-analysis was restricted to programs delivered in groups, but this is a minor limitation since virtually all such programs for offenders are conducted in group formats. A more interesting aspect of this meta-analysis is the range of offenders represented in the studies it included—some applied CBT programs to general samples of offenders; others treated only specialized types of offenders, for example, sex offenders, drug offenders, driving under the influence cases, or batterers. Much of the variability in effects found across studies may have been due to differences in the responses of these different types of offenders, though there were too few studies in any one category for Wilson, Allen, and MacKenzie to closely examine this factor.

The only other meta-analysis of the effectiveness of CBT programs on the reoffense rates of offenders of which we are aware is Pearson and his colleagues (no date). This meta-analysis included 69 research studies but covered both behavioral (for example, contingency contracting, token economy) and cognitive-behavioral programs. Pearson and his colleagues found that the cognitive-behavioral programs were more effective in reducing recidivism than the behavioral ones were, with a mean recidivism reduction for treated groups of about 30 percent. Moreover studies of higher methodological quality showed the largest effect sizes. The criteria for identifying cognitive-behavioral programs in this meta-analysis were rather broad, however. They included not only interventions directed specifically toward altering cognitions but also social skills training and problem-solving programs for which cognitive change was not the main focus.

These two meta-analyses provide strong indications of the effectiveness of CBT for reducing the recidivism of offenders. Both, however, encompass considerable diversity within their scope, including a range of offender types, quality of study design, and (especially in Pearson et al. no date) variations in what is counted as a CBT. Against this background, it seems wise to confirm the effectiveness of CBTs for offenders with an analysis of the set of available studies that most directly and

convincingly tests this promising program approach.

In this article, we present another meta-analysis of research on the effects of cognitive-behavioral programs on the reoffense rates of offenders. To provide a clear view of the best evidence available on the effectiveness of this specific treatment modality, we have restricted the studies eligible for inclusion in the analysis in four important ways. First, we have selected only studies with experimental or strong quasi-experimental designs so that the most methodologically credible evidence is represented. Second, to better isolate the distinctive feature of CBT, we have adopted a relatively narrow definition of CBT that requires the intervention to focus centrally on cognitive change. Third, we have included only studies that applied CBT to samples of the general offender population and excluded those using samples of specialized offenders. While the issue of the effectiveness of CBT for different types of offenders is important, the broader issue is whether CBT can be used with good results in routine correctional practice with typical mixed samples. Last, we have focused the analysis exclusively on reoffense recidivism as an outcome variable. Though disciplinary infractions within a correctional institution, technical parole violations, and other such outcomes may be proxies for criminal behavior, the effects of CBT on subsequent criminal behavior is best shown by results on such direct measures as rearrest and reconviction.

METHOD

The criteria used to select the studies for this meta-analysis are as follows.

Interventions. The treatment under investigation is directed toward changing offenders' distorted or dysfunctional cognitions or toward teaching new cognitive skills in areas where offenders have deficits. The therapeutic techniques consist of specific, relatively structured learning experiences designed to affect such cognitive processes as interpreting social cues, reasoning about right and wrong behavior, and making decisions about appropriate behavior. When the program also includes other elements, the cognitive-behavioral component is centrally featured rather than being only a secondary component.

Participants. The recipients of the intervention are criminal offenders, either juvenile (ages 12 to 21) or adult, who are treated while on probation, incarcerated, or in aftercare/parole. They are drawn from a general offender population and are not selected for, or restricted to, a specific type of offense (for example, sex offenses, driving under the influence) or problem behavior (for example, drug use).

Outcome measures. The study reports subsequent delinquent or criminal offenses as an outcome variable and presents quantitative data or statistical information that permits computation or reasonable estimation of an effect size statistic representing the contrast between the subsequent criminal behavior of treated versus untreated offenders.

Research methods. The study uses a design in which participants are assigned to intervention and control conditions either randomly or with a nonrandom procedure that does not involve manifest differential selection. That is, if nonrandom assignment is used, the selection procedure must not involve treatment-related differentiation (for example, volunteers versus nonvolunteers, treatment completers versus dropouts), and the groups must be matched explicitly or implicitly on key demographic variables and/or prior offense histories or evidence must be provided that demonstrates initial equivalence between the groups. Control groups can represent placebo, waiting list, no-treatment, or treatment-as-usual conditions.

Other considerations. Both published and unpublished studies are eligible, but only studies from English-speaking countries that are reported in English are included.

Search strategy for identification of studies

Candidate study reports were located first through the authors' existing delinquency intervention database (Lipsey 1992) and the references in recent meta-analyses and research reviews covering cognitive-behavioral interventions. Additional studies were then sought through computer searches of a wide range of bibliographic databases (for example, Psychological Abstracts, National

Criminal Justice Reference Service, Sociological Abstracts, Dissertation Abstracts International, Educational Resources Information Clearinghouse, and Medline) and examination of the bibliographies of studies retrieved for screening. Copies of promising study reports were obtained, and determination of their eligibility for the meta-analysis was made by one of the authors.

Coding procedures

Each study judged eligible for inclusion in the meta-analysis was coded into a database by one of the authors. The coding scheme recorded general information about the study report (for example, date and type of publication) and a range of specific characteristics of the intervention, the participating offenders, and the study methods (Table 1 shows some of the coding categories used).

The most critical portion of the coding dealt with the findings reported by the studies on reoffense recidivism outcomes. In all but one instance, those outcomes were reported as the simple proportion or percentage of offenders in each research group who recidivated. This information was coded in odds ratios representing the odds of recidivating among the treatment group relative to the odds among the control group. For dichotomous outcomes, the odds ratio provides an effect size statistic for meta-analysis that has favorable statistical properties and yields readily interpretable results (Lipsey and Wilson 2001). The one study (Walters 1999) that did not report recidivism outcomes as proportions provided information from which an

odds ratio could be imputed, using the median control group recidivism base rate from the other studies.

RESULTS

Fourteen studies that met the eligibility criteria were located and coded. We consider this a work in progress and are continuing to search for additional studies, but we are confident that our search to this point has been reasonably thorough. The characteristics of these studies are summarized in Table 1. As Table 1 shows, all of these studies were conducted in the United States or Canada and were published in 1985 or later. The interventions were conducted as demonstration programs for half the studies and, in the other half, constituted ongoing programs in a criminal justice context. All the treatments were provided in group format, and nearly two-thirds took place in custodial institutions. The intervention typically lasted from 11 to 20 weeks, meeting one to two times per week, for a total of 10 hours or less average weekly contact time.

The offenders who participated in the interventions were about evenly divided between juvenile groups with a mean age of 15 to 18 years and adult groups with a mean age in the 20 to 30 years range. The group composition was usually all or mostly male and white or mixed race (though in half the studies information on ethnicity was not provided). Of the 14 studies, 8 used a random-assignment design, with the remaining ones involving mainly matched or waiting list controls, and most of the study samples consisted of 100 or

TABLE 1

**CHARACTERISTICS OF THE STUDIES
INCLUDED IN THE META-ANALYSIS**

Characteristic	Number of Studies	Proportion of Studies
Study reports		
Type of publication		
Journal article, book chapter	8	0.57
Book	2	0.14
Technical report, thesis	4	0.29
Date of publication		
1985-1990	5	0.36
1991-2000	9	0.64
Country of origin		
United States	9	0.64
Canada	5	0.36
Treatment program		
Circumstances of implementation		
Demonstration program	7	0.50
Ongoing practical program	7	0.50
Setting		
Correctional institution	9	0.64
Probation or parole	5	0.36
Treatment format		
Individual	0	0.00
Group	14	1.00
Treatment duration		
5-10 weeks	4	0.29
11-20 weeks	8	0.57
> 20 weeks	2	0.14
Total hours of treatment		
5-15	3	0.21
30-40	4	0.29
60-80	4	0.29
> 100	3	0.21
Frequency of sessions		
1-2 times per week	7	0.50
2-4 times per week	2	0.14
Daily	5	0.36
Hours per week		
1-2	6	0.43
3-10	6	0.43
> 10	2	0.14
Offenders in treatment samples		
Mean age		
15-18	7	0.50
20-30	6	0.43
> 30	1	0.07

TABLE 1 Continued

Characteristic	Number of Studies	Proportion of Studies
Gender mix		
All female	1	0.07
Mostly male	5	0.36
All male	8	0.57
Ethnic mix		
Most/all Anglo	3	0.21
Most/all black	1	0.07
Mixed, none predominates	3	0.21
Cannot tell	7	0.50
Research methods		
Design		
Randomized	8	0.57
Nonrandom	6	0.43
Control condition		
Treatment as usual	14	1.00
Other	0	0.00
Sample size (treatment plus control)		
20-45	3	0.21
55-100	6	0.43
100-300	4	0.29
> 2,000	1	0.07
Outcome variable		
Rearrest	8	0.57
Reconviction	6	0.43
Weeks posttreatment when measured		
13-26	6	0.43
30-52	3	0.21
> 52	5	0.36

fewer offenders in the treatment and control groups combined. The control condition in all studies was treatment as usual, that is, regular probation, parole, or prison as received by the intervention participants, but without the intervention program. The reoffense recidivism outcome variables selected for effect size coding were either rearrest or reconviction and, most commonly, were measured 13 to 16 weeks posttreat-

FIGURE 1
LOGGED ODDS RATIOS FOR RECIDIVISM EFFECTS

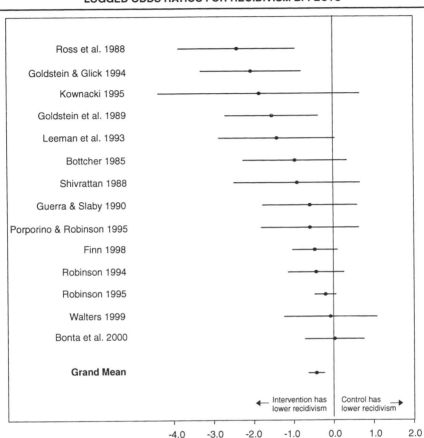

Log of Odds Ratio with 95% Confidence Interval

ment, though about one-third were measured more than a year after treatment was completed.

Intervention effects

Figure 1 shows the logged odds ratios and their confidence intervals for the treatment versus control group differences in reoffense recidivism across the 14 studies. The odds ratio represents the odds of recid-ivism among treated offenders relative to the odds among offenders in the control group, where the odds are defined as the number recidivating divided by the number not recidivating. Thus an odds ratio of .50 means that the ratio of recidivists to nonrecidivists among treated offenders was half that of the control group. The logged odds ratio is more convenient for statistical computations and takes negative values when the treatment group recidivates less than the control does, positive values when the control recidivates less than the treatment group does, and zero when recidivism rates are the same for both groups.

Figure 1 shows that with one slight exception, the odds ratios from these 14 studies all indicate lower recidivism for the offenders receiving CBT than for those in the control groups with whom they were compared. As the confidence intervals reveal, however, only a few of these odds ratios are statistically significant (that is, the confidence interval around the logged odds ratio does not include zero). The weighted[1] mean odds ratio across all 14 studies, computed as .66 (log = −.42), however, takes advantage of the statistical power of the full set of studies and is statistically significant ($p < .05$).

Of the 14 studies, 1 (Robinson 1995) had an exceptionally large sample size (more than 2000; next largest was less than 300) and thus exercised a disproportionate influence on the weighted mean odds ratio. With the weight on the odds ratio from that study scaled back to match the next highest, the weighted mean across studies was .55 (log = −.59), which gives a more generally representative value for this collection of study findings. This value indicates that on average, the odds of recidivating for offenders receiving CBT programs were almost half those for offenders in the control groups who did not receive CBT. More specifically, the weighted mean recidivism rate for the intervention groups was .26 compared with .38 for

the control groups (that is, 26 percent versus 38 percent recidivating in the respective groups). Thus only about two-thirds as many offenders receiving CBT recidivated as did offenders in the control groups.

The grand mean odds ratio and treatment versus control recidivism rates, however, do not take into account the variation in treatment effects across the 14 studies. A Q test of the homogeneity of the logged odds ratios (Lipsey and Wilson 2001; Shadish and Haddock 1994) showed that even with only 14 studies, the variation in findings was statistically significant. Adjusting the weighting for the one large sample reduced the heterogeneity but still left it marginally significant ($p = .07$). Before drawing any conclusions about the overall effectiveness of CBT from these studies, therefore, some investigation is warranted of the potential sources of this variability in findings across studies.

One potentially important moderator of effect sizes is the type of research design. Although only the strongest quasi-experimental designs were eligible for inclusion in the meta-analysis, they still might be sufficiently biased to yield findings systematically different from those resulting from randomized experiments. This did not prove to be the case, however. The mean odds ratio from the six nonrandomized designs (.62) was not significantly different, $Q(1) = .75, p = .39$, from the mean for the eight randomized designs (.50). Of the remaining coded variables dealing with important study characteristics, exploratory analysis suggested that as many as half a dozen might be significantly associated with effect size. Some of these were correlated among themselves, however, making simple bivariate breakdowns potentially misleading.

With only 14 studies, on the other hand, there was little scope for multivariate analysis. To generate some insight about the study characteristics most closely associated with larger and smaller intervention effects, therefore, a simple categorical procedure was used. The 14 studies were sorted by effect size and divided into the groups with the highest, middle, and lowest effect sizes. The dividing points were set inductively at gaps in the effect size distribution and with an eye on contrasts in the study characteristics between groups. The coded study characteristics (shown in Table 1) that were not already binary items were then dichotomized at the median or the nearest break in the respective distribution. Next, a chi-square test was applied to the simple cross-tabulation of each study characteristic and the three effect size groupings for the 14 studies.

Table 2 shows the study characteristics that were significantly associated with the grouping of studies by effect size. The characteristics most distinctive of each grouping are shown in boldface. Table 2 also reports the mean odds ratios and treatment versus control group recidivism rates for each group of studies.

The four studies that reported the largest effects of CBT on recidivism were demonstration programs set up by researchers and applied to offenders on probation or parole (that is, not incarcerated). These studies tended to measure short-term recidivism outcomes (6 months or less posttreatment) and use relatively small samples. The recidivism effects they reported were quite substantial. Offenders receiving CBT in these studies had a mean recidivism rate of .15 compared to .52 for the controls.

The four studies yielding in-between effects on recidivism were also demonstration programs, with one exception, but these were applied to juvenile offenders in institutional settings. They tended to examine longer-term recidivism (more than 6 months posttreatment) and use larger samples. The mean recidivism rate for the offenders receiving CBT in these studies was .37 compared to .53 among offenders in the corresponding control groups.

The six studies that produced the smallest effects were ongoing practical programs for which the researcher was primarily the evaluator. These programs used CBT with adult offenders in correctional institutions (with one exception). They also tended to examine longer-term recidivism outcomes and use larger samples. Most of these studies were reported since 1995, whereas most in the other two categories were published before then. The recidivism rates for the offenders in the control groups in these studies were notably lower than for the other two categories of studies, with a mean of .31. The treatment groups still showed a lower recidivism rate than their respective control groups, but at .26 it was not very much lower.

TABLE 2
CHARACTERISTICS OF STUDIES WITH DIFFERENT
MAGNITUDES OF RECIDIVISM EFFECTS

Treatment Program		Offender		Research Method		Study Report	
Type	n	Type	n	Type	n	Type	n
Studies showing largest effects (n = 4); Mean odds ratio = .16 (log = −1.85); Weighted mean recidivism rate; Treatment groups = .15; Control groups = .52							
Demonstration	4	Juveniles	2	**Posttest < 6 months**	4	Published before 1995	3
Practical	0	Adults	2	Posttest ≥ 6 months	0	Published in or after 1995	1
Institutional	0			**Sample N < 75**	4		
Probation/parole	4			Sample N ≥ 75	0		
Studies showing in-between effects (n = 4); Mean odds ratio = .41 (log = −.89); Weighted mean recidivism rate; Treatment groups = .37; Control groups = .53							
Demonstration	3	**Juveniles**	4	Posttest < 6 months	1	Published before 1995	4
Practical	1	Adults	0	**Posttest ≥ 6 months**	3	Published in or after 1995	0
Institutional	4			Sample N < 75	1		
Probation/parole	0			**Sample N ≥ 75**	3		
Studies showing smallest effects (N = 6); Mean odds ratio = .76 (log = −.28); Weighted mean recidivism rate; Treatment groups = .26; Control groups = .31							
Demonstration	0	Juveniles	1	Posttest < 6 months	1	Published before 1995	1
Practical	6	**Adults**	5	**Posttest ≥ 6 months**	5	Published in or after 1995	5
Institutional	5			Sample N < 75	1		
Probation/parole	1			**Sample N ≥ 75**	5		

NOTE: Boldface entries identify the characteristics most distinctive of the respective category of studies.

CONCLUSION

This meta-analysis encompasses only a small set of studies, but they were selected by criteria that make them the best available evidence about the effectiveness of CBT programs for reducing the reoffense recidivism of criminal offenders. Taken as a group, these studies show rather clearly that CBT is indeed an effective intervention—treated offenders on average recidivated at a rate of about two-thirds that of the offenders in the treatment-as-usual control groups with which they were compared. Moreover, the most effective programs reduced recidivism rates to about one-third of the rate for untreated controls.

The meta-analysis findings are not all good news for use of CBT in rehabilitation programs for offenders, however. Most of the large recidivism reductions shown in the research studies were produced by demonstration programs set up by researchers for the limited time required to mount an evaluation of their effects. Such programs involve levels of training for treatment personnel, adherence to treatment protocols, and strength and fidelity of implementation that are not likely to be typical of routine practice in criminal justice settings. The effects found in the six evaluation studies of ongoing CBT programs implemented by correctional institutions clustered at the bottom of the effect size distribution, and though positive, they were quite modest.

It is encouraging, on one hand, that practical programs implemented on a more or less routine basis in correctional facilities can produce measurable, even if modest, recidivism reductions. Such effects, multiplied over the volume of offenders to whom CBT programs can be administered in correctional facilities, may well be worthwhile, for instance, in cost-benefit terms (though none of the studies reviewed here provided cost data). On the other hand, the gap between the small effects of the practical programs and the substantial effects of the demonstration programs suggests that a great deal of improvement may be possible in the administration of effective CBT programs by criminal justice agencies. At the same time, it must be noted that the relatively large effects achieved by demonstration programs came from studies conducted in institutional settings with juvenile offenders or studies with adult and juvenile offenders on probation or parole. These differences raise a question as to whether the strong results from the demonstration programs can be generalized to incarcerated adults. Until studies of demonstration programs of CBT delivered to adults in jail or prison are available, it would be premature to conclude that this setting or offender population is either more or less conducive to effective treatment than the others that have been studied with such programs.

The most promising findings from the research reviewed here apply to juvenile offenders. Demonstration programs with juveniles both on probation/parole and in custodial institutions produced sizeable reductions in recidivism, with treated offenders showing only one-third to two-thirds the recidivism rates of untreated controls. However, no research studies of practical programs using CBT with juvenile offenders were found that met the methodological standards of this meta-analysis. The very positive results found in these demonstration programs, therefore, have not yet been confirmed with research studies of CBT administered to juvenile offenders in routine juvenile justice circumstances. In short, the best available research evidence supports the concept of CBT as an effective intervention for offenders, at least for juvenile offenders. Whether that concept can be translated into effective routine practice, however, is an open question.

Note

1. All statistical calculations were conducted with the logged odds ratios weighted by the inverse of their conditional variances to reflect the differential statistical precision stemming from their different sample sizes (Lipsey and Wilson 2001; Shadish and Haddock 1994).

References

Andrews, Don A., Ivan Zinger, Robert D. Hoge, James Bonta, Paul Gendreau, and Francis T. Cullen. 1990. Does Correctional Treatment Work? A Clinically-Relevant and Psychologically Informed Meta-Analysis. *Criminology* 28:369-404.

Beck, Aaron T. 1999. *Prisoners of Hate: The Cognitive Basis of Anger, Hostility, and Violence*. New York: HarperCollins.

*Bonta, James, Suzanne Wallace-Capretta, and Jennifer Rooney. 2000. A Quasi-Experimental Evaluation of an Intensive Rehabilitation Supervision Program. *Criminal Justice and Behavior* 27:312-29.

*Bottcher, Jean. 1985. *The Athena Program: An Evaluation of a Girl's Treatment Program at the Fresno County Probation Department's Juvenile Hall*. Sacramento: California Youth Authority.

Dodge, Kenneth A. 1993. Social-Cognitive Mechanisms in the Development of Conduct Disorder and Depression. *Annual Review of Psychology* 44:559-83.

*Finn, Peter. 1998. *The Delaware Department of Correction Life Skills Program*. Washington, DC: U.S. Department of Justice, Office of Justice Programs.

Goldstein, Arnold P. and Barry Glick. 1987. *Aggression Replacement Training: A Comprehensive Intervention for Aggressive Youth*. Champaign, IL: Research Press.

*———. 1994. *The Prosocial Gang: Implementing Aggression Replacement Training*. Thousand Oaks, CA: Sage.

*Goldstein, Arnold P., Barry Glick, Mary J. Irwin, Claudia Pask-McCartney, and Ibrahim Rubama. 1989. *Reducing Delinquency: Intervention in the Community*. 1st ed. New York: Pergamon.

*Guerra, Nancy G. and Ronald G. Slaby. 1990. Cognitive Mediators of Aggression in Adolescent Offenders: 2. Intervention. *Developmental Psychology* 26:269-77.

*Kownacki, Richard J. 1995. The Effectiveness of a Brief Cognitive-Behavioral Program on the Reduction of Antisocial Behaviour in High-Risk Adult Probationers in a Texas Community. In *Thinking Straight: The Reasoning and Rehabilitation Program for Delinquency Prevention and Offender Rehabilitation*, ed. Robert R. Ross and Roslynn D. Ross. Ottawa, Canada: Air Training and Publications.

*Leeman, Leonard W., John C. Gibbs, and Dick Fuller. 1993. Evaluation of a Multi-Component Group Treatment Program for Juvenile Delinquents. *Aggressive Behavior* 19:281-92.

Lipsey, Mark W. 1992. Juvenile Delinquency Treatment: A Meta-Analytic Inquiry into the Variability of Effects. In *Meta-Analysis for Explanation: A Casebook*, ed. Thomas D. Cook, Harris Cooper, David S. Cordray, Heidi Hartmann, Larry V. Hedges, Richard J. Light, Thomas A. Louis, and Frederick Mosteller. Newbury Park, CA: Sage.

Lipsey, Mark W. and David B. Wilson. 1998. Effective Intervention for Serious Juvenile Offenders: A Synthesis of Research. In *Serious and Violent Juvenile Offenders: Risk Factors and Successful Interventions*, ed. Rolf Loeber and David P. Farrington. Thousand Oaks, CA: Sage.

———. 2001. *Practical Meta-Analysis*. Thousand Oaks, CA: Sage.

Little, Gregory L. and Kenneth D. Robinson. 1986. *Juvenile MRT: How to Escape Your Prison*. Memphis, TN: Eagle Wing Books.

*References marked with an asterisk indicate studies included in the meta-analysis.

Lösel, Friedrich and Peter Köferl. 1989. Evaluation Research on Correctional Treatment in West Germany: A Meta-Analysis. In *Criminal Behavior and the Justice System: Psychological Perspectives*, ed. Hermann Wegener, Friedrich Lösel, and Jochen Haisch. New York: Springer-Verlag.

Palmer, Ted. 1994. *A Profile of Correctional Effectiveness and New Directions for Research*. Albany: State University of New York Press.

Pearson, Frank S., Douglas S. Lipton, Charles M. Cleland, and Dorline S. Yee. N.d. *The Effects of Behavioral/Cognitive-Behavioral Programs on Recidivism*. Unpublished manuscript, National Development and Research Institutes, Inc., New York.

*Porporino, Frank J. and David Robinson. 1995. An Evaluation of the Reasoning and Rehabilitation Program with Canadian Federal Offenders. In *Thinking Straight: The Reasoning and Rehabilitation Program for Delinquency Prevention and Offender Rehabilitation*, ed. Robert R. Ross and Roslynn D. Ross. Ottawa, Canada: Air Training and Publications.

Redondo, Santiago, Julio Sanchez-Meca, and Vicente Garrido. 1999. The Influence of Treatment Programmes on the Recidivism of Juvenile and Adult Offenders: An European Meta-Analytic Review. *Psychology, Crime, and Law* 5:251-78.

*Robinson, David. 1995. *The Impact of Cognitive Skills Training on Post-Release Recidivism Among Canadian Federal Offenders*. Ottawa: Correctional Service of Canada.

*Robinson, Sue C. 1994. Implementation of the Cognitive Model of Offender Rehabilitation and Delinquency Prevention (Cognitive Skills Training). Ph.D. diss., University of Utah. Abstract in *Dissertation Abstracts International* 55(08):2582A. (University Microfilms No. 95-02199)

Ross, Robert R. and Elizabeth A. Fabiano. 1985. *Time to Think: A Cognitive Model of Delinquency Prevention and Offender Rehabilitation*. Johnson City, TN: Institute of Social Sciences and Arts.

*Ross, Robert R., Elizabeth A. Fabiano, and Crystal D. Ewles. 1988. Reasoning and Rehabilitation. *International Journal of Offender Therapy and Comparative Criminology* 32:29-35.

Shadish, William R. and C. Keith Haddock. 1994. Combining Estimates of Effect Size. In *The Handbook of Research Synthesis*, ed. Harris Cooper and Larry V. Hedges. Thousand Oaks, CA: Sage.

*Shivrattan, Jacob L. 1988. Social Interactional Training and Incarcerated Juvenile Delinquents. *Canadian Journal of Criminology* 30:145-63.

Walters, Glenn D. 1990. *The Criminal Lifestyle: Patterns of Serious Criminal Conduct*. Newbury Park, CA: Sage.

*———. 1999. Short-Term Outcome of Inmates Participating in the Lifestyle Change Program. *Criminal Justice and Behavior* 26:322-37.

Walters, Glenn D. and Thomas W. White. 1989. The Thinking Criminal: A Cognitive Model of Lifestyle Criminality. *Criminal Justice Research Bulletin* 4:1-10.

Wilson, David B., Leana C. Allen, and Doris L. MacKenzie. 2000. *A Quantitative Review of Structured, Group-Oriented, Cognitive-Behavioral Programs for Offenders*. Unpublished manuscript, University of Maryland, College Park.

Yochelson, Samuel and Stanton E. Samenow. 1976. *The Criminal Personality*. Vol I, *A Profile for Change*. New York: Aronson.

ANNALS, *AAPSS*, **578**, November 2001

Toward an Evidence-Based Approach to Preventing Crime

By BRANDON C. WELSH and DAVID P. FARRINGTON

ABSTRACT: This article brings together the main conclusions from the previous articles in this issue and identifies priorities for moving toward an evidence-based approach to preventing crime. The Campbell Collaboration Crime and Justice Group has begun the important task of preparing systematic reviews of the effectiveness of a wide range of criminological interventions. Alongside the Campbell initiative, a program of research of new crime prevention and intervention experiments and quasi-experiments needs to be launched. Efforts must also be made to confront the challenges of getting research evidence into policy and practice. Here, political and policy considerations need to be faced.

Brandon C. Welsh is an assistant professor in the Department of Criminal Justice, University of Massachusetts–Lowell.

David P. Farrington is Professor of Psychological Criminology at the Institute of Criminology, University of Cambridge and Jerry Lee Research Professor of Criminology at the Department of Criminology and Criminal Justice, University of Maryland.

U NFORTUNATELY, "crime prevention today as in the past has a tendency to be driven more by rhetoric than reality" (Visher and Weisburd 1998, 238). However, effective public policy and practice need to be based on scientific evidence. This is an approach that has garnered much support in medicine (Millenson 1997) and other fields dedicated to the betterment of society. This is not, however, the practice usually adopted in criminology or criminal justice. Anecdotal evidence, program favorites of the month, and political ideology seemingly drive much of the crime policy agenda. As a result, we are left with a patchwork of programs that are of unknown potential in preventing crime. Crime prevention programs may or may not work or worse yet may produce harmful or iatrogenic results. We are not suggesting that the public is being intentionally misled by lawmakers and policy makers who are funding programs with no scientific evidence of effectiveness but rather that lawmakers and policy makers are shirking their responsibility to the taxpaying public by not funding only those programs with evidence of effectiveness in preventing crime.

In writing on the subject of evidence-based policing, Sherman (1998) noted that "most police practice, like medical practice, is still shaped by local custom, opinions, theories, and subjective impressions" (6). But "evidence-based policing challenges those principles of decision making and creates systematic feedback to provide continuous quality improvement in the achievement of police objectives" (Sherman 1998, 6). This is equally applicable to the larger field of crime prevention, whether it be for police, courts, or corrections or for alternative, non–criminal justice approaches such as violence prevention programs in schools or gang intervention programs in communities. As noted by Petrosino (2000), "an evidence-based approach requires that the results of rigorous evaluation be rationally integrated into decisions about interventions by policymakers and practitioners alike" (635).

This final article brings together the main conclusions of the eight previous articles in this special issue of *The Annals* and identifies priorities for moving toward an evidence-based approach to preventing crime. It is divided into four parts. In the first part, we examine the main review methods for assessing what works in light of their (potential) contribution to evidence-based crime prevention. In the second part, we review key features of impact evaluation research, focusing on the highest-quality research designs (experimental and quasi-experimental designs); discuss the relationship between research design and program effects; and make some recommendations for improving the state of evaluation research in criminology. In the third part, we briefly summarize the main findings and discuss policy implications of the four systematic reviews reported in this special issue, and in the final part, we discuss a number of important political and policy considerations that influence an evidence-based approach to preventing crime.

ASSESSING WHAT WORKS

Efforts to assess whether a particular crime prevention strategy (for example, developmental, criminal justice), intervention modality (for example, parent training), or some other subset of crime prevention programs works—that is, has a reducing effect on crime (or alternatively, if it is promising, has no effect, or is harmful)—can take many different forms. Some of these are the single study method, the narrative review method, the vote-count method, the meta-analytic review, and the systematic review. Each of these is discussed in light of its (potential) contribution to evidence-based crime prevention (Sherman et al. forthcoming).

Not only is the single study method self-explanatory, but its limitations—in comparison with the other methods—are blatantly evident. Here, a single evaluation study, usually of high quality methodologically (for example, randomized controlled experiment), is used to represent a body of research on a particular type of intervention. The well-known Perry Preschool program (Schweinhart, Barnes, and Weikart 1993) has long been used by advocates of early childhood intervention to show the beneficial results this type of intervention can have on delinquency and later offending. Despite its beneficial results, as well as findings from cost-benefit analyses that showed that it returned to society savings far in excess of the costs to run the program (see Barnett 1996; Greenwood et al. 2001), it is by no means representative of other early childhood interventions that have measured effects on criminal activity (see Farrington and Welsh 1999).

Narrative reviews of the literature quite often include many studies and may be very comprehensive. Their main drawback, however, is researcher bias. This bias, whether intentional or not, typically starts right from the beginning with a less than rigorous methodology for searching for studies. More often than not, the researcher will limit his or her search to academic sources or even self-select studies to be included, based on the researcher's familiarity with them. This can lead to an incorrect interpretation of the interventions' effects on crime; for example, what should have been presented as a positive effect is instead reported as an uncertain effect (that is, unclear evidence of an effect).

The vote-count method adds a quantitative element to the narrative review, by considering statistical significance. In essence, this method tallies up the "number of studies with statistically significant findings in favor of the hypothesis and the number contrary to the hypothesis (null findings)" (Wilson 2001 [this issue], 73).

A more comprehensive vote-count method was developed by Sherman and his colleagues (1997) to help them draw conclusions about what works, what does not work, what is promising, and what is unknown in preventing crime (see our appendix) in seven major institutional settings: families, communities, schools, labor markets, places (for example, urban centers, homes), police agencies, and courts and corrections. In addition to statistical significance, their vote-count method integrated a scientific methods scale that was based on the work of Cook and Campbell (1979) and described research designs that are most effective in eliminating threats to internal validity (that is, alternative plausible explanations of observed effects). As shown in our appendix, level 3 studies (presence of before and after crime measures in comparable experimental and control conditions) were used as the minimum cutoff point for inclusion of studies. This decision was based largely on the existing state of scientific knowledge. Their vote-count method also took into account the preponderance of evidence of the crime prevention program type (for example, home visitation for disadvantaged mothers, closed circuit television in town centers) in the relevant setting being investigated.[1]

One of the main strengths of this vote-count method is that it goes beyond the use of statistical significance in drawing conclusions about what works or does not work. It also has great utility as part of meta-analytic and systematic reviews. However, some of the limitations of the vote-count method include not accounting for the influence of larger studies and not taking account of the size of the observed effects. (For a more complete discussion of the vote-count method's limitations, see David Wilson's [2001] article.)

The systematic review and the meta-analytic review are the most rigorous methods for assessing the effectiveness of criminological interventions and have the most to offer to evidence-based crime prevention. Systematic reviews use rigorous methods for locating, appraising, and synthesizing evidence from prior evaluation studies, and they are reported with the same level of detail that characterizes high-quality reports of original research. Systematic reviews, according to Johnson and his colleagues (2000), "essentially take an epidemiological look at the methodology and results sections of a specific population of studies to reach a research-based consensus on a given study topic" (35). They have explicit objectives, explicit criteria for including or excluding studies, extensive searches for eligible evaluation studies from across the world, careful extraction and coding of key features of studies, and a structured and detailed report of the methods and conclusions of the review. All of this contributes greatly to the ease of their replication by other researchers.

The "foremost advantage of systematic reviews," as noted in the article by Anthony Petrosino and his colleagues (2001 [this issue]), "is that when done well and with full integrity, they provide the most reliable and comprehensive statement about what works" (20). Systematic reviews are not, however, without their limitations, although these limitations or challenges appear to be more closely linked with administrative and dissemination issues (see the article by Petrosino et al. 2001). The challenges that face the substance of systematic reviews include the transparency of the process (for example, the need to state the reasons studies were included or excluded) and the need to reconcile differences in coding of study characteristics and outcomes by multiple researchers (that is, interrater reliability).

As noted in the article by David Farrington and Anthony Petrosino (2001 [this issue]), in systematic reviews, "quantitative techniques are used, when appropriate and possible, in analyzing results" (37). The use of quantitative techniques such as meta-analysis may not be suitable due to a small number of studies, heterogeneity across studies, and different units of analysis of the studies (that is, a mix of area- and individual-based studies). Another instance in which a meta-analysis does not equal a systematic review is when the former fails to conform to the methodology of systematic review, for example, using biased search strategies to locate relevant studies. (For other situations in which a meta-analysis should not be performed, see David Wilson's [2001] article.)

High-quality systematic reviews are the core ingredient of the newly created Campbell Collaboration. Named after the influential experimental psychologist Donald T. Campbell, the Campbell Collaboration was set up for the purpose of preparing, maintaining, and disseminating evidence-based research on the effects of interventions in the three fields of education, social welfare, and crime and justice. The Campbell Collaboration Crime and Justice Group aims to prepare and maintain systematic reviews of criminological interventions and to make them accessible electronically to scholars, practitioners, policy makers, and the general public.

A meta-analysis involves the statistical or quantitative analysis of the results of prior research studies. Since it involves the statistical summary of data (for example, effect sizes), it requires a reasonable number of intervention studies that are sufficiently similar to be grouped together. For example, there may be little point in reporting a mean effect size based on a very small number of studies. Nevertheless, quantitative methods can be very important in helping the reviewer determine the average effect of a particular intervention.

David Wilson's (2001) article reviews meta-analysis in the context of criminological interventions. He identifies a number of strengths and limitations in the use of meta-analysis. Among the strengths, he lists its transparent nature—the explication of its methods and the studies involved—which makes it easily replicated by other researchers and its ability to handle a very large number of studies that may be overwhelming for other review methods, and he notes that the "statistical methods of meta-analysis help guard against interpreting the dispersion in results as meaningful when it can just as easily be explained as sampling error" (84). Limitations of meta-analysis include, on a practical side, its time-consuming nature and its inability to synthesize "complex patterns of effects often found in individual studies" (Wilson 2001, 84). Overall, as David Wilson notes, "meta-analysis provides a defensible strategy for summarizing crime prevention and intervention efforts for informing public policy" (85).

One issue that is central to each of the types of review methods discussed above (and discussed in all of the articles in this special issue of *The Annals*) is the importance of including only the highest-quality studies, that is, those studies that used the most methodologically rigorous evaluation designs (experimental and quasi-experimental designs) to assess criminological outcomes. We take up this important issue next.

EXPERIMENTAL AND
QUASI-EXPERIMENTAL
EVALUATION DESIGNS

The subtitle of this special issue of *The Annals* makes clear the types of evaluation research that are of interest to the discussion of systematic reviews reported throughout. Our interest in the use of experimental (randomized and nonrandomized) and quasi-experimental research designs in evaluating criminological interventions is largely threefold. First, they represent the most methodologically rigorous approaches to evaluating the impact of the independent variable (the program) on the dependent variable (crime or offending). Second, in the field of criminology, unlike in medicine, for example, there is not a long history of randomized controlled experiments, and by limiting systematic reviews to this type of evaluation design there would be very little to say (for most intervention modalities). Third, limiting systematic reviews to randomized experiments would mean the

exclusion of area-based interventions (for example, closed circuit television and many types of community crime prevention programs) (see Hope 1995; Welsh and Hoshi forthcoming). This part reviews key features of impact evaluation research, discusses the relationship between research design and program effects, and makes some recommendations for improving the state of evaluation research in criminology.

Intervention studies differ in methodological quality (see Farrington and Petrosino 2001). Two of the most important features of methodological quality are internal and external validity (Cook and Campbell 1979). Internal validity refers to how well the study unambiguously demonstrates that an intervention (for example, parent training) had an effect on an outcome (for example, offending). External validity refers to how well the effect of an intervention on an outcome is generalizable or replicable in different conditions: different operational definitions of the intervention and various outcomes, different persons, different environments, and so on.

It might perhaps be argued that the gold standard design should be the randomized experiment, which is the most convincing method of evaluating crime prevention programs (Farrington 1983). The key feature of randomized experiments is that the experimental and control groups are equated before the experimental intervention on all possible extraneous variables. Hence any subsequent differences between them must be attributable to the intervention. The randomized experiment, however, is the most convincing method of evaluation only if it is implemented with full integrity. To the extent that there are implementation problems (for example, problems of maintaining random assignment, differential attrition, cross over between control and experimental conditions), internal validity could be reduced in it.

Another important feature of the randomized experiment is that a sufficiently large number of units needs to be randomly assigned to ensure that the treatment group is equivalent to the comparison group on all extraneous variables (within the limits of statistical fluctuation). As a rule of thumb, at least 50 units in each category are needed (Farrington 1997). This number is relatively easy to achieve with individuals but very difficult to achieve with larger units such as communities, schools, and classrooms (see below).

Other things being equal, an intervention study in which experimental and control units are matched or statistically equated (for example, using a prediction score) prior to intervention—what is called a nonrandomized experiment—has less internal validity than a randomized experiment. An intervention study with no control group has even less internal validity since it fails to address many threats to internal validity, such as history, maturation, regression to the mean, and testing or instrumentation effects (Cook and Campbell 1979).

In area-based studies, the best and most feasible design usually involves before and after measures in comparable experimental and control conditions, together with statistical control of extraneous variables. This is an example of a quasi-experimental evaluation design. Even better, the effect of an intervention on crime can be investigated after controlling (for example, in a regression equation) not only for prior crime but also for other factors that influence crime. Another possibility is to match two areas and then to choose one at random to be the experimental area. Of course, several pairs of areas would be better than only one pair. These are the best ways of dealing with threats to internal validity when random assignment of units to experimental and control conditions cannot be done.

Regarding systematic reviews including studies with different high-quality research designs, instead of being limited to studies with only randomized experimental designs, an important question needs to be asked: Does the type of research design affect study outcomes? This is the subject of the article by David Weisburd, Cynthia Lum, and Anthony Petrosino (2001 [this issue]), which is further elaborated by the following:

Assuming that experimental designs are the gold standard for evaluating practices and policies, it is important to ask what price we pay in including other types of studies in our reviews of what works in crime and justice. Are we likely to overestimate or underestimate the positive effects of treatment? Or conversely, might we expect that the use of well-designed nonrandomized studies will lead to about the same conclusions as we would gain from randomized experimental evaluations? (52)

Both medical and social science (criminal justice included) literatures on the subject of research design affecting study outcomes are mixed, with some systematic reviews reporting that nonrandomized studies produce results with significantly larger effect sizes than randomized studies while other reviews report the opposite. Using a sample of criminal justice studies with outcome measures of crime ($N = 308$) from the University of Maryland report (Sherman et al. 1997), Weisburd, Lum, and Petrosino (2001) find "a moderate inverse relationship between the quality of the research design, defined in terms of internal validity, and the outcomes reported in a study" (64). A number of different analyses (for example, highest-quality nonrandomized versus randomized experimental studies, excluding quasi-experimental studies) confirm the results. The main implication of this finding, despite the authors' noting that their work is preliminary and hence that the findings should be interpreted with caution, is that the findings of systematic reviews may be biased by the inclusion of nonrandomized studies. More research is needed on this subject, examining different intervention modalities (for example, parent training, hot spots policing) and settings in which crime prevention takes place (for example, families, communities), as well as examining if research design affects study outcomes differently for individual- and area-level studies.

In their article, Farrington and Petrosino (2001) note that the criterion of methodological quality that is used for including (and excluding) studies is perhaps the "most important and controversial" (42) in conducting systematic reviews. How high to set the bar of methodological rigor as part of a review of the literature, systematic review method or otherwise, is a question that all researchers face. (For a brief discussion of this issue in the context of the vote-count review method, see the note 1 and MacKenzie 2000.) We support the inclusion of intervention studies that use experimental or quasi-experimental designs in systematic reviews. Systematic reviews of criminological interventions conducted under the name of the Campbell Collaboration should, however, set as a minimum for inclusion studies with before and after measures in comparable experimental and control conditions, together with statistical control of extraneous variables. Of course, for certain intervention modalities like multisystematic therapy for chronic and violent young offenders and cognitive-behavioral skills training for offenders, it will be possible for researchers to use only randomized experiments because of the comparatively large number of experimental evaluations in these areas.

More high-quality research designs of this sort and, of course, randomized experiments are needed in criminology. Experiments and quasi-experiments should have large samples, long follow-up periods, and follow-up interviews (Farrington 1999). As noted above, sample size is particularly important for both individual- and area-based studies. Long-term follow-ups are needed to assess how long effects persist after the intervention ends. This information may point to the need for booster sessions. Long follow-ups are a rarity in criminological interventions and should be a top priority of funding agencies.

Research is needed to identify the active ingredients of successful (and promising) crime prevention programs (Farrington 2000). Many programs are multimodal, making it difficult to isolate the independent effects of different components. Future experiments that attempt to disentangle the effects of different elements of the most successful programs are needed. Although not a specific focus of this special issue, it is also important that programs include, as part of the original research design, provision for an economic analysis—either a cost-benefit or cost-effectiveness analysis—to allow for an assessment of the economic efficiency of the program (see Welsh and Farrington 2000; Farrington, Petrosino, and Welsh 2001; Welsh, Farrington, and Sherman 2001).

USING WHAT WORKS AND
STOPPING USING WHAT DOES
NOT AND WHAT IS HARMFUL

In an evidence-based society, government crime prevention policy and local practice would be based on interventions with demonstrated effectiveness in preventing crime and offending. Equally important, governments would put an end to those interventions that do not work and, more important, to those that are harmful or iatrogenic. The key

here, of course, is fostering high-quality research—using experimental and quasi-experimental evaluation designs—on the effects of interventions. Another important process, likely (but disappointingly) to be even more important than the research product, which we take up in the next section, is the political and policy considerations that are made about what evidence gets used and what does not.

Systematic reviews are the most comprehensive method to assess the effectiveness of crime prevention measures and, in an evidence-based society, they would be the source that governments would turn to for help in the development of policy. This issue of *The Annals* reports on four systematic reviews of different criminological interventions. Each follows as closely as possible the methodology for conducting systematic reviews as advocated by the Campbell Collaboration, although it is important to note that none of these reviews (or their research protocols) has yet been approved by the Campbell Collaboration. In this part we briefly summarize the main findings and discuss policy implications of these four systematic reviews.

In the systematic review of parent training and support before age 3 by Odette Bernazzani, Catherine Côté, and Richard Tremblay (2001 [this issue]), seven studies were included, and effectiveness was assessed on the outcome measures of disruptive behavior (for example, opposition to adults, truancy, aggression) and delinquency. The authors found that three of the studies reported some beneficial effects on disruptive behavior or delinquency (one also reported some harmful effects), while the remaining four studies reported no evidence of effectiveness. The authors call for caution in interpreting the results (for example, due to modest effect sizes of the beneficial studies) and recommend further intervention studies in these areas.

In Anthony Braga's (2001 [this issue]) systematic review of hot spots policing—targeting of police enforcement measures in high-crime areas—nine studies were included, and effectiveness was assessed on the outcome measures of crime and disorder. Findings suggested that targeted police actions can prevent crime and disorder in hot spots. Braga also investigated the effects of the studies on the displacement of crime and the diffusion of crime control benefits and found that evidence of displacement was rare and some programs produced unintended crime prevention benefits in areas that did not receive the treatment. Braga concluded that "results of this systematic review support the assertion that focusing police efforts at high-activity crime places can be used to good effect in preventing crime" (121).

In the systematic review of correctional boot camps by Doris MacKenzie, David Wilson, and Suzanne Kider (2001 [this issue]), 44 studies were included, and effectiveness was assessed on recidivism. The authors found beneficial effects on recidivism for 9 studies, harmful effects for 8 studies, and no effects for the remaining 27 studies. A meta-analysis found there to be "no overall significant differences in recidivism" (126)

between boot camp participants and their control group counterparts. On the basis of the evidence, the authors concluded that "boot camps do not reduce the risk of recidivism relative to other existing criminal justice system forms of punishment and rehabilitation" (131).

In the systematic review of cognitive-behavioral programs for offenders by Mark Lipsey, Gabrielle Chapman, and Nana Landenberger (2001 [this issue]), the authors bring together 14 of the highest-quality studies with outcome measures of recidivism. The authors find that all but 1 of the studies reports beneficial effects on recidivism, and a meta-analysis reveals that the grand mean effect size across all 14 studies is statistically significant. The authors also investigate the effectiveness of cognitive-behavioral treatment on recidivism for those studies carried out as "research-oriented demonstration programs" (144) ($n = 8$) and those carried out as part of ongoing criminal justice practice ($n = 6$). Findings from the meta-analysis show that the former find the largest recidivism reductions of the total sample of studies.

When viewed together, these four systematic reviews suggest three main courses of action:

1. Increase funding of police initiatives targeted at crime hot spots (to reduce crime and disorder) and cognitive-behavioral programs for offenders (to reduce recidivism);

2. Stop funding of correctional boot camps designed to reduce recidivism; and

3. Initiate a program of research to test the effects of parent training and support programs during early childhood on disruptive behavior and delinquency.

Acting on this evidence could arguably make a difference to preventing crime, both now and in the long run. In the first place, police enforcement of street-level crime and correctional treatment account for a large share of criminal justice expenditure on preventing future offending in the community, and increasing the use of hot spots policing and cognitive-behavioral treatment for offenders as part of the overall police and correctional programming activities, respectively, could produce impressive effects on crime. Such a shift in police enforcement efforts has been shown to be a promising approach to preventing crime (Eck and Maguire 2000).

Second, the elimination of boot camp programs from correctional practice would free up public dollars that could be used on interventions with proven effectiveness in reducing recidivism. The ending of boot camp programs would also have the positive benefit of eliminating one source of harmful or iatrogenic effects among correctional practice, which is an important aim in itself (see Dishion, McCord, and Poulin 1999).

Third, future demonstration trials that test the effects of parent support and training during early childhood on disruptive behavior and delinquency offer to contribute to a more

extensive knowledge base on these types of interventions. Information on the effects on delinquency from these new trials will of course take some time to become available. However, updates of this systematic review may produce more information on delinquency in the short term. This is because, of the seven studies included in the present systematic review, a number are longitudinal trials and are approaching the age of the participants (or the participants' children) when delinquency can be measured.

POLITICAL AND POLICY
CONSIDERATIONS

In any discussion about implementing new crime prevention programs, expanding existing ones, or putting an end to ineffective or harmful ones, political and policy considerations are dominant. In fact, it is all too common that the strength of the programmatic evidence under consideration for developing policy becomes secondary to the political and policy considerations of the day. Certainly, some of these considerations are important. Other government priorities such as military defense spending, environmental protection, and lower costs of prescription drugs for seniors are competing for scarce public resources. National polls may show that the public is more concerned with matters of public policy other than crime prevention or community safety. Other political considerations that are more germane to crime prevention include the perception on the part of politicians that they are being soft on crime by supporting non–criminal justice crime prevention efforts, as well as the short time horizons of politicians (Tonry and Farrington 1995), which makes programs that show results only in the longer run less appealing to politicians who are trying to get elected every few years.

How to overcome some of the misconceived political and policy barriers in order to get more of what works in preventing crime into policy and practice is by no means an easy task, but fortunately it has received some attention in criminology (for example, Cullen forthcoming), public management (for example, Nutley and Davies 2000; Nutley, Davies, and Tilley 2000), public health care (for example, Millenson 1997; Halladay and Bero 2000), and evaluation science (for example, Weiss 1998), to name a few of the academic disciplines that have been investigating the subject.

According to Weiss (1998), getting research evidence to be utilized by decision makers may be facilitated under any one of the following four scenarios:

1. "If the implications of the findings are relatively non-controversial, neither provoking rifts in the organization nor running into conflicting interests";
2. "If the changes that are implied are within the program's existing repertoire and are relatively small-scale";

3. "If the environment of the program is relatively stable"; and
4. "When the program is in a crisis or paralysis, and nobody knows what to do." Here the decision maker "may turn to evaluation." (24-25)

In commenting on evaluation research on gun control policy (equally applicable to crime prevention policy in general), Rosenfeld (2000) illuminated one of the hopeful outcomes of an evidence-based approach to policy development: "although political considerations will always play a prominent role in policy development, politics that has to contend with the results of good science should produce better policy than politics based on poor science or none at all" (616).

APPENDIX
STUDY INCLUSION CRITERIA
FOR UNIVERSITY OF MARYLAND
REPORT

The scientific methods scale ranks evaluation studies from 1 = *weakest* to 5 = *highest* on overall internal validity:

1. Correlational evidence (low offending correlates with the program at a single point in time);
2. No statistical control for selection bias but some kind of comparison (for example, program group compared with nonequivalent control group; program group measured before and after intervention, with no control group);
3. Moderate statistical control (for example, program group compared with comparable control group, including pre-post and experimental-control comparisons);
4. Strong statistical control (for example, program group compared with control

group, with control of extraneous influences on the outcome, by matching, prediction scores, or statistical controls); and

5. Randomized experiment: units assigned at random to program and control groups prior to intervention.

What works. These are programs that the authors (Sherman et al. 1997) were reasonably certain prevent crime or reduce risk factors for crime in the kinds of social contexts in which they have been evaluated and for which the findings can be generalized to similar settings in other places and times. For a program to be classified as working, there must be a minimum of two level 3 studies with significance tests demonstrating effectiveness and the preponderance of evidence in support of the same conclusion.

What does not work. These are programs that the authors were reasonably certain fail to prevent crime or reduce risk factors for crime, using the identical scientific criteria used for deciding what works. For the classification of not working, there must be a minimum of two level 3 studies with significance tests showing ineffectiveness and the preponderance of evidence in the same direction.

What is promising. These are programs for which the level of certainty from available evidence is too low to support generalizable conclusions but for which there is some empirical basis for predicting that further research could support such conclusions. For the classification of promising, at least one level 3 study is required with significance tests showing effectiveness and the preponderance of evidence in support of the same conclusion.

What is unknown. Any program not classified in one of the three above categories is considered to have unknown effects.

Note

1. Here, Sherman and his colleagues (1997) were faced with a dilemma in deciding how high the threshold of scientific evidence should be set for determining program effectiveness. A very conservative approach might require at least two level 5 studies (that is, randomized controlled experiments) showing that a program is effective (or ineffective), with the preponderance of the remaining evidence in favor of the same conclusion. Employing a threshold that high, however, would have left very little to say about crime prevention, based on the existing science. There was a clear tradeoff between the level of certainty in the answers that can be given about program effectiveness and the level of useful information that can be gleaned from the available science. Sherman and his colleagues took the middle road between reaching very few conclusions with great certainty and reaching very many conclusions with very little certainty. This is a dilemma that also faces other social science disciplines such as education and social work.

References

Barnett, W. Steven. 1996. *Lives in the Balance: Age-27 Benefit-Cost Analysis of the High / Scope Perry Preschool Program.* Ypsilanti, MI: High/Scope Press.

Bernazzani, Odette, Catherine Côté, and Richard E. Tremblay. 2001. Early Parent Training to Prevent Disruptive Behavior Problems and Delinquency in Children. *Annals of the American Academy of Political and Social Science* 578:90-103.

Braga, Anthony A. 2001. Effects of Hot Spots Policing on Crime. *Annals of the American Academy of Political and Social Science* 578:104-125.

Cook, Thomas D. and Donald T. Campbell. 1979. *Quasi-Experimentation: Design and Analysis Issues for Field Settings.* Chicago: Rand McNally.

Cullen, Francis T. Forthcoming. Rehabilitation and Treatment Programs. In *Crime and Public Policy.* 2d ed., ed.

James Q. Wilson and Joan Petersilia. San Francisco: Institute of Contemporary Studies Press.

Dishion, Thomas J., Joan McCord, and François Poulin. 1999. When Interventions Harm: Peer Groups and Problem Behavior. *American Psychologist* 54:755-64.

Eck, John E. and Edward R. Maguire. 2000. Have Changes in Policing Reduced Violent Crime? An Assessment of the Evidence. In *The Crime Drop in America*, ed. Alfred Blumstein and Joel Wallman. New York: Cambridge University Press.

Farrington, David P. 1983. Randomized Experiments on Crime and Justice. In *Crime and Justice: An Annual Review of Research*. Vol. 4, ed. Michael Tonry and Norval Morris. Chicago: University of Chicago Press.

———. 1997. Evaluating a Community Crime Prevention Program. *Evaluation* 3:157-73.

———. 1999. A Criminological Research Agenda for the Next Millennium. *International Journal of Offender Therapy and Comparative Criminology* 43:154-67.

———. 2000. Explaining and Preventing Crime: The Globalization of Knowledge—The American Society of Criminology 1999 Presidential Address. *Criminology* 38:1-24.

Farrington, David P. and Anthony Petrosino. 2001. The Campbell Collaboration Crime and Justice Group. *Annals of the American Academy of Political and Social Science* 578:35-49.

Farrington, David P., Anthony Petrosino, and Brandon C. Welsh. 2001. Systematic Reviews and Cost-Benefit Analyses of Correctional Interventions. *The Prison Journal* 81:338-58.

Farrington, David P. and Brandon C. Welsh. 1999. Delinquency Prevention Using Family-Based Interventions. *Children and Society* 13:287-303.

Greenwood, Peter W., Lynn A. Karoly, Susan S. Everingham, Jill Houbé, M. Rebecca Kilburn, C. Peter Rydell, Matthew Sanders, and James Chiesa. 2001. Estimating the Costs and Benefits of Early Childhood Interventions: Nurse Home Visits and the Perry Preschool. In *Costs and Benefits of Preventing Crime*, ed. Brandon C. Welsh, David P. Farrington, and Lawrence W. Sherman. Boulder, CO: Westview.

Halladay, Mark and Lisa Bero. 2000. Implementing Evidence-Based Practice in Health Care. *Public Money & Management* 20:43-50.

Hope, Tim. 1995. Community Crime Prevention. In *Building a Safer Society: Strategic Approaches to Crime Prevention*. Vol. 19, *Crime and Justice: A Review of Research*, ed. Michael Tonry and David P. Farrington. Chicago: University of Chicago Press.

Johnson, Byron R., Spencer De Li, David B. Larson, and Michael McCullough. 2000. A Systematic Review of the Religiosity and Delinquency Literature: A Research Note. *Journal of Contemporary Criminal Justice* 16:32-52.

Lipsey, Mark W., Gabrielle L. Chapman, and Nana A. Landenberger. 2001. Cognitive-Behavioral Programs for Offenders. *Annals of the American Academy of Political and Social Science* 578:144-157.

MacKenzie, Doris Layton. 2000. Evidence-Based Corrections: Identifying What Works. *Crime & Delinquency* 46:457-71.

MacKenzie, Doris Layton, David B. Wilson, and Suzanne B. Kider. 2001. Effects of Correctional Boot Camps on Offending. *Annals of the American Academy of Political and Social Science* 578:126-143.

Millenson, Michael L. 1997. *Demanding Medical Excellence: Doctors and Accountability in the Information Age.* Chicago: University of Chicago Press.

Nutley, Sandra and Huw T. O. Davies. 2000. Making a Reality of Evidence-Based Practice: Some Lessons from the Diffusion of Innovations. *Public Money & Management* 20:35-42.

Nutley, Sandra, Huw T. O. Davies, and Nick Tilley. 2000. Editorial: Getting Research into Practice. *Public Money & Management* 20:3-6.

Petrosino, Anthony. 2000. How Can We Respond Effectively to Juvenile Crime? *Pediatrics* 105:635-37.

Petrosino, Anthony, Robert F. Boruch, Haluk Soydan, Lorna Duggan, and Julio Sanchez-Meca. 2001. Meeting the Challenges of Evidence-Based Policy: The Campbell Collaboration. *Annals of the American Academy of Political and Social Science* 578:14-34.

Rosenfeld, Richard. 2000. Tracing the Brady Act's Connection with Homicide and Suicide Trends. *Journal of the American Medical Association* 284:616-18.

Schweinhart, Lawrence J., Helen V. Barnes, and David P. Weikart. 1993. *Significant Benefits: The High/Scope Perry Preschool Study Through Age 27.* Ypsilanti, MI: High/Scope Press.

Sherman, Lawrence W. 1998. Evidence-Based Policing. In *Ideas in American Policing.* Washington, DC: Police Foundation.

Sherman, Lawrence W., David P. Farrington, Brandon C. Welsh, and Doris Layton MacKenzie, eds. Forthcoming. *Evidence-Based Crime Prevention.* London: Routledge.

Sherman, Lawrence W., Denise C. Gottfredson, Doris Layton MacKenzie, John E. Eck, Peter Reuter, and Shawn D. Bushway. 1997. *Preventing Crime: What Works, What Doesn't, What's Promising.* Washington, DC: U.S. Department of Justice, National Institute of Justice.

Tonry, Michael and David P. Farrington. 1995. Strategic Approaches to Crime Prevention. In *Building a Safer Society: Strategic Approaches to Crime Prevention.* Vol. 19, *Crime and Justice: A Review of Research*, ed. Michael Tonry and David P. Farrington. Chicago: University of Chicago Press.

Visher, Christy A. and David Weisburd. 1998. Identifying What Works: Recent Trends in Crime Prevention Strategies. *Crime, Law and Social Change* 28:223-42.

Weisburd, David, Cynthia M. Lum, and Anthony Petrosino. 2001. Does Research Design Affect Study Outcomes? Findings from the Maryland Report Criminal Justice Sample. *Annals of the American Academy of Political and Social Science* 578:50-70.

Weiss, Carol H. 1998. Have We Learned Anything New About the Use of Evaluation? *American Journal of Evaluation* 19:21-33.

Welsh, Brandon C. and David P. Farrington. 2000. Monetary Costs and Benefits of Crime Prevention Programs. In *Crime and Justice: A Review of Research.* Vol. 27, ed. Michael Tonry. Chicago: University of Chicago Press.

Welsh, Brandon C., David P. Farrington, and Lawrence W. Sherman. 2001. Improving Confidence in What Works and Saves Money in Preventing Crime: Priorities for Research. In *Costs and Benefits of Preventing Crime*, ed. Brandon C. Welsh, David P. Farrington, and Lawrence W. Sherman. Boulder, CO: Westview.

Welsh, Brandon C. and Akemi Hoshi. Forthcoming. Communities and Crime Prevention. In *Evidence-Based*

Crime Prevention, ed. Lawrence W. Sherman, David P. Farrington, Brandon C. Welsh, and Doris Layton MacKenzie. London: Routledge.

Wilson, David B. 2001. Meta-Analytic Methods for Criminology. *Annals of the American Academy of Political and Social Science* 578:71-89.

Book Department

INTERNATIONAL RELATIONS AND POLITICS

BROOKER, PAUL. 2000. *Non-Democratic Regimes*. Pp. viii, 288. New York: St. Martin's. Paperbound, $21.95.

Despite advances in governance, the world remains characterized by a host and variety of tyrannical and oppressive regimes. Today the concepts of authoritarian and totalitarian are routinely and indiscriminately employed by commentators interested in all-inclusive generic labels to various autocracies, despotism, dictatorships, satraps, or tyrannies. Paul Brooker's book provides a current and thoughtful examination of modern nondemocratic regimes that in their various forms, dominated the twentieth century and continue to thrive in the twenty-first century.

Two opening chapters effectively draw the reader in, examining how classic and leading theorists have sought to explain and categorize nondemocracies. Brooker's careful and thorough literature review illustrates how totalitarianism emerged as an analytic concept during the World War II as a generation of social scientists attempted to understand the distinctive characteristics of the Hitler, Stalin, and (to a lesser extent) Mussolini regimes. Examining the works of Hannah Arendt, Carl J. Friedrich, Michael Curtis, Juan Linz, Amos Perlmutter, Leonard Shapiro, and others, Brooker shows how and why various systems of classification help scholars think clearly about important differences between totalitarianism and authoritarianism. Elements common to most taxonomies include the role of the supreme leader, the nature and ideology (if any) of the official party (if such a party exists), the degree of political terror, social mobilization, and societal penetration.

The core of the book adopts a thematic approach analyzing the most common form of dictatorships in modern times: military and party dictatorships. Brooker's careful schema brings out the novel aspects of modern nondemocracies relating to political control and social organization and expertly clarifies these concepts by comparative cross-national analysis. Included in this are case studies of Chile's General Pinochet, Paraguay's Alfredo Stroessner, and Iraq's Saddam Hussein, who transformed theirs into personalist dictatorships; also considered is how dictatorships make and implement policies and whether they are effective in promoting economic growth.

Penultimate chapters examine the challenge of democratization and how some modern semidemocracies/semidictatorships (such as Mexico's PRI/Presidentialist regime, or Peru's Albert Fujimori) have sought to disguise themselves as democratic regimes. Brooker's concluding chapter cautions current, conventional wisdom that democratization is inevitable everywhere and that dictatorships are headed for the historical scrap heap. Democratically disguised, bureaucratic semidictatorships of Mexico's or Peru's ilk, rather than blatant military regimes, are probably the future models.

Brooker's book is a well-documented, sobering analysis of the oldest and most common form of government: non-democracy. His book also has important foreign policy implications for the United States in its relationships with a plethora of less than democratic systems around the world. This is an excellent book for upper-division or graduate courses in political science.

PAUL C. SONDROL

University of Colorado
Colorado Springs

DOBROWOLSKY, ALEXANDRA. 2000. *The Politics of Pragmatism. Women, Representation, and Constitutionalism in Canada.* Pp. xii, 320. Don Mills, Canada: Oxford University Press. Paperbound, Canada$24.95.

The Politics of Pragmatism recounts the activism of national women's groups in Canada as they attempted to influence the series of constitutional changes proposed in the years 1980 to 1992. These proposals, which first fascinated and then appalled even the mavens of Canadian politics, are hardly familiar to anyone else. Even fewer are aware of the role played by women and women's groups in the process. As Alexandra Dobrowolsky is able to demonstrate, in Canada as elsewhere, women's groups are now active, continuously, in all forms of conventional and unconventional politics. If anything, the book's focus on national groups (as well as the identity of those interviewed) understates the amount and variety of feminist activism across Canada.

Dobrowolsky's topic includes one of the icons of contemporary Canadian feminism, the successful enshrinement in the Canadian constitution of equality rights superior to what the Equal Rights Amendment would have provided for the United States. This was in 1982; the relevant sections of the Canadian Charter of Rights would have been significantly weaker without the intervention of women activists. A second attempt at constitutional revision, the decentralizing, Quebec-focused Meech Lake Accord, failed to achieve the necessary provincial ratification in 1987, partly because of opposition by women's groups. Then, in 1992, a national referendum rejected a packet of constitutional amendments that would, among other things, have subordinated women's rights to communal claims. Canada's largest national women's organization, the National Action Committee on the Status of Women, was conspicuous among the many opponents of the Charlottetown Accord; other women and women's groups were among the prominent supporters.

The role of women activists in the first of these episodes has already been studied at some length, but Dobrowolsky has been able to add previously unpublished material from interviews and private archives. Women's political responses to the Meech Lake Accord have had almost no attention, and their organized involvement with the campaign to defeat the Charlottetown Accord has had little more, so most of the relevant, detailed discussion in this book is new. Dobrowolsky shows that as we might expect, there has been continuing attention to the constitutional process from national women's groups. She also interestingly demonstrates how media and politicians have lumbered women's activism with labels that would delegitimize its political role: the women's movement is only a special interest group (therefore elitist and unrepresentative) or a social movement (therefore with no political or policy standing).

As its title and subtitle suggest, *The Politics of Pragmatism* is inclined to draw rather sweeping theoretical conclusions from its case study material. Certainly, a more experienced scholar would not be so surprised to learn of excellent efforts by women's groups—and less excellent results. Nor would she feel obliged to refute the many monocausal theories that abstract from the complex realities of political action. For example, it is hardly necessary to prove that women's organizations in Canada have, in spite of misgivings, worked with and through political parties. In addition, the knowledgeable reader will look at *The Politics of Pragmatism* and remember what the protagonists are like as individuals. Tact and self-protection together probably dictated the absence of such a personal dimension, but it is important for the study of politics in a large country with a small population of activists.

Feminism is not extinct, and the women's movement has not been rendered obsolete; these facts make a difference for mainstream politics. This book is therefore to be recommended to those interested in constitutional politics as well as that more obvious audience whose concern is the involvement of women with politics.

NAOMI BLACK

York University
Toronto
Canada
Mount Saint Vincent University
Halifax
Canada

FLERAS, AUGIE and PAUL SPOONLEY. 1999. *Recalling Aotearoa: Indigenous Politics and Ethnic Relations in New Zealand*. Pp. xiv, 288. Auckland, NZ: Oxford University Press. $29.95.

The meaning and nature of nation-states, national identity, and social cohesion are becoming increasingly contested as global forces and internal challenges produce competing claims for entitlements, recognition, and resources. Few states are exempt from such tensions. However, crises related to sovereignty pose a special significance for nations that are struggling to acknowledge and redefine their relationships with indigenous populations. Augie Fleras and Paul Spoonley, in an insightful and provocative recent book, highlight critical dimensions of these challenges for New Zealand (Aotearoa) and its relations with Maori.

Fleras and Spoonley present a convincing case for a reconstituted vision of New Zealand through "multiculturalism with a bi-national framework," which acknowledges in substantive ways the need to create effective spheres of Maori self-government within a nation constituted by increasing diversity. While their position is rooted in an understanding of details specific to the history, composition, and dynamics of New Zealand society, their analysis carries implications that extend even beyond the most obvious referents to comparable societies like the United States, Canada, and Australia in which recent changes in immigration patterns are layered on a white settler colonialism imposed over long-standing forms of social organization among indigenous peoples.

Fleras and Spoonley begin with a rethinking of New Zealand history from a Maori perspective to highlight contending visions that accompany efforts to realize a meaningful postcolonial state. They do not define the issue by whether there is any legitimacy to claims to indigenous self-determination, since indigenous rights are recognized and guaranteed in a legal and historical framework; they define an issue of disagreement over the nature, scope, and specific manifestations of Maori sovereignty in relation to the sovereignty of the nation-state. The British crown's recognition of indigenous sovereignty (formalized in the 1840 Treaty of Waitangi), even if asserted to accomplish immediate colonial objectives to exercise dominion over land, labor, and resources, has had the contradictory impact of leaving indigenous people and their societies vulnerable to marginalization and subordination at the same time as they are ensured a special status as distinct collectivities whose rights and identities derive from their entitlements as original occupants of the land. The true challenges are embedded along the pathways leading to realization of meaningful forms of Maori sovereignty within contemporary political economies.

A major strength of the book lies in the authors' willingness to embrace and discuss key contradictions or paradoxes implicated in efforts to negotiate indigenous rights, sovereignty, and national identities. These include extended discussions of relations among individual and collective rights, socially cohesive and divisive forces, colonialism and postcolonial resistance, internal differentiation within distinct social groups, and the politics of multiculturalism and ethnic identity. In particular, Fleras and Spoonley integrate the analysis of indigenous politics with an understanding of the material and ideational circumstances within which they are played out. Whereas academic literature and policy frameworks alike tend either to subsume consideration of indigenous peoples under broader attention to race and ethnic relations or to isolate the analysis of issues relevant to indigenous people from those that pertain to immigrants and racialized minorities, the authors here emphasize the complex dynamics involved in strategies to ensure social cohesion amid competing pressures generated by racial and multicultural diversity, indigenous rights and sovereignty, broader state objectives, and global challenges.

The book is not without problems. A more direct and integrated discussion of the key issues, especially in the early chapters, would make the work more accessible to an extended readership (especially those with a limited knowledge of New Zealand issues) to whom the book should be made available. A more focused analysis of socioeconomic conditions, internal population differentiation, and key institutional domains that characterize Maori-state relations, comparable to that devoted in chapter 6 to the Tagata Pasifika—New Zealanders with South Pacific origins—would also be beneficial. Nonetheless, *Recalling Aotearoa* is an important book with respect to both its explicit focus on the politics of indigeneity in New Zealand and its wider contributions to an understanding of tensions and issues related to sovereignty, diversity, and identity.

TERRY WOTHERSPOON

University of Saskatchewan
Saskatoon
Canada

LAMMERS, WILLIAM W. and MICHAEL A. GENOVESE. 2000. *The Presidency and Domestic Policy: Comparing Leadership Styles, FDR to Clinton*. Pp. xii, 383.

"Could it be that Roosevelt, Johnson, or Reagan were actually underachievers?" William Lammers and Michael Genovese ask in the early pages of their work. Their question is posed not so much to buck conventional wisdom but rather to make the point that presidents should be evaluated and compared based on the relative climate of opportunities that they faced. To do this, the authors divide the presidents since Franklin D. Roosevelt into three categories: Roosevelt,

Johnson, and Reagan are categorized as high-opportunity presidents; Truman, Eisenhower, and Kennedy are classified as moderate-opportunity presidents; and Nixon, Carter, Bush, and Clinton are considered low-opportunity presidents. The major part of the book consists of an individual chapter on each of these presidents, assessing their effectiveness in domestic policy making given their relative opportunity for leadership.

Chapter 1 outlines Lammers and Genovese's strategy for assessing presidents. Four dimensions of presidential activity are compared: approaches to advisory processes and decision making, administrative strategies, public leadership, and congressional leadership. Although many of the indicators of presidential skills and dimensions of the political environment are not new, they are assembled in an innovative way. Lammers and Genovese effectively summarize helpful influences and major limitations facing the last 10 presidents.

Chapters 2 through 10 examine each presidency, beginning with Roosevelt and the high-opportunity presidents and ending with Clinton and the low-opportunity presidents. Each chapter combines a wide-ranging array of information on each chief executive in addition to the factors listed above: personal characteristics, career path, personality traits, policy views, major challenges, major legislative enactments, and success with Congress. Looking at this sweeping array of factors for 10 presidents while keeping this book to less than 400 pages necessitates a certain degree of superficiality in coverage, particularly for the taste of presidential scholars. For example, rarely is more than a page devoted to such complex questions as psychological factors and presidential personality. For students and those new to the presidency literature, however, it is an excellent

overview. Particularly important is the emphasis on policy outcomes and results as a major component of comparing presidential effectiveness in policy making.

The last chapter compares the accomplishments and the effectiveness of the presidents since Franklin D. Roosevelt. It is both the best chapter of the book and the one most subject to dispute as presidents are ranked within their opportunity level. Among the high-opportunity presidents, Roosevelt is ranked first, followed by Johnson, with Reagan last. Of the moderate-opportunity presidents, Truman is first, Eisenhower second, and Kennedy third. Among the four low-opportunity presidents, Nixon is rated highest, Clinton second, and Carter and Bush are tied for last. Many readers may dispute these conclusions or even the categorization of certain presidents. For example, one could argue that Clinton's opportunity levels were closer to Eisenhower's than to Bush's. Nixon's high ranking among low-opportunity presidents is also questionable, given that his rather substantial legislative record was largely pushed by Congress.

Studies of individual presidencies are often detailed and rich but usually too idiosyncratic for meaningful comparisons. Conversely, all presidential typologies oversimplify to some extent, and that is the case here. Overall, however, this book largely succeeds and is a fine addition to the literature on the presidency. Perhaps no other book covers as much ground on twentieth-century presidents and the policy achievements of their administrations in a truly comparative fashion. As explained in the preface, this book is primarily the work of William Lammers, who submitted a draft of the manuscript shortly before his death. Michael Genovese, his former student and colleague, saw the manuscript through to publication. It is a fine tribute to the scholarship and broad perspective of Lammers and is recommended to readers.

LANCE T. LeLOUP

Washington State University
Pullman

MacMANUS, SUSAN A. 2000. *Targeting Senior Voters: Campaign Outreach to Elders and Others with Special Needs.* Pp. xxi, 225. Lanham, MD: Rowman & Littlefield. $59.00. Paperbound, $21.95.

Susan MacManus provides a comprehensive analysis of the importance, role, and influence of senior citizens in American politics. Political candidates and consultants have long recognized the importance of senior Americans. Indeed, they vote, they contribute funds, they stay informed of issues, and they voice their opinions. In the next two decades, the baby boomers will continue to contribute to the graying of America. By 2030, those older than 65 will comprise more than 20 percent of the population. Thus anyone who wishes to seek an electoral office or work as staff members for politicians, political parties, or special interest groups must target senior citizens in terms of message and issues.

The volume is a comprehensive resource guide to understanding senior citizens by including original survey information on how to talk with them, how they view important issues, and how to help them maximize civic participation. The analysis goes beyond simple techniques of pandering to full appreciation of the values and contributions elder Americans may provide the political process. For example, there is a full chapter dedicated to the issue of helping senior citizens register and vote. MacManus addresses such topics as registration site accessibility, registering the disabled,

transportation to the polls, ballot access, and alternative voting arrangements. There is another chapter full of do's and don'ts relative to telephone interviews, focus groups, campaign literature, television ads, campaigning among disabled senior voters, and how to make voting easier and more secure.

There are seven chapters in the book with nearly 100 tables and figures. More specifically, the book describes the growing size and influence of senior voters, reports on national survey results on what seniors think about a variety of social issues, and identifies the best ways to target and communicate with senior citizens. Thus one feature that makes this book rather unique is the combination of descriptive and prescriptive material. It provides both an in-depth analysis of the attitudes, opinions, and political behaviors of senior voters and a descriptive guide on how to target them.

In light of the 2000 presidential election and the problems with voting in many jurisdictions of Florida, *Targeting Senior Voters: Campaign Outreach to Elders and Others with Special Needs* should be mandatory reading for all election officials. In addition, this book would be a valuable resource guide for political candidates, office holders, consultants, special interests groups, and members of the media.

ROBERT E. DENTON, JR.

Virginia Polytechnic Institute and State University
Blacksburg

AFRICA, ASIA, AND LATIN AMERICA

KOLSTØ, PÅL. 2000. *Political Construction Sites: Nation-Building in Russia and the Post-Soviet States.* Pp. xi, 308. Boulder, CO: Westview. $65.00. Paperbound, $24.00.

The first thing that should be noted about this book is that it is primarily historical and descriptive. Despite the intriguing conceptualization that is contained in the title, University of Oslo professor Pål Kolstø is primarily concerned with the background conditions that gave former Soviet republics the historic opportunity to become nation builders. His survey is more far reaching than comparable studies published in recent years. The countries examined include Russia (the Russian diasporas found in the other new independent states are treated in a separate chapter), Latvia, Ukraine, Belarus, Moldova, and Kazakhstan. A decade after Soviet disintegration, few authors are brave enough to draw comparisons between so many and such diverse former Soviet republics.

To be sure, Kolstø is writing for undergraduate students and a general readership. As an introductory text, this book has much to recommend it. Instead of simply a sequence of case studies of select new states, it begins with useful overviews of such topics as nation building, construction of historiography, and religious pathways. Certainly a more robust chapter on theorizing about nation building and social integration would be desirable. As it is, the attention given to a handful of experts (Walker Connor, Karl Deutsch, Ernest Gellner, and Arend Lijphart are the featured scholars) does not do credit to this exceptionally fertile field.

Kolstø's major achievement is to alert the reader to the diversity between and within the new states. His accounts of minorities in the new countries are particularly informative and also idiosyncratic. He piques the interest of the reader with references to the ethnic complexities of Moldova (for example, the recently established Gagauz Yeri territory) and of Ukraine (Transcarpathia, Northern

Bukovina, the Donbass, and much studied Crimea and Galicia). There is slightly more than one page on Chechnya and six pages on Tatarstan. Even a specialist on the Baltic region would appreciate Kolstø's study of the Latgale province of Latvia.

Another refreshing feature of this book is its Scandinavian perspective. Whether it is invoking the pioneering work of Norwegian Stein Rokkan, citing the research results of not-well-known Danish and Swedish academics, or drawing comparisons to the unique status of Finland's Åland islands, the North American reader will be enriched by exposure to new ideas. Indeed Kolstø's work is just one example of the high-quality scholarship produced in recent years by Scandinavian academics studying former Soviet republics. The anecdotal information that Kolstø relates on national airlines, postage stamps, soccer matches, and Olympic athletes in the new states should not be treated as trivia. Rather they confirm his extensive knowledge about the societies he writes about. Moreover he demonstrates the degree to which nation building has been micromanaged in these new countries.

The last chapter of *Political Construction Sites* attempts to test certain theories of nation building (such as consociationalism and ethnic democracy) in light of Kolstø's empirical findings about the new states. Kolstø concludes, rightly, that not all of them will be successful in nation building. But he infers, confusingly, that there is "good reason to expect that at least some of them will join the international community of nation-states. Even if they may qualify only as quasi-states today, that does not mean they are doomed to remain in this category forever." The contemporary international system already comprises quasi states from several continents. This unofficial status does not affect their legal status. Nor do quasi states consist only of failed nation builders.

RAY TARAS

Tulane University
New Orleans
Louisiana

LOMNITZ, LARISSA ADLER and ANA MELNICK. 2000. *Chile's Political Culture and Parties, An Anthropological Explanation*. Pp. ix, 161. Notre Dame, IN, University of Notre Dame Press. $26.00. Paperbound, $14.00.

This is an English-language version of a study published in Chile in 1998 by the Fondo de Cultura Economica. The authors, one a naturalized Mexican citizen who lived in Chile for many years, and the other a Chilean, both teach at Universidad Nacional Autónoma de México but frequently work on Chilean topics. In this essay/study, they analyze two political parties, the avowedly secular and entirely middle-class Radical party, and the multiclass and largely Catholic Christian Democratic party, from the vantage points of their respective political cultures. In their view, political parties cannot be understood independent of the subjective attitudes of their leaders, militants, and rank-and-file members and supporters. But they do not believe that such attitudes are adequately captured by survey data alone and opt for studying the formative experiences and relationships that in their view give them meaning and legitimacy.

Lomnitz and Melnick view party cultures as emerging from formative social networks (which are clubs, regions, schools, and family settings) to which leaders and activists are initially attracted or exposed, and by which their subsequent initiatives, decisions, factional developments, and ultimate successes and failures are conditioned. To describe these networks, and to trace their ongoing impacts, they draw on the abundant secondary literature on Chilean parties and politics and on open-ended interviews of leaders, militants, and members of both parties that they conducted during the 1980s and early 1990s. On these bases, they describe in often rich detail the origins, early development, and coming of age of these parties and nicely capture the flavor of their respective projects and their contributions to pre-1973 Chilean politics, although in each instance they largely reinforce the images or portraits that the existing literature provides of these parties.

It is not clear to me, however, that Lomnitz and Melnick really test their approach or show its superior explanatory power (vis-à-vis alternative perspectives) in dealing with either Chilean parties generally or their evolution beyond 1973. They argue that contrasting Radical and Christian Democratic identities have endured over the years thanks to the continuing vitality of underlying social networks, the ongoing appeal of values and symbols associated with their respective subcultures, and their successful and not so successful electoral and political experiences. They further contend that horizontally linked networks continue to provide the basis for internal tendencies and factions within the parties and that they enable party members to restrain or hold their party leaders more accountable in Chile than in countries like Mexico. But I do not believe that Lomnitz and Melnick look carefully enough at either the distant or the not-so-distant past to establish connections among social networks, party tendencies, and party life. Although claiming to explain key party choices (of candidates, alliances, or platforms) at crucial junctures, they do not look closely enough at any of these events, at the changing contexts in which they take place, or at the other factors that may or may not have played important roles. And it is therefore difficult to compare their assertions or conclusions with those reached by other analysts.

In fact, aside from asserting that factions or tendencies do exist and are based on underlying social networks, Lomnitz and Melnick tend to treat these parties as monoliths. In the case of the PDC, for example, Lomnitz and Melnick emphasize its strong identification with the progressive social Christian tradition but fail to note that both the meaning and content of this social Christian tradition were vigorously debated from the late 1940s on (when a second generation of activists entered the Falange), and rival internal tendencies have attempted to fuse social Christianity with things as dissimilar as neocapitalist and development (Frei Montalva), purist independence from both Left and Right (Castillo), and Christian socialism in alliance with the traditional left (Silva, Chonchol, and others) as early as the PDC's 1959 founding congress.

MICHAEL FLEET

Marquette University
Milwaukee
Wisconsin

RONIGER, LUIS and MARIO SZNAJDER. 1999. *The Legacy of Human Rights Violations in the Southern Cone, Argentina, Chile and Uruguay.* Oxford Studies in Democratization. Pp. xvi, 367. Oxford, UK: Oxford University Press. $82.00.

Argentina, Chile, and Uruguay, the three temperate countries of South America, were considered the most prosperous, socially progressive, and Europeanized republics in Latin America. During the 1970s, these characteristics were supplemented by an unflattering one: all three were governed by authoritarian regimes that exercised repression as a preferred tool of political control and social intimidation.

This book recounts the events leading to the installation of dictatorial rule and the subsequent use of repression against political activists and dissenters. When authoritarian rule ended (1983 in Argentina, 1985 in Uruguay, and 1989 in Chile) these nations entered a period of democratization during which societies and political elites had to deal with the restoration of civil government and simultaneously engage in a critical examination of what occurred in the past. To different degrees, in each of these countries the politics of reconciliation had to balance the search for truth and justice with the urgent need to establish viable democratic regimes. Public agendas had to incorporate a necessary commitment toward human rights protection, but for the sake of keeping the state functioning, a compromise had to be established between memory and oblivion. Obviously, this threw into question the primacy that the human rights discourse held in the public affairs and private lives of individuals. Not dealing with the crimes of the past and allowing for impunity disturbed the sensitivities of many who held that collective morality was an integral part of the national soul. On the other hand, the majority sentiment was that indulging in recriminations or fueling revenges did little to appease the national social conscience.

Although all three countries share many common sociocultural traits, their historical and political paths diverge considerably, so it is erroneous to assume that repression and expiation ran similar courses in each of them. Argentina was shaken most by both processes, as lack of accountability and an attitude of disrespect for the powerless nurtured a defiance and cynicism that made recognition of past atrocities more difficult and contrition less frequent. Consequently, the healing process has taken longer and has been more bitter than in its sister republics. Uruguay's use of violent repression during the dictatorship years (1972-1985) was less encompassing, and the subsequent reconciliation was carried out in a spirit of compromise. The conciliatory and pragmatic character of Uruguayans permitted the resumption of political dialogue, and redemocratization proceeded without the antagonistic tones found in Argentina. Developments in Chile followed a different course from those of the Platine countries. The dictatorship of General Augusto Pinochet was accompanied by an economic development not mirrored in the other two countries, which contributed to a greater acceptance of military rule by the rich and middle-class segments. The poor and the Left suffered so deeply that their forgiveness of authoritarian abuses has been more difficult to achieve. The legalistic character of Chileans and their belief that institutions and public actors are accountable for their actions explains the ongoing search for justice and punishment.

One can dispute the propriety of using the term "legacy of human rights violations," referenced in the title, when referring to the postauthoritarian political events in Argentina, Chile, and Uruguay. Even Roniger and Sznajder find difficulties in specifying what is meant by this expression that certainly represents an unpleasant bequest to the countries in question. Despite the improper use of the term "legacy," this work is a well-documented account and a credible interpretation of the sad events that occurred in the recent history of Argentina, Chile, and Uruguay. The book is structured in a way that permits a clear understanding of the issues involved, and the abundant background information substantiates every aspect of the redemocratization and reconciliation processes. Moreover, in the discussion of the transgressions committed, Roniger and Sznajder invoke enlightening interpretations that come from current theories explaining authoritarianism, political abuse, and violations of civil rights. Such frameworks allow for a theory-informed view of the issues at play in the Southern Cone during these troubled years. In this light, the abuses do not appear as unique South American configurations but figure as recurrent themes in contemporary history from which, it is hoped, general lessons can be drawn.

CESAR N. CAVIEDES

University of Florida
Gainesville

SWAINE, MICHAEL D. and ASHLEY J. TELLIS. 2000. *Interpreting China's Grand Strategy: Past, Present and Future.* Pp. xx, 283. Santa Monica, CA: RAND. $35.00. Paperbound, $20.00.

Of the many large unknowns facing the United States in the new century, China is perhaps the most tangible, though not the most predictable. *Interpreting China's Grand Strategy* is a comprehensive attempt by two senior RAND Corporation analysts to fit China—past, present, and future—into a general pattern of predictability. The result is not convincing, but it is the best-argued pessimistic estimate of China's security trajectory.

Swaine and Tellis take structural realism as their analytic approach, arguing that China, like other nations, wants to maximize its interests and power, and therefore its strategic posture is set by its situation of relative power. Since power is "ultimately a function of a state's capability to coerce other states," the argument is relevant to current American policy toward China, and since China's capacity is likely to continue to grow in both absolute and relative terms, it will be even more critical for the United States after 2020. Despite their expectation that China will become more assertive as it approaches great power capacity, Swaine and Tellis recommend a long-term policy of engagement rather than one of preemptive containment.

The book begins with a lengthy discussion of China's history, arguing that China has not been reluctant to use violence in the past. China's wars were usually on its periphery, and they were often limited and defensive, but there were many of them. The second major part of the book concerns China's strategic posture since Deng Xiaoping's reform era began in 1979. Swaine and Tellis describe a foreign policy that is based on economic progress, requires peaceful international relations, and does not unduly concentrate resources on the military. This peaceful posture is explained as a "calculative strategy," one based on the fact that China is currently weak as a modern military power and therefore its current purposes are best served by nonmilitary means. Moreover, economic growth is a necessary prerequisite of global military prominence, so China's shortest path to great power status is through peaceful expansion of its economy for the next two decades.

The final third of the book discusses possible future trajectories for China's security strategy. The possibility that China will eliminate itself as contender through catastrophe or internal dissension is considered and dismissed. The possibility that the global context of a future powerful China will constrain it to be cooperative is considered and rebutted in some detail. We are left with an assertive China, one whose interests are more concentrated on its periphery but whose memories of imperial glory and confidence of new strength lead it to view the existing global order as an old one.

Any book of this scope requires generalizations and judgments that can be disputed, but two deeper questions should be raised. First, the book is not an interpretation of China's grand strategy, if strategy involves intent, and by *interpretation* we mean the effort to understand another's intent. In contrast to such classics by RAND alumni as Allen Whiting's *China's Calculus of Deterrence* or Mel Gurtov's *China and Southeast Asia*, there is little careful analysis of Chinese diplomacy here. Indeed, the five principles of peaceful coexistence, China's major diplomatic mantra since 1954, is not mentioned. The book argues that China is not an exception from the predictable behavior of power-sensitive states, and therefore its grand strategy is a question of capacity, not intent.

A second problem is that while the book is well researched and presents enough data to make its argument plausible, China contains sufficient ambiguous and contradictory data that a contrary argument could also be made plausible. In such a situation an analyst must be careful not to ride a tangent too far. For example, Swaine and Tellis say that "if all the territories claimed, occupied, or directly controlled by China since its unification in the 3rd century BC were matched against its current physical holdings, the presently disputed territories would fade into insignificance." True, but not true enough. After all, cozily within the same time frame the same could be said of Greece, Italy, Great Britain, the Iroquois, and Peru.

BRANTLY WOMACK
University of Virginia
Charlottesville

VERÁSTIQUE, BERNARDINO. 2000. *Michoacán and Eden: Vasco de Quiroga and the Evangelization of Western Mexico*. Pp. xviii, 194. Austin: University of Texas Press. $40.00. Paperbound, $19.95.

Utopia is an alluring but dangerous idea that, in its heyday since 1789, often slopes steeply into authoritarian nightmares. Now Mexico's best-loved utopian experiment under Vasco de Quiroga, Michoacán's first bishop during the second third of the sixteenth century, is receiving more skeptical attention. Quiroga is resurfacing as an authoritarian zealot more than the benign, idealistic bishop long celebrated as the apostle of the New World. In this new critical spirit, James Krippner-Martínez has examined how views of Tata Vasco have been shaped by the times since the eighteenth century, and Fernando Gómez has given us Quiroga the *letrado* (expert in law), a Foucaldian hospital administrator who combined monastic rigor with a chillingly letter-of-the-law conception of a Christian republic.

Michoacán and Eden offers a more balanced and ample vision of Bishop Quiroga within this new criticism, a vision that springs from Verástique's grounding in the Chicago history of religions school, with a dash of liberation theology added. Quiroga emerges here as the agent of colonialism he undoubtedly was—capable of the actions of a benevolent pastor bent on protecting native *Purhépecha* people from abusive Spanish *encomenderos*, but substituting his own authoritarian practices and unable to

achieve just what he intended. Verástique's Quiroga was no soul mate of Bartolomé de las Casas, the energetic protector of the Indians who regarded native peoples of Mesoamerica as fully the equals of Spaniards (arguably their superiors, he thought, given Spaniards' bestial behavior in the conquest). Rather, Quiroga saw them as crude, ignorant people who resembled untamed animals in their behavior. Teachable, perhaps, but definitely in need of teaching and radical transformation. Only in his conflicts with Spanish rivals did Quiroga begin to see *Purhépecha* as a potentially active citizenry. Even his Santa Fe de la Laguna community project "was ultimately a form of coercion."

The strength of this book is in Verástique's own balanced, humane vision, his interest in *Purhépecha* culture, and his aims to bring a more historical Quiroga and the question of religious change in Michoacán after the conquest to a general audience. He concludes that there was, in fact, a social and religious transformation of native society, but not a neat conversion to Christianity and European ways of living.

Unfortunately, we are given too little solid information about Quiroga's actions and their results or *Purhépecha* participation in and resistance to his plans and view of conversion to judge whether this view is more than plausible. Half of the very short text up to the epilogue is given over to background discussions of Spanish and *Purhépecha* history, geography, and religion before Spaniards reached Michoacán, little of which is put to any direct use in the 50 or so pages that actually address Quiroga and his New World Eden. Verástique gives Quiroga a somewhat different twist than did Benedict Warren in his earlier pioneering research on Quiroga and the early colonial history of Michoacán, but he adds virtually nothing new to Warren's information. That *Purhépechas* may have viewed their forced removal into hospital-villages as a circumstance in which they could "create a native network that would preserve their religious and cultural autonomy" seems likely, but again, there is practically nothing in the book to establish this view.

WILLIAM B. TAYLOR

University of California
Berkeley

EUROPE

GLOVER, JONATHAN. 2000. *Humanity: A Moral History of the Twentieth Century*. Pp. xiv, 464. New Haven, CT: Yale University Press. $27.95.

"The chief business of twentieth-century philosophy," wrote R. G. Collingwood, "is to reckon with twentieth-century history." And what a bloody century it was—almost beyond imagination. The flower of a generation of European youth was wasted in the muddy trenches of Flanders during World War I. British and American bombing of Germany and Japanese cities during World War II led to the death of hundreds of thousands of noncombatants. The victims of Stalin's tyranny numbered in the millions. The number of Mao's victims was greater. And Pol Pot killed a higher proportion of his own population than either Stalin or Mao. More recently, there was the terrible bloodbath in Rwanda. Yet even after taking stock of all of these brutalities, to ponder Hitler's campaign of genocide against the Jews of Europe is to look into the very heart of darkness. No explanation or apology is needed for giving the unprecedented inhumanity of the twentieth century a central place in recent history.

This is what Jonathan Glover, director of the Center of Medical Law and Ethics at King's College in London, does in his sustained and thoughtful mediation on the (im)moral history of the twentieth century. Glover tackles the central and troublesome question of modern man's inhumanity to his fellow man by using ethics to pose questions of history and by exploring those parts of human nature that are relevant to ethics—all in the hope that by understanding more about our world and ourselves, we can create a world with less misery and perhaps prevent the long nightmare of the twentieth century from spilling over into the twenty-first.

Glover gives us a detailed catalog of the horrors of the last century—a reminder of the evil of which humans are capable. But he does more than this. He also explores what produced this unprecedented brutality. Mankind has always had a capacity for cruelty. He quotes Dostoyevsky's character Ivan Karamazov: "no animal could ever be so cruel as a man, so artfully, so artistically cruel." The atrocities of the twentieth century, he argues, resulted from coupling this capacity for cruelty with modern technology's terribly efficient machinery of destruction and death. To Glover, the lesson is clear: contemporary societies must resuscitate morality from the ground up by placing greater emphasis on sympathy and respect for other humans; this is what prevents cruelty between people. The task is especially urgent because of the vast and terrifying efficiency with which all jobs of murder can now be carried out. People must be persuaded to think and act differently toward one another—there is no real and sustainable alternative. "It is too late to stop the technology," he points out, so "it is to the psychology we should now turn."

Glover identifies several reasons for hope: we possess the moral resources to fight inhumanity, we can nurture the moral defenses that restrain cruelty, and we can remember. The latter may be the easiest and the most important. In a speech to SS camp guards going to the extermination camps of Poland in the 1940s, Hitler told them to kill men, women, and children without pity—their acts would be forgotten. "Who remembers now the massacres of the Armenians?" he sneered. There is a chilling similarity between Hitler's words and Stalin's comment while signing death warrants during the Great Purge of the 1930s: "Who's going to remember all this riff-raff in ten or twenty years' time? No one."

BRIAN VanDeMARK

United States Naval Academy
Annapolis
Maryland

GONEN, JAY Y. 2000. *The Roots of Nazi Psychology: Hitler's Utopian Barbarism.* Pp. 224. Lexington: University of Kentucky Press. $25.00.

After the collapse of Yugoslavia, the way in which Serbian leaders Slobodan Milosevic and Radovan Karadzic revived historical traumas and enflamed malignant nationalism has increased contemporary scholars' interest in the relationship between such leaders and their millions of followers. How is political propaganda related to the psychology of the masses? Nazi Germany still remains an arena for further exploration of this question. In *The Roots of Nazi Psychology: Hitler's Utopian Barbarism*, Jay Gonen focuses on Nazi ideology to illustrate the contact points between the Führer and the German people. Adolf Hitler often used the repetition of short slogans to feed his followers Nazi ideology, including ideas on race, the Jewish threat, living space, world domination, the folkish state, the femininity of masses, and the omnipotence of the leader. Hitler was able to sell this ideology in part because, after being traumatized during World War I, Germans were looking for an omnipotent savior. As a reaction against

their hurt and humiliation, the public turned to old myths from German culture. Such myths helped them to explain, for example, their indigestible defeat in World War I and their having been stabbed in the back by evil doers, that is, Jews. The German people reactivated a group fantasy of rebuilding a Holy Roman Empire of the German nation (a concept that requires a closer look).

Gonen rightly tells us that Hitler was a borrower of ideas. He states that Hitler borrowed ideas on the psychology of crowds from the French Gustave Le Bon who was a racist himself and was admired by the fascist leadership in Italy. While there is no proof that Hitler himself read Le Bon, the Nazi literature suggests that Joseph Goebbels was familiar with Le Bon's writings. Interestingly, Gonen does not focus on cronies of Hitler such as Goebbels. Perhaps future studies will explore the importance of the psychology between a leader and his or her entourage as a factor in the success of propaganda campaigns. Nevertheless, Gonen should be complimented on his illustration of how a leader's internal needs dovetail with the primitive desires and fears of the masses. Leaders, even absolute dictators like Hitler, do not exist in a vacuum. The psychology of both sides, leaders and followers, needs to be taken into account for a comprehensive view of history.

At the end of his book, Gonen looks at present-day Germany and notes, for example, that the reunification of East and West Germany did not bring back old dreams of malignant nationalism. This makes him optimistic that Germans' acknowledgment of responsibility for the past will secure a future that is neither utopian nor barbaric. This reviewer, as a clinician, would point out that it has taken Jewish people several decades to fully recognize the transgenerational transmission of trauma and its influence on the second and third generations, whether adaptive or pathological. Accordingly, the trauma that the German people experienced in the Nazi period and its influence on the second and third generations likewise needs to be opened up further. Despite the social, legal, and intellectual safeguards against recreating malignant nationalism and anti-Semitism, there are hints that the influence of the Third Reich continues beneath the surface. Clinical studies of Nazi skinheads and German individuals in psychoanalysis whose ancestors were Nazis tell us a great deal about how the relationship between the Führer and his people is still being played out at the unconscious level.

VAMIK D. VOLKAN

University of Virginia
Charlottesville

QUINN, FREDERICK. 2000. *The French Overseas Empire*. Pp. xx, 336. Westport, CT: Praeger. $65.00.

This book is an excellent example of a genre all too rare in our day: a broad historical canvas painted by a scholar-diplomat, who has served in the places he writes about. In this instance, North Africa, Black Africa, West Indies, and Vietnam—the most important places in the old French overseas empire.

Because of his service, Quinn is compelled to ask, how did this far-flung empire come about? His plan is ambitious: to take us on a tour of five centuries of French expansion and contraction, culminating in the twentieth century when the empire reached its apogee. He gives a well-balanced, thoughtful account, starting with the fishing empire, followed by the traders' empire, the eighteenth-century duel with Britain, and the nineteenth-century advent of the military and missionaries. He then focuses on the establishment and expansion of the new empire, its vicissitudes from 1900 to 1945, and finally its demise during decolonization with the 1962 loss of Algeria.

One is struck by how much of the French experience falls in the shadow of Great Britain. The nineteenth century escalated what Walter Dorn called "the competition for empire," and in 1763, the French lost Canada and India. In the nineteenth century, however, the French outflanked the other powers interested in the Far East by taking Indochina and making a comeback in North and Black Africa to rival Britain. Quinn points out the irony of the Third Republic of *liberté*, *égalité*, and *fraternité* presiding over an empire whose subjects had few rights.

Quinn emphasizes that France could never hope to match Britain, since its navy and merchant marine were always inferior; since France was primarily a land power, politics always favored the Continent; and finally, the fact is that the French body politic, despite enthusiastic visits to colonial expositions, was never much interested in the colonies. Algeria, enshrined in the myth of being a part of mainland France, was the most tragic chapter of all and provides a sober ending to five centuries of imperial rule.

Why, then, did France play an international game of expansion? Except for Algeria (and early Canada) there were no settler colonies (prompting Bismarck's remark, "France has colonies but no colonists"); French commerce was never greatly involved in overseas trade as compared to Britain. Was it the Napoleonic quest for glory? Or was it (at a later stage) national prestige? It is here that Quinn abandons ship: we are waiting for a grand conclusion, an analytical overview of what all of this activity meant, but he prefers to bail out. I hope that Quinn will publish such an overview, which he is well qualified to write, in a journal article in the near future.

The strengths of the volume are its comprehensiveness, which makes it useful for teachers and students, and its attention to detail. Its broad scope fills a need to have an up-to-date narrative of the French empire; while imperial studies are out of fashion in some quarters, they are essential if we are to understand the modern postindependence world. Quinn is at his best when he brings personal insights to bear on his material, such as his arriving in Vietnam to be given a library of Victor Hugo's works hidden since colonial days.

One problem for Quinn is that of sources. Generally, it is a fully documented work. He was well advised to peruse the most relevant French sources, which he has done, but in the process, his notes show a lack of familiarity with works by British and American scholars of the French empire. For instance, the African materials do not reflect the relevant works of Crowder, Wallerstein, Morgenthau, Austen, Foltz, and others. Part of the problem is that his French experts themselves often do not cite the English-speaking sources, which Quinn needed to pick up.

One of the empire's most important legacies of empire in our century was the formation of political parties, which from the 1920s onward played a capital role in the decolonization process. This subject area, as well as the evolution of elites (who eventually took over the empire), needed fuller coverage. We learn about Bourguiba and Ho Chi Minh but not much about Blaise Diagne or Ferhat Abbas.

Last, more copyediting was needed—misspellings of Henri Brunschwig, *spahi*, Lamine Guèye, Ousmane Sembène, and so forth mar an otherwise literate and readable text. On the positive side, Quinn's sections on the literary aspect of colonial life add a sensitive touch often missing in purely political narratives. And his quip from *Casablanca*, the Claude Rains line, of the French "to round up the usual suspects," adds a marvelous light touch to the proceedings.

G. WESLEY JOHNSON

Brigham Young University
Provo
Utah

UNITED STATES

ALTSCHULER, GLENN and STUART BLUMIN. 2000. *Rude Republic: Americans and Their Politics in the Nineteenth Century.* Pp. xii, 316. Princeton, NJ: Princeton University Press. $35.00.

In the 1960s political historians developed what has become an enduring paradigm of nineteenth-century American history. In its elemental form this interpretation holds that politics after 1840 was pervasive, interesting, and accessible to large numbers of Americans who displayed their commitment to the process by voting in the frequent elections that mark this period, by joining the political parties that became institutionalized, and by participating in the campaign rituals that grew to large-scale celebrations such as parades and pole raisings. "Politics," in the cliché that now summarizes this period, "was in the air everywhere," as the American electorate created a golden age of politics.

Glenn Altschuler and Stuart Blumin, in their remarkable study *The Rude Republic: Americans and Their Politics in the Nineteenth Century*, challenge this ruling wisdom. Theirs is not so much a heads-on confrontation as it is a flanking operation that seeks to demonstrate the variability and different levels of political activity among nineteenth-century Americans. "Even to the most active and interested, politics was only part of life, and at that not always the most important part."

Among their insights is that the evidence of the so-called party period of American politics has come from insiders who glorify their own political engagement, which is by no means representative of their fellow Democrats and Republicans. In fact, outsiders ranged from the apathetic to the intermittently interested (mostly during presidential elections and during the Civil War) to the silents about whom even the research of Altschuler and Blumin reveals little to the engaged disbelief of skeptical Americans who considered politics as they might a Barnum circus. Neglected by the practitioners of the "New Political History" whose application of statistics was much heralded 30 years ago, write Altschuler and Blumin, was "any sustained analysis of the nature and depth of popular political engagement."

Altschuler and Blumin provide such an analysis. Using representative towns in various sections of the United States, which are changed over time because of demographic transformations, they have constructed a list of those men mentioned by newspapers as engaged in some form of public activity. The numbers involved in this sample are not paltry; for example, their data include thousands of activists whom they track for political and civic involvement and whom they use to determine the social structure of political activism. For Augusta, Georgia, before the war they find 866 Augustans, although most of these did not participate in the nominating system of conventions, which takes in *The Rude Republic* quite a beating in terms of interest. Cross-reference to the U.S. census provides a social profile of the elite nature of partisan leaders, at least before the war.

But newspapers, so famously useful for the argument that Americans were interested in politics, offer only insider information in the Altschuler-Blumin model. In a back-breaking and eye-straining use of sources, Altschuler and Blumin look at the world beyond politics through fiction, diaries, and iconography, the former written by those who were outsiders with varying interest in the world inhabited by the partisans whom we have heretofore taken as typical Americans.

Altschuler and Blumin pursue their hypothesis through the nineteenth century. In this thick description specialists will take issue with some of their conclusions. For example, they argue that before the Civil War "slavery was not in itself a matter of national policy," and in their demotion of voting after the war they entirely neglect the agonizing efforts of women to obtain an instrumental right. Still the range of this book, its sophisticated use of sources, and its evidence is striking. Inevitably *The Rude Republic* points to a comparison with today's politics. While we may be comforted that things have not declined as much as we may think, still this important, superbly researched and argued book may make us wonder whether our democracy was ever a government by the people.

JEAN H. BAKER

Goucher College
Baltimore
Maryland

DIGGENS, JOHN PATRICK. 2000. *On Hallowed Ground: Abraham Lincoln and the Foundations of American History*. New Haven, CT: Yale University Press. No price.

At the core of American society resides a body of liberal ideals that has realized itself in every generation and in every historical era. The present generation of historians, distinguished by its obsession with the sins of America's past, convinced that the function of any dominant ideology is to exclude minorities, and blind to anything about which Americans agree, have utterly distorted American history. Such is John Diggens's claim.

Diggens summons the example of Abraham Lincoln to illustrate his point. The real Abraham Lincoln was not the man now admired by politically correct television documentaries and their Left-looking talking heads. The real Lincoln was the ultimate capitalist. Embracing the liberalism of the founders, Lincoln believed in the morality of the free market and the sanctity of property. John Locke, one of the founders' ideological sages, defined property as the lynchpin of the good society. When man mixes his labor with his soil, Locke declared, the product must be his to possess. Owners and workers alike, from the very creation of the American state, believed that the right to produce and accumulate property is a natural right subsisting independently of the consent of others. For Lincoln, "the nation is worth fighting for, to secure such an inestimable jewel." Lincoln never studied Locke closely, but Locke was part of the political atmosphere in which he lived and breathed. Unqualified recognition of the will to work and to succeed in the race of life oriented Lincoln's life because it oriented America's political culture. And when Lincoln invoked "liberty to all" he meant not only political rights but, above all, "*enterprise*, and *industry* to all." The very purpose of life, Lincoln believed, "is to improve one's condition."

The right to accumulate property and influence comprises the liberal consensus that contemporary historians deny. African Americans, more than any other group, Diggens stresses, have been excluded from the liberal consensus, but many black spokesmen retard their in-

clusion by rejecting liberalism. A long strand of African American writing, from Frederick Douglass and Booker T. Washington to Thomas Sowell and Shelby Steele, all influenced by Locke, sees the marketplace as the mechanism of social integration. On the other side, W.E.B. Du Bois, Martin Luther King, Jr., Cornel West, and Henry L. Gates seek to integrate African Americans into the mainstream of life through the political arena. Diggens's stand on this issue leaves nothing to the imagination: one cannot bask vicariously in the glow of victimhood, celebrate the politics of difference, and expect to keep up with history.

> Those with the will to work and the ambition to prosper have always made up the liberal consensus—a consensus that includes women, laborers, blacks and other ethnic minorities, all those who believe in the gospel of work and try to live for conviction as well as comfort. Call them Lincoln's heirs. (291)

Diggens's book is distinguished by its relentless and effective criticism of multiculturalism, poststructuralism, and other imbecilities of the academic Left, but it does not warrant its subtitle: *Abraham Lincoln and the Foundations of American History*. Readers who think they are buying a book about Lincoln will be very disappointed, for only a small portion of its pages actually deals with him. Lincoln is Diggens's vehicle for an analysis of liberalism in American intellectual history. Historians, in this regard, will find plenty to criticize, including Diggens's overestimating Locke by glossing over Montesquieu and Blackstone, and his ignoring Lincoln's realization that northerners' fear of freed slaves glutting the labor market superceded Lockean ideals. Diggens's argument, however, withstands such details. True, he says nothing new about the cultural Left, but his commentary on Lincoln's values, however brief, is fresh and provocative. In truth, John Locke, mentioned rarely by American historians, suffused Lincoln's life and America's history. The time to bring liberalism back into the study of Lincoln and his America is now. *On Hallowed Ground* is a good start.

BARRY SCHWARTZ

University of Georgia
Athens

FISHER, LOUIS. 2000. *Congressional Abdication on War & Spending*. Pp. xv, 220. College Station: Texas A&M University Press. $34.95. Paperbound, $17.95.

Louis Fisher, senior specialist in the Congressional Research Service and distinguished author of dozens of scholarly works on interbranch relations, probes more profoundly than ever two of his prime subjects: war powers and the budget process. Partly, *Congressional Abdication* takes war and budget decision making from the framers to the eve of the new administration, reviewing against the backdrop of history, recent events such as the military interventions in Yugoslavia and the Supreme Court's line item veto decision. Most interestingly, Fisher expounds and defends a challenging thesis: that for all the vital need of democracy for a vigorous legislature and institutional checks, Congress of late has conducted an "abject surrender of legislative prerogatives to the president."

As to war powers, the framers intended only to empower the sacrifice-wary Congress, not the martially inclined president, to engage the nation in combat. Until 1950, Congress declared, expressly authorized, or at least impliedly ratified virtually all major military actions. The Korean War, Vietnam, and the initiatives of President Reagan (for example, Iran-Contra) marked a surge in presidential war making. Fisher's survey of these serves primarily as the prologue

for scrutinizing the military operations by President Bush as to Panama and Iraq, and Clinton as to Somalia, Haiti, Bosnia, Iraq redux, and Yugoslavia (Kosovo). To illustrate how recent Congresses let presidents make war decisions, Fisher marshals fresh and thought-provoking evidence, from Professor Ezra Y. Siff's 1999 study of the Tonkin Gulf Resolution in the Vietnam War, to how the Clinton administration quietly reprogrammed—that is, spent without Congress' fully voting—a billion previously appropriated dollars in 1996 to finance the Bosnia commitment.

Next, as to the budget process, Congress had largely kept the power of the purse in its own hands from the framers' time to the 1960s. However, Fisher finds that congressional enactment of the Budget Act of 1974 as a riposte to President Nixon's impoundments relinquished more legislative power than it recovered. The now-centralized budget process itself strengthened presidents in the wrestling for budget control, from President Reagan's 1981 Omnibus Act with his domestic agenda aboard, through the Gramm-Rudman-Hollings Law. Again, the book builds on pre-1990s prologue to explore its abdication thesis, this time to the self-straitjacketing spending caps of the 1990s and the enactment of the Line Item Veto Act as an ultimate "abdication of spirit and institutional self-respect" eliciting Supreme Court invalidation in 1998.

Fisher writes with a lively nonpartisan style, his well-footnoted critiques lambasting Presidents Bush and Clinton and Democratic and Republican Congresses alike, the former pair for stealing or at least receiving stolen power, the latter for cravenly surrendering it. The reader will enjoy his occasional first-person accounts, such as a few of his 37 (!) appearances at congressional hearings where he often first field tests warnings about (then-)impending outrages.

Scholars and students of interbranch relations, with interests quickened in 2001 by the first inauguration in a half century of a unified Republican government, will find in *Congressional Abdication* a lucid work providing deep perspective on real-time controversies.

CHARLES TIEFER

University of Baltimore
Chevy Chase
Maryland

STARK, ANDREW. 2000. *Conflict of Interest in American Public Life*. Pp. x, 331. Cambridge, MA: Harvard University Press. $49.95.

From Whitewater and Hillary Clinton's cattle futures to the makeup of the Food and Drug Administration's advisory panels, issues of governmental ethics have been steady front-page news for years. Add to this the growing list of corporate ethics consultants, think tanks and advocacy groups devoted to ethical issues of various kinds, and even the occasional efforts to force the adoption of a scholarly code of ethics for academics, and it would seem that we must live in the most ethical age in history. Yet this is hardly the way most people feel.

One reason for this, notes Andrew Stark in his new book *Conflict of Interest in American Public Life*, is that we have been experiencing a sort of ethical bracket creep. We have raised our standards from those of subjective ill intent to create a vast array of prophylactic laws designed to forbid any circumstances that might lead to inner conflict. Yet such rules cover so much conduct that violations are sure to be found, regardless of the intent of those they cover. The end result, as others have pointed out, is that the regulation of ethics becomes a game for technicians, drained of moral content.

Stark's book provides an in-depth survey of the many different varieties of conflict-of-interest regulation, continually returning to a single theme: that the replacement of laws regulating *mala in se* (those acts that are wrong in themselves) with regulations of acts innocent in themselves but forbidden for prophylactic reasons and thus classed as *mala prohibita*, has created a dilemma. As Stark notes, "the problem with conflict-of-interest law is that it has become a moral stigmatizer when, in reality, it is just law."

Nonetheless, Stark is not an enemy of conflict-of-interest law. His attitude might be better described as that of a concerned friend: because Stark believes that it is important to regulate conflicts of interest, he wishes to see such regulation kept within its proper scope, where it might do good. Such pragmatic modesty is, unfortunately, rare in scholarship these days.

Stark's defense of regulations based on preventing an appearance of impropriety (or, perhaps more accurately, on maintaining an appearance of propriety) is more problematic. The essence of an appearance violation, of course, is that it is not actually wrong but that it might look bad, at least to the ill informed. Stark conscientiously raises the point that the public deserves a share of the blame here (if citizens bothered to know more, they would attend less to appearances and more to substance) but ultimately favors a strict-liability approach in such cases. One might wonder (in fact, I do wonder) whether this approach, with its inevitable injustices and absurdities in practice, really does anything to promote public confidence, but Stark sets forth the best possible case for his position.

Appropriately enough, the book does not end with a checklist of cut-and-dried approaches for ending problems with governmental ethics for all time. The problem, as Stark frankly admits, is as much one of culture as of legality: so long as we want governmental officials to possess great authority and wide discretion, and so long as we find the notion of deep inquiry into individuals' thoughts and motivations repellently totalitarian, we will be forced to enact objective regulations that will often be a poor fit with individual cases. Though this conclusion will not satisfy those who yearn for simple (or at least simplistic) solutions, it is correct. In *Conflict of Interest in American Public Life*, Stark has given us a clear and insightful guide to the features, flaws, and purposes of today's political ethics laws.

GLENN HARLAN REYNOLDS

University of Tennessee
Knoxville

STEPHAN, ALEXANDER. 2000. *"Communazis": FBI Surveillance of German Emigre Writers.* Trans. Jan van Heurck. Pp. xxi, 384. New Haven, CT: Yale University Press. $29.95.

The title is somewhat misleading since Stephan deals not only with the FBI but also with two other organizations equally interested in the activities of expatriates during World War II and the 1950s: the Office of Strategic Services (OSS) (before it was phased out of existence and evolved into the CIA) and the INS. Stephan's is a sobering study even to those familiar with the extent to which government agencies were obsessed with the minutiae of the lives that under ordinary circumstances, would never have merited such scrutiny. But these were not ordinary times; Emma Lazarus's welcome to the "huddled masses yearning to breathe free" was given lip service during World War II and the McCarthy era, when the great triumvirate—the FBI, OSS, and INS—decided, more or less in-

dependently, that emigre = intellectual = left wing (at least) = Communist/fellow traveler/dupe/nationalist/maybe-not-commie-but-probably-un-American. Never mind that neither Communist Party USA members nor the emigres, most of whom were not Communists, constituted a threat to the internal security of the United States. In theory they did.

In a perverse way, the theory was not all that farfetched, although it was misapplied. The reasoning was not so much simple as simplistic: since Communism was a German invention, and the two greatest threats to democracy were the German brand of fascism (Nazism) and Communism, there was virtually no difference between them. Thus Herbert J. Hoover called Communists "Red fascists," even though through the 1940s and 1950s, *Fascism* and *Communism* were considered antonyms—the difference being that ideologically, the former was right wing; the latter left wing. Although it took leftists a long time to realize it, there was no difference between the extreme Right and the extreme Left, each having its own way of enforcing conformity and settling scores.

What is ultimately saddening about Stephan's painstaking study, enriched by excerpts from files that Stephan has acquired through the Freedom of Information Act (which in itself makes his book invaluable), is the amount of time and money wasted on investigations that reveal more about the investigators than the investigated—for example, the FBI's fear that Thomas Mann might become a member of the Free Germany Committee, which was perceived as comprising Stalinist Germans. The FBI assumed that emigres cherished a dream of a Germany guided by Social Democrats (translate: Socialists or worse) but not by the principles of American democracy. And why were the sexual propensities of Mann's son, Klaus, of such concern except that the equation had been extended to include homosexuals, so that any expatriate gay is a potential (or actual) subversive. All that is missing is a pink triangular stamp on the file transcript.

Although most of the book is devoted to the more colorful and famous Los Angeles community (Thomas Mann, Bertolt Brecht, Franz Werfel, Erich Maria Remarque, Emil Ludwig), there are chapters on the New York and Mexico expatriates. Especially instructive is Stephan's reminder that Mexico was quite liberal in its immigration policies and welcomed those who supported the Spanish republic during the Spanish civil war. One of the most fascinating of the Mexican emigres was Bodo Uhse, a Communist writer and Spanish civil war veteran. Although Stephan does not mention Lillian Hellman, it should be noted that her prophetically antifascist play, *Watch on the Rhine* (1941), deals with a family that has returned from Germany to Washington, DC, via Mexico. The husband's politics are never specified except as antifascist, but he fought in Spain and is about as far to the Left as a character could be in a Broadway play. Interestingly, the younger son's name is Bodo, a rather unusual one (the other children are called Joshua and Babette). Given Hellman's politics (supposedly she belonged to the Communist Party for a very short time) and the prodigious research she did for the play, the choice of name was not accidental.

"Communazis" is the kind of book that adds to our knowledge and illuminates what we already know. If I had not known I was reading a translation, I would have congratulated the author on writing such readable prose. Instead, I must commend Jan van Heurck for a translation that does not sound like one.

BERNARD F. DICK

Fairleigh Dickinson University
Teaneck
New Jersey

SUMMERS, MARK WAHLGREN. 2000. *Rum, Romanism, & Rebellion: The Making of a President, 1884.* Pp. xv, 377. Chapel Hill: University of North Carolina Press. $55.00. Paperbound, $19.95.

In *Rum, Romanism, & Rebellion*, Mark Wahlgren Summers, author of two earlier estimable books, deals with more than *The Making of a President, 1884*; indeed, as he himself notes, his study "sprawls across the map and over eight years." James G. Blaine (Republican) and Grover Cleveland (Democrat) are not nominated for president until chapters 8 and 9, respectively, this after coverage of gilded age political culture, campaigns, and elections; the disputed presidential election of 1876 and its aftermath; the Democrats' ruthless consolidation of power in the South; Republican party factionalism; cultural issues (Protestant-Catholic conflict and prohibition); the tariff issue; and the revival of Democratic fortunes before 1884.

The political campaigns of 1884 are treated exhaustively by Summers, including state contests held prior to the presidential canvass. Minor parties receive their due, as do other groups of significance, particularly (though by no means exclusively) in New York State, which would decide the outcome of the national election—Mugwumps, Irish politicians, and Irish nationalists. Campaign episodes with which readers are likely to be familiar—scandals, most famously Grover Cleveland's fathering a child out of wedlock; the Reverent Samuel Burchard's alliterative but impolitic indictment of the Democratic Party as the party of "rum, Romanism, and rebellion" at a large ministerial rally for Blaine; and the controversial fund-raising dinner for Blaine ("Belshazzar's Feast") at Delmonico's restaurant—take on new significance as Summers carefully places them in their contexts. Like earlier chapters, those on the unfolding events of the presidential election year rest on diligent and remarkably wide research in manuscript collections, newspapers, and magazines of opinion. Summers's familiarity with relevant scholarship, unpublished as well as published, further strengthens his study.

In the end, Summers concludes that "Cleveland's election marked a significant moment in Gilded Age politics in several ways"—"real issues were at stake in 1884"; "politics remained the mainstream politicians' game"; the demonstrated need of the parties for campaign funds would influence their subsequent behavior." Likewise, the Democrats' tightening grip on the South and recapture of the presidency meant that the Republicans would seek to strengthen further their position in the North by sharpening their protective tariff rhetoric and by seeking admission of Western states. Summers's arguments merit close attention by political historians, particularly those of us who have stressed the significance of developments and elections during the 1890s and perhaps failed to appreciate fully the importance of those of the previous decade.

Rum, Romanism, & Rebellion stands as a fine work of historical analysis, but it is not without limitations and weaknesses. Summers writes well, very well, but occasionally he strikes me as trying too hard for effect. He is a master of detail, but some of that detail could have been deleted without serious loss, indeed perhaps with benefit. The generally high standard of writing to the contrary notwithstanding, a handful of sentences contain gaffes that should have been caught. Summers appears more comfortable analyzing the behavior of politicians and other public figures than analyzing that of the electorate. Quantitative election analyses are generally adequate, no more; for the most part they focus on selected districts rather than illuminate broader patterns in the period. One gen-

eral presentation (p. 300, Table 10), ranking the states in which Blaine fared worst and indicating his "Gain/Loss over 1880," somehow generally confuses 1876 to 1884 percentage point shifts with those of 1880 to 1884. Certainly James A. Garfield carried neither Louisiana nor South Carolina. (A final—and idiosyncratic—concern: I wonder whether "the cotton fields of Iowa" were not fields of dreams).

My caveats notwithstanding, I strongly endorse *Rum, Romanism, & Rebellion: The Making of a President, 1884*.

SAMUEL T. McSEVENEY
Vanderbilt University
Nashville
Tennessee

WEBBER, MICHAEL J. 2000. *New Deal Fat Cats: Campaign Finances and the Democratic Party in 1936*. Pp. xiii, 208. New York: Fordham University Press. $39.95. Paperbound, $19.95.

The rise and fall of Franklin D. Roosevelt's New Deal coalition has captured the imagination of generations of historians, political scientists, and sociologists. For most, the story begins with FDR's impressive victory in the 1932 general election and continues with the Democratic president's skill in solidifying his broadbased coalition in the 1936, 1940, and 1944 electoral contests.

In *New Deal Fat Cats*, Michael Webber, chair of the Department of Sociology at the University of San Francisco, offers a powerful and convincing social scientific analysis of one of the century's most important elections. Noting an abundance of literature on class conflict and the rise of labor unions, Webber focuses his study of the 1936 election on the interactions between business, organized labor, and political parties. "The guiding thread of this study," Webber argues, "is the assumption that campaign finance contributions can be a reliable empirical indicator of the political preferences of people following their real material interests." Campaign donations, he explains, "act as an important 'tracer element' marking the tracks of business and labor influence in the political system."

In an eight-chapter book, Webber offers a historiographic overview of New Deal writings in both the social sciences and humanities fields, reviews the role of business between 1932 and 1936, discusses the mass-consumption sector and Democratic party finances, evaluates the investment theory of politics, offers a fascinating and novel investigation of the 1936 Democratic convention book soft money scandal, points out important differences among business leaders in New York City and the South, and closes with a study of FDR and the unions.

For Webber, the story of business and the 1936 election reaffirms the importance of FDR's far-reaching political coalition. "If there is a lesson to be learned from the New Deal," Webber explains, "it is that the Democratic party successfully mobilized groups outside the mainstream of the American power structure to bring about far-reaching changes in how government responded to the needs of the American people."

Webber, in one of his most important observations, discovered strong pro-FDR sentiment among business leaders from New York City, the South, and the alcohol industry. Avoiding a common tendency to blur all business leaders together, Webber showed how Jews in New York City, southern Democrats, and opponents of prohibition dissented from the old-line Protestant corporate elite. In this sense, marginalized business leaders mirrored the political attitudes of the larger electorate. "The presidential election of 1936," as Webber notes in his conclusion, "was, in many respects, a referendum on

the activist role taken by the federal government since the inception of the New Deal."

New Deal Fat Cats offers a powerful and convincing mix of social scientific data and historical narrative. Webber's ability to translate the theoretical to the real makes this an excellent book for both the specialist and the interested observer. His opening chapter surveying existing New Deal scholarship was especially useful and informative. Webber's use of secondary sources from across disciplinary lines also demonstrated great attention to detail and respect for competing methodological approaches.

MARC DOLLINGER

Princeton University
New Jersey

SOCIOLOGY

BAYOR, RONALD H. [1996] 2000. *Race and the Shaping of Twentieth Century Atlanta.* Pp. xvi, 334. Chapel Hill: University of North Carolina Press. Paperbound, $19.95.

The publication of a paperback edition of Ronald H. Bayor's book on race in twentieth-century Atlanta is a welcome event. Bayor is a careful scholar who writes with clarity and insight, and he deserves a wide reading.

Historians, journalists, and social scientists have perhaps studied and written about Atlanta more than any other city in the South. Site of Booker T. Washington's famous speech at the Cotton States and International Exposition, and just a few years later scene of a particularly violent riot precipitated by inflammatory anti-black newspaper rhetoric, birthplace of Martin Luther King, Jr., a one-time center of Klan activity, headquarters for many progressive organizations seeking to disestablish the Jim Crow system and diminish its legacy, and the only Southern city whose mayor testified in favor of the public accommodations section of the 1964 Civil Rights Act, Atlanta has a racial history with twists and turns unmatched by any other city in the nation.

In the second half of the twentieth century, Atlanta, with its widely celebrated biracial coalition, was known as the city too busy too hate. Yet, as Bayor shows, such a simple slogan fails to capture the complexity of Atlanta in that period, and it overlooks the weight of the city's racial past. Bayor's book provides needed depth to the story of how racially motivated policy actions taken at an earlier time resound through the growth and change of a city that has often prided itself on rising to new heights out of the ashes of its past. Georgia is a deep South state, and for the first half of the twentieth century there were few checks on white disregard for and antagonism toward the interests of Atlanta's black citizens. Black Atlanta proved adept at making use of limited resources, but in harsh circumstances adeptness can only carry a group so far.

Focusing on public policy, Bayor shows how large a part the drive to establish and maintain a Jim Crow system played in the shaping of the city, not just in the first half of the twentieth century, but through that early legacy in the second half as well. The biracial coalition was not so much a thorough triumph of enlightenment as a new arena in which Atlanta's African American community could ply its efforts to end old practices and cope with their consequences. To be sure, electoral enfranchisement and other federal civil rights actions came to play a major part in giving black Atlantans a larger body of resources with which to pursue their own attempt to rise from the ashes, in their case the ashes of oppression. Nevertheless, early patterns

of land-use policy and a continuing drive by whites to distance their commercial and residential lives from African Americans remained a substantial force throughout the second half of the twentieth century.

In mid-century, when the Civil Rights movement challenged the racial order of the South, apologists for the status quo often spoke of that order as resting on local custom. Historian Ronald Bayor sets the record straight. The status quo of the mid–twentieth century rested on a policy past constructed by a multitude of government actions. Once constructed, as subsequent events demonstrated, that past could not be undone by a simple shift of political power and a wave of policy decisions based in that shift. Contemporary conservatives who complain that African Americans look too much to past grievances reveal a superficial grasp of history. They would do well to read Ronald Bayor's book and reflect on its lessons. There is much that a deeper understanding of history can teach.

CLARENCE N. STONE

University of Maryland
College Park

BROWDER, LAURA. 2000. *Slippery Characters: Ethnic Impersonators and American Identities*. Pp. xii, 312. Chapel Hill: University of North Carolina Press. $49.95. Paperbound, $18.95.

An elderly WASP man poses as a Latino youth, a colored Southern janitor goes native as a Cherokee Indian, and the daughter of a Welsh Baptist mother creates an identity as an orthodox Jew. These are only three of the many "ethnic impersonators" whose lives are discussed by Laura Browder in this intriguing study.

Browder's guiding premise is that the autobiographical narrative is a key genre in American culture, which has been used for a variety of personal and political purposes. She argues, convincingly, that popular autobiographies have come to claim a moral authority, as "the power of individual testimony can help reshape public thinking and public discourse," in this case about race and ethnicity. Browder traces these autobiographies from white-authored slave narratives to contemporary accounts of individuals passing from one ethnic category to another.

An irony that unites them all is that autobiographies by impersonators were often greeted with greater public enthusiasm than those by real members of the groups concerned. A case in point is the now-notorious 1976 memoir, *The Education of Little Tree*, written under a pseudonym by Forrest Carter, a former Ku Klux Klansman and speechwriter for Alabama Governor George Wallace. In the persona of the Cherokee Little Tree, Carter wrote of being raised by saintly, spiritual grandparents before enduring torment in a brutal orphanage and finally being rescued. The book fit perfectly with the new age mood of the time and became a huge best seller. As Browder explains, *Little Tree* was a fantasy about Indian spirituality, and "it is also a fantasy perfectly attuned to an American public well versed in the rhetoric of self-actualization and the recovery movement." In the wake of the success of Carlos Castaneda's equally spurious Yacqui medicine man Don Juan (whom Browder does not mention), *Little Tree* epitomized the noble savage image, and the cruel irony is that "Carter succeeded in his impersonation by trading on his deep knowledge of racial and ethnic stereotypes."

While Carter used his impersonation to escape his racist past, Sylvester Long became an Indian to escape his racial identity as a colored man in the 1930s South. In a series of calculated steps, Long became Chief Buffalo Child Long Lance, and carved out a successful career as an "authentic" Indian, starring in both fictional and ethnographic films. In earlier chapters, Browder carefully describes how Indian representations in theatre, museums, and Wild West shows laid the groundwork for the mélange of imagery that came to define Indian identity and on which both Carter and Long traded.

Turning to black identity, Browder traces the use of fictional slave narratives by abolitionists to make the case for the essential humanity of African Americans. Yet abolitionists also perpetuated the stereotypes: "unwilling to trust the slaves to tell their own stories, these writers created slave personae who were disgusted by black bodies . . . and unable to see the truth about slavery without the intercession of the abolitionists." Later, she discusses the development of blackface entertainers, and describes how groups like the Symbionese Liberation Army took on blacker-than-thou personae in an attempt to demonstrate their radical authenticity in the 1970s.

Throughout, Browder makes a good case for the primacy of the personal narrative in American cultural history and explores the complicated and ever-changing notions of race and ethnicity. She strains her argument when she includes a chapter on hoboes, asserting that "poverty behaves as an ethnicity," and I would have liked to see a discussion of a major autobiographical genre, the Indian captivity narrative, but these are quite minor flaws in an innovative and engaging book.

S. ELIZABETH BIRD

University of South Florida
Tampa

COSTA, DORA L. 1998. *The Evolution of Retirement: An American Economic*

History, 1880-1990. Pp. xiii, 234. Chicago: University of Chicago Press. $40.00. Paperbound, $19.00.

Dora Costa's book on retirement is very much in the cliometric tradition, containing much evidence and statistical analysis. The big issue she tackles is explaining the well-documented withdrawal from the labor force of men 65 and older in the United States, a trend that started in the late nineteenth century. The key factors she examines are rising real income, improvements in health, and changes in the structure of occupations. It is based in part on several of her previously published papers combined with some new material that covers the political history of retirement and speculates about future patterns of retirement. While it is filled with charts, graphs, and econometrics, her story is still quite accessible to the careful, noneconomist reader.

The core of her evidence comes from a large sample of the military pension records of Union Civil War veterans. She supplements these samples with samples drawn from the 1900 and 1910 Public Use Microdata Samples of the Decennial Censuses. The Union Army Veteran Sample allows the observation of how increases in real income, a pure income effect, affected the labor force behavior of veterans. As the sample of veterans is representative of the general population, Costa is able to show that the income from the pension was large enough to induce many older men to withdraw from the labor force and that until recently, rising real income was central in reducing the labor force participation of men 65 and older.

Rising real income has been key in spurring the withdrawal from the labor force, particularly before social security and other government pensions were put in place. The sensitivity to changes in income on the part of older men, however,

has decreased over time, or as economists would put it, the elasticity of demand for retirement with respect to income has decreased. Costa concludes that rising income was important perhaps up until 1940, after which other factors became more important in the labor force withdrawal decision. This result is important for academic researchers, but it is also very important for policy makers who will be increasingly faced with a growing number of retirees as the baby boom generation ages. An example of such a policy issue is, How much of the retired population should social security retirement benefits cover? Has income, and indirect saving, become high enough that some restrictions on coverage or even means testing become sensible? Likewise, what would the impact of partial privatization of social security be on labor force activity?

Given the scope of Costa's subject, some questions arise. Equating declining labor force participation rates with increasing retirement rates is troublesome, as retirement has strong voluntary connotations to it, while being out of the labor force can include withdrawal owing to disability, injury, or unemployment. I also suspect that labor force activity of older men may start increasing as the relatively smaller supply of labor coming from the cohort following the baby boom generation puts pressure on the labor market, increasing real wages. Perhaps the substitution effect, as economists put it, will induce older men to stay in the labor force longer now that health issues are less of an issue than they were earlier in the twentieth century. This book, nevertheless, provides the basis from which most economic analysis of retirement should proceed.

JON R. MOEN

University of Mississippi
University

ECONOMICS

FISKE, EWARD B. and HELEN F. LADD. *When Schools Compete: A Cautionary Tale.* Pp. xvii, 342. Washington, DC: Brookings Institution. $47.95.

This book provides a detailed history and analysis of one of the broadest and most radical reforms in education decentralization in the world. The New Zealand reforms may be of even more interest than are similar reforms in Great Britain, Chile, or the United States because they occurred throughout the country and they transformed a system that was extremely centralized before the reforms began in 1989. Thus the degree of change appears to be truly revolutionary.

Written by a husband and wife team combining the theoretical and statistical skills of an economist (Ladd) with the historical and qualitative eye of a journalist (Fiske), *When Schools Compete* is thorough and precise yet reads extremely well. The reader obtains the degree of background, historical, and context material to understand thoroughly the New Zealand experience. The statistical presentation is simple and descriptive, with more complex presentations being reserved for academic journals. Thus the book should have broad appeal for both classrooms and interested general audiences.

Roughly the first third of the book presents the context, history, assumptions, and logic of reforms in New Zealand. It alone is worth the price of the book. Fiske and Ladd focus on three philosophical currents behind the reforms: democratic-populism, managerial-business, and new-right-market currents. This combination leads Fiske and Ladd to believe that "New Zealand thus became a laboratory for testing the extent to which principles deduced from the economic marketplace are relevant to the delivery of education."

The reforms they describe, to use American parlance, amount to a combination of open enrollment and extreme site-based management. These reforms moved the delivery of education in New Zealand an enormous distance from the prior attendance-area, Wellington-run system in which principals needed permission to buy pencils.

A great deal of information in the book will be useful to education reformers in other countries. First, the effects of open enrollment were as one would anticipate. There was dramatic shift of students from lower to higher socioeconomic schools. And *Pakeha* (European descendants) were more likely to take advantage of this movement than Maori or Pacific Island minorities. The derivative results were more racial isolation and more segregated schools by class and race. Thus one of the downsides of choice, echoed in Scotland, England, and Chile, is the tendency of parents and schools to select what each sees as better options. This is exactly what market models would predict, and the inequality that results is also easy to anticipate.

The real question is whether that same competition will also improve the lot of all schools, by forcing bad ones to get better. Here, unfortunately, the Fiske-Ladd book can tell us very little. There was no real effort in New Zealand to systematically study this phenomenon. There is nothing like value-added standardized testing available, and the researchers are forced to use student movement to try to distinguish successful from unsuccessful schools. This obviously confounds the two critical questions concerning choice, and thus the effects of competition on student learning are essentially unknown.

Finally, a fascinating feature of the New Zealand reforms is the battle over teacher salaries and assignments. Fiske and Ladd realize this is crucial and devote considerable space to proposed teacher salary block grants to schools. This would have changed the practice of assigning and paying teachers directly from the national Ministry of Education. The idea was to allow schools to use these and operating grants in a flexible fashion. Unions strongly resisted, and after 10 years and continuous sweetening of the pot, there still were a number of schools not participating in this funding scheme. The model and implementation problems are important because many education systems in former Eastern and Soviet states are going through the process of devolving education responsibilities to local and school levels. Some variant of the New Zealand model may well allow these states to continue funding schools on a national level while devolving authority and responsibility to localities and schools. Policy makers in those and other countries would be well advised to read this wonderful book.

JOHN F. WITTE

University of Wisconsin
Madison

INDEX

BUY RECYCLED.

AND SAVE.℠

Thanks to you, all sorts of everyday products are being made from materials you've recycled. But to keep recycling working to help the environment, you need to buy those products.

So look for products made from recycled materials, and buy them. It would mean the world to all of us. For a free brochure, please write *Buy Recycled*, Environmental Defense Fund, 257 Park Ave. South, New York, NY 10010, or call 1-800-CALL-EDF.

&EPA

ENVIRONMENTAL DEFENSE FUND EDF

SAGE CONTENTS ALERT

STAY CURRENT ON THE LATEST RESEARCH...
FREE.

Sage Publications is pleased to announce **SAGE CONTENTS ALERT** a pre-publication alerting service **FREE** to all subscribers. If you have e-mail, you can now receive the table of contents for any journal you choose, delivered by e-mail directly to your PC.

You can automatically receive:

- Future Article Titles and Author(s)
- Volume and Issue Number
- Journal Title and Publication Date

Plus:

- Calls for Papers
- Special Issue Announcements
- News from the Editor

Registration is simple – just give us your name, the journal title(s) you want to receive, and your e-mail address.

E-mail: contents.alert@sagepub.com
Visit our Website: www.sagepub.com
Or mail to: Sage Contents Alert
Sage Publications
2455 Teller Road
Thousand Oaks, CA 91320

F999015

You aren't looking at
a future pilot.

You're looking at YOUR
future pilot.

Higher academic standards are good for everyone.

What a child learns today could have a major effect tomorrow. Not just on him or her, but on the rest of the world. Your world. Since 1992, we've worked to raise academic standards. Because quite simply, smarter kids make smarter adults. For more information, call 1-800-38-BE-SMART or visit www.edex.org.

The Business Roundtable • U.S. Department of Education • Achieve
American Federation of Teachers • National Alliance of Business
National Education Association • National Governors Association

Education Excellence Partnership